NOTES

without

MUSIC

Da Capo Press Music Reprint Series

GENERAL EDITOR
FREDERICK FREEDMAN
VASSAR COLLEGE

NOTES

without

MUSIC

An Autobiography

Darius

MILHAUD

𝄞 *Da Capo Press · New York · 1970*

A Da Capo Press Reprint Edition

This Da Capo Press edition of Darius Milhaud's *Notes without Music* is an unabridged republication of the first edition published in New York in 1953.

Library of Congress Catalog Card Number 72-87419

SBN 306-71565-1

Published by Da Capo Press
A Division of Plenum Publishing Corporation
227 West 17th Street, New York, N.Y. 10011

Manufactured in the United States of America

NOTES

without

MUSIC

Darius

MILHAUD

An Autobiography

NOTES

without

MUSIC

Alfred A. Knopf: 1953: New York

The body of this book was translated from the French by DONALD EVANS *and edited by* ROLLO H. MYERS; *the final chapter, written especially for the American edition, was translated by* ARTHUR OGDEN *and edited by* HERBERT WEINSTOCK.

L. C. catalog card number: 52–12205

THIS IS A BORZOI BOOK,
PUBLISHED BY ALFRED A. KNOPF, INC.

Originally published in France as NOTES SANS MUSIQUE, *copyright 1949 by René Julliard.*

PRELUDE

How many times have I been told: "You ought to write your memoirs!" "Impossible—I have such a bad memory." "That doesn't matter; you've known so many artists and musicians and been everywhere. . . ." "Yes, but so many others have described all these things better than I could. Besides, except for the catalogue of my works, which might help me supply a few exact dates, I don't possess a single letter or document." "Well, then, talk about yourself." It is true there is so much misunderstanding between the public, the critics, and myself that I should be pleased to clear some of it away. That decided me.

It was August 25, 1944. Paris had just been liberated, and, for the first time, after four dramatic years during which our despondency contrasted with the hospitality and comfort we enjoyed in the United States, it was possible at last to foresee final victory. After being ill for seven months I was obliged to rest and recuperate at the Stanford Hospital at San Francisco, and had time to look back over the half-century that had been my life.

I am going to conjure up memories of my friends and of my travels. I am going to try to describe the course of my musical development without going into technicalities and without any literary pretensions. This book, jotted down in fits and starts, will perhaps help to throw light upon certain aspects of musical history during the last thirty-five years in the form of "notes"—but this time without music.

CONTENTS

ILLUSTRATIONS

ix

x

NOTES

without

MUSIC

1

ORIGINS

I AM a Frenchman from Provence, and by religion a Jew. The establishment of the Jews in the south of France dates back to remote antiquity. Six hundred years before Christ, when the city of Marseille was founded, the Phocæans, the Greeks, and the Jews set up their counting-houses on the shores of the Mediterranean in France, and so came there not as emigrants, but as traders. There are tombstones showing that there were Jews in the Rhône valley before the Christian era. At that time the Jewish religion was the only one that was monotheistic, and conversions among the Gauls were very numerous. After the second destruction of the Temple the Jews emigrated from Palestine to Italy, Spain, and Provence. In Provence they amalgamated with the Jewish colony living there under comparatively peaceful conditions. Nevertheless, early in the twelfth century King René, Count of Provence, threatened them with exile unless they all became converted to Christianity. According to the archives of the Museum of Old Aix, two noble families of Aix, who pride themselves on never having allowed a Jew to cross the threshold of their house, would seem to be, by a charming irony of fate, the descendants of Jews forced to embrace the Christian faith. And yet a large number of Israelites refused to forswear their faith, and preferred exile at Avignon or elsewhere in the county (*comtat*) of Venaissin.

The county belonged to the popes after 1274, and the Jews under their jurisdiction were admirably treated. They were, indeed, so well aware of their good fortune that they were afraid of losing it, and it was for this reason that they refused hospitality to the wandering tribes of Ashkenazi Jews (Russians, Poles, or Germans fleeing from persecution), whose manners and customs differed from their own. The library at Carpentras possesses a request presented to the Cardinal Bishop for four sergeants to guard the gates of their "quarry" (the popular name for the Jewish quarter) so as to prevent the vagabonds from entering there. Their request was granted in return for a few sacks of saffroñ.

The Jews used to speak a jargon consisting of a mixture of Hebrew and Provençal. A little Jewish-Provençal dictionary containing a fairly complete list of these expressions, which are still used in the south of France by a few persons respectful of tradition, was published in Paris about 1860 in a Hebrew almanac. Armand Lunel found several folklore texts written in Hebrew-Provençal dialect, very humorous and outspoken in style—carols in the form of dialogues, with one strophe in Provençal favoring the conversion of the Jews, and another in Hebrew refuting the arguments of the Christians; some *Pioutims* (circumcision songs); a little eighteenth-century comedy describing a visit paid by the Jews Arcanoth and Barcanoth to the Bishop; and a "Tragedy of Queen Esther."

Like most of their coreligionists the Mediterranean Jews bore the names of towns: Lunel, Milhaud, Bédarrides, Monteux, Valabrègue. The county was the only place where their names were entered in the official archives, and their genealogy can be traced down to the Middle Ages. The library at Carpentras and the Calvet Museum at Avignon possess some interesting documents of this kind. I have seen there a sixteenth-century picture representing a view of Carpentras, with its ramparts, belfries, and low-built houses, and its quarry, where the houses sometimes were fifteen stories high because there was not enough space for the growing population. Each tenant in the quarry became the owner of the floor he lived on, looked upon the pope as the head of the state, and hung his portrait on the wall opposite the traditional print representing Moses and the Tables of the Law. Prayers were also said for the pope in the synagogues.

The Provençal rite resembles, in its pronunciation of liturgical Hebrew, that of the Sephardim, or Latin Jews; but the services are slightly different. There are only two synagogues in France which date from before the Revolution: one at Cavaillon, in Louis XV style, and the other at Carpentras, whose foundations, as well as the women's ritual bathing pool, date from the Middle Ages. This one was rebuilt under Louis XVI, and is decorated with finely worked wood paneling and enchanting chandeliers more suggestive of an elegant salon than of a sacred edifice. Thanks to the generosity of Mme Fernand Halphen and the Fine Arts Administration, these two temples have been restored and classified as "historical monuments." The Temple at Aix-en-Provence was founded in 1840. The speech at the inauguration was delivered by my great-grandfather, at that time president of the Consistory and Administrator of the Temple, who was succeeded in this position by his sons and grandsons. I intended to celebrate with my father the centenary of this little synagogue, and composed a cantata, *Couronne de Gloire*, on three texts by Gabirol, a Jewish Renaissance poet, and three texts taken from the "Comtadin" (Provençal) liturgy translated by Armand Lunel: *Prière pour le Pape, Prière pour les Ames des Persécutés*, and *Chant pour le Jour de la Réclusion*. Unfortunately the sad events of 1940 prevented us from carrying out our project.[1]

My paternal ancestors came from the Venaissin "Comtat." I found among the family archives some old papers, stamped with the pontifical arms dating from the fifteenth century, in which mention is made of a Milhaud from Carpentras in connection with some lawsuit. I have also been told that when Mirabeau needed four thousand pounds to go to Paris he asked my great-great-grandfather Benestruc Milhaud for the money, promising in exchange "to make a man of him." He kept his word, for the Jews acquired their citizenship rights after the Revolution. My great-grandfather Joseph Milhaud was born in the reign of Louis XVI, and as he lived to a great age he witnessed all the different regimes that followed the Revolution, and died as the Third Republic was born. Of a profoundly religious nature, he wrote works of religious exegesis, including a study of the Pentateuch and another on Deuteronomy and a life of Jethro. He was made responsible for establishing a census of all the Israelites who returned to France after the Revolution. I have unearthed some of these lists; many of the names are followed by a note: "Naturalized French after the restoration of the Venaissin Comtat." My grandmother Précile Valabrègue came from a numerous family living at Carpentras. One of her brothers was in the madder-dyeing business—madder

---

[1] This work was a sequel to *Prières Journalières à l'usage des Juifs du Comtat Venaissin*, composed in 1929, and to *Cinq Chants de Rosch Haschanna (Liturgie Comtadine)*, authentic liturgical melodies that I harmonized freely.

6

being the color used for French soldiers' trousers until it fell into disuse after the invention of chemical dyes.

My mother, Sophie Allatini, was born at Marseille. Her parents, who came from Modena, were descendants of the Sephardic Jews who have been established in Italy for centuries, and one of her ancestors in the fifteenth century was medical adviser to the Pope. Her family was very numerous and had vast business interests all over the world. Her grandfather owned the tobacco monopoly in Austria, a Bank at Marseille, mines in Serbia, and flour-mills at Salonika, run by French engineers on the model of those at Corbeil. My mother had spent a year in Turkey when she was a child and had a fund of stories and memories of her stay there which she used to tell me when I was small. She described the customs of the Jews who had been at Salonika ever since their expulsion from Spain in the fifteenth century and still spoke Spanish as it used to be spoken then.[2]

My mother used to tell me, too, stories about adventures and misdeeds of the brigands who lived in caves in the mountains, and of how the brigand chief once called on my grandfather to ask him for one of his estates, in return for which he promised protection, not only for him, but for all his family. And as my grandfather was on such friendly terms with the brigand chief, he was often able to help those who were captured and to arrange for them to be ransomed. My mother used to speak of horseback riding with her father; sometimes they would be rudely disturbed by herds of wild buffalo. She recalled, too, the visits paid them by pashas, to whom, according to Oriental custom, you had to offer anything to which they took a fancy, and the "Khavas," armed

[2] In Paris there is a little Temple, in the rue Saint-Lazare, still frequented by the Salonika Jews. There I have heard, at the Feast of Purim, the *Story of Esther* sung in old Spanish. It is a fine language, rather harsh and primitive, but very impressive.

7

to the teeth, who stood sentinel outside the doors. But what I liked best to dream about, being a spoiled and greedy child, were the rose-flavored syrups that the Turkish servants used to bring to my mother, on silver trays, after the siesta.

CHAPTER

2

MY CHILDHOOD

AFTER THEIR marriage my parents settled at Bras d'Or in Aix-en-Province. It was in this old house that my childhood was spent. When I was still very young I was already sensitive to my surroundings and to familiar noises. Bras d'Or was in the center of the town, on a little square that was the terminus of both the Avignon road and the Cours Sextius. From my window I could see the whole length of the Cours Sextius as far as the Hydropathic Institute, which on market days especially was very entertaining. It was thronged with farm-carts and mules and provisions of every kind; and, just as you see them in pictures by Cézanne, there were blue-bloused peasants drinking and playing cards in the cafés.

The "south room," opposite my bedroom, was specially kept for me; it was, in turn, playroom, schoolroom, and music-room. How often did I linger there, watching the distant trees that lined the road to Marseille and the soft curve of the hills on the horizon outlined in the setting sun!

But what attracted and fascinated me most was "the station"—a freight depot situated behind our house and nearly always deserted, being used only when the main station was too congested. It was at its best during military

9

maneuvers, when it was crowded with soldiers in their red and blue uniforms, guns, trucks, ambulances, and horses. An officer would shout orders and the train would—sometimes—steam out. But more often than not, there was no engine attached during these entrainment exercises.

We occupied the whole of the first floor of the Bras d'Or. My father, who was the director of a firm exporting almonds (founded by his grandfather in 1806), had his offices on the ground floor. Mornings, when still half asleep, I could hear the women pushing their trolleys laden with sacks, the conversation of the men loading and unloading the trucks, the noise of the trucks being driven away drawn by a couple of powerful horses, and, dominating everything else, the exclamations of the drivers swearing in Provençal!

The sounds I heard from the south room were quite different: the hum of conversation and scraps of song that floated up to me were mingled with the soft sound of fruit falling into the baskets and the monotonous and soothing drone of the machines for sorting the almonds: the *flots*, the *béraudes*, the *cassées*, and the *avolas*. Sometimes in the evenings too the same sounds could be heard again, and I would lie listening to echoing voices, distant singing, and the rumble of trucks until I fell asleep.

I was a well-behaved but rather neurotic child, continually subject to nervous attacks brought on by the slightest thing—a fright, a noise in the dark, a shadow. I shall always remember the shadow cast by the huge alabaster vase that stood on the mantelpiece in my parents' room, magnified in the wavering light of my bedside lamp. And how many times when we were traveling did I force them to change our hotel bedroom because I could not detach my eyes from the flowers on the wallpaper intertwined with geometrical figures, at which I would gaze unceasingly until overcome with terror.

And nothing could relieve my anguish until my mother appeared to give me a dose of bromide.

The three daughters of my uncle David Milhaud, who was my father's partner, were like sisters to me, especially the eldest, Rosine. She was almost the same age as I was, and we used to go out together every day. She was vivacious and charming, and led me into all kinds of mischief that I would never have thought of alone. My grandmother Précile Milhaud lived opposite us in the same house as my cousins. She was sensitive, reserved, and shy; she did not like going out very much, and we used to lunch with her every Saturday. At Passover the family circle was almost complete; our uncles and aunts used to come from Lyon for the holidays and joined us at the traditional dinner, during which my father read prayers in Hebrew while we ate *coudoles* (the local name for the unleavened bread that the Jews eat at Passover). These *coudoles* came from Carpentras and were of many different kinds. My uncle Michel Milhaud, who was a solicitor in Paris, used to come with his wife and two children, Étienne and Madeleine. The latter, who was ten years my junior, had a mischievous little face framed in golden curls. Even when she was quite small she used to amuse us by imitating Sarah Bernhardt and reciting the fables of La Fontaine.

My uncle Michel had very definite ideas about hygiene, and Rosine and I were always much amused by the row of gloves that they used for their toilet hanging out to dry on the balcony; for the "Parisians" changed them every day and used a different pair for each part of their bodies. Their luxurious ways, their elegance, and their little foibles excited in my cousins and me a feeling of inferiority mixed with a touch of irony.

Every summer my parents left their house, and we went to

11

stay with Grandmother Précile on the outskirts of the town, on an estate that had belonged to my great-grandfather. I always liked going there, and it is one of the places where I have done my best work. L'Enclos, built level with the earth and without any basement, like most Provençal houses in the country, was deliciously cool and fresh inside in summer if one was careful to keep all the doors and windows shut. There was a big garden, divided in two by a path lined with chestnut trees, and a terrace where my parents liked to sit in the shade of four huge plane trees. In certain years it became a rendezvous for sparrows; there they indulged in their mysterious games and made the air thrum with the flutter of their wings. Little paths fringed with spindle trees, laurel, Abraham's balm, Japanese medlar, and arbutus, wound in and out among these trees, and this was my chosen domain, where I would read and work under an arbor of honeysuckle, looking out over the kitchen-gardens and the vines that clambered over the trellis around the tennis court. A little row of quince trees and hazel, above which towered a tall cypress, a pine, and two cedars, ran alongside the Vauvenargues road as far as the little entrance to our grounds. Every day I used to perch in the topmost branch of one of the cedars and watch for the carriage in which my father would drive home to lunch. His punctuality was so proverbial that many people used to set their watches when they saw Monsieur Milhaud drive along the Cours Mirabeau. The garden at L'Enclos seemed huge to me, and this was not the only favorite corner of mine that it contained; there was a little paddock with a pretty fountain and all kinds of trees—magnolias, acacias, lime trees of the kind known as muscat, and a crape myrtle whose slightly draped foliage bowed beneath the weight of pink, almost purple flowers. As a precaution against drought, my grandfather had built an enormous ornamental pond quite out of proportion to the size of our garden, and there I loved to lie and watch the swallows lured by its waters, or to clamber up on its stone parapet to catch a glimpse of the surrounding countryside.

The meadow abutting on one of the boundary walls of L'Enclos was owned by the municipal authorities of Gardanne, whose townsfolk pastured their flocks there during the transhumance. At the beginning of summer all the inhabitants of the villages in the district sent their sheep to the mountains. In a noisy mass the flocks pushed along the road to the Alps, and the familiar sounds of L'Enclos were submerged in a flood of continuous baaing. At night the long, modulated notes of the nightingales filled me with anguish until they were resolved in a short, deliciously careless trill. A little later a regular full-throated chorus of frogs would strike up. Sometimes a sharp sound rather like a sudden click of shears rang through the night air. Was it an insect or a bird? I have never been able to find out. Even as I lay in bed I could see a tiny gray owl in one of the tall cedars, and hear its plaintive hoot. Dawn was an explosion of cockcrows mingled with the shrilling of the locusts and the sound of bells, for we were surrounded on all sides by convents.

I could hear the Angelus from the Convent of St. Thomas chiming out in triple time a major sixth that hung in the air nearly as long as the note whose harmonic it was. Far off, like an echo, the bells of the Cathedral Church of St. Saviour and of St. Mary Magdalen faintly answered; but how near the tocsin from the Mairie hammering out like a feverish pulse its warning note that announced a hillside afire or a house ablaze!

These were the sights and sounds which awaited me each year at L'Enclos.

One by one the carefree summers flowed peacefully by. When the weather was too hot, we would go off to the mountains for a few weeks. It was on coming back from one such stay that I first manifested signs of my musical vocation. Mother told me that she heard someone playing *"Funiculi, funicula"* on the old piano in the drawing-room. She thought it was my grandmother, who occasionally amused herself by picking out old tunes, but she could not understand where she had learned that particular melody, or why she was playing it so hesitantly. So she went into the drawing-room to clear up the mystery, and found me all alone, perched on a stool and absorbed in groping after the tune I had heard some little Italians singing under our window a few weeks before. When my father came home from the office, I played him "my tune," to which, to my delight, he immediately hummed an accompaniment. Thereafter he helped me to remember tags of melody I had heard, and encouraged me to play duets with him, which awakened my sense of rhythm. He was a born musician, endowed with a very sure musical instinct; he was the pillar of the Musical Society of Aix, and accompanied all its vocalists. My mother had a powerful contralto voice, and up to the time I was born had studied in Paris under Duprez, who taught her to interpret operatic arias. Thus music was already a familiar friend in our house.

Léo Bruguier, son of an old dancing teacher who accompanied his pupils on a *pochette* or pocket violin, was a delightful musician. A former pupil of Massart, and a laureate of the Conservatoire, he devoted his life to giving violin lessons in Aix, where with the help of his wife he organized chamber-music recitals. His marriage to one of his pupils, which had scandalized some of the inhabitants of Aix, led to a permanent breach with the Fabri family. Yet this marriage between "an artist" and "a young lady of society" was an extremely happy one, and for many years the Bruguiers were a living symbol of marital bliss. When it came to Bruguier's ears that Gabriel Milhaud's son was playing duets with his father although he was not yet four, he offered to give me lessons. My parents were willing, but so many doctors had recommended complete rest and tranquillity for me—one of them, the famous Dr. Grasset, had even specifically said: "No music!"—that they thought it wise to wait a few years.

I had started to learn the violin when I was seven. Bruguier's method might well serve as an example for all teachers. When teaching me the elementary principles of the instrument, he made me read and play easy little pieces. He had realized from the outset that he would get nothing out of me by forcing me to do exercises that were too dull. He wished to avoid rubbing me the wrong way and inspiring in me a dislike for the violin; he wanted to make a musician of me, not a virtuoso. Thanks to his teaching, I made rapid progress and could soon play sonatas with my father, and transcriptions of classical symphonies.

Until I went to the lycée at the age of ten, I had been having private lessons. Afterward Mother made me submit to a system of regular discipline, which turned me into a model pupil of the sort that wins all the prizes year after year. No sooner had I started school than she began to supervise my homework and see that I learned my lessons, which she read over to me next morning at breakfast. To avoid all danger of overstrain, she made me revise all my work long before the dates prescribed for writing essays. If I had a few pages of verbs to write out, she wrote them for me, imitating my handwriting. Thanks to her care, and to Bruguier's, I was able to go on with my studies and still put in a few hours' daily practice on my violin. Already I could play virtuoso pieces, but what I liked best of all was to play music with my father when he came home from the office. As he could read music with ease, he used to accompany me during my sight-reading lesson on Sundays. Every Thursday I went to Bruguier's on my own, and played to him in his drawing-room, littered with trinkets and rare violins. In the summer he would come to L'Enclos, for he owned a charming house near ours. He was one of the first in our part of the country to have an automobile, one of those vehicles standing as high as a wardrobe, and fiendishly difficult to start. After my lesson, we used to take leave of him before going home to lunch, and often we would find him on the pavement, brandishing a crank and cranking desperately.

In 1904, Bruguier asked me to take part in a string quartet, consisting of himself, Monsieur Pourcel, a professional cellist and teacher at the Conservatoire of Aix, and a local carpenter, Ségalas, who was an accomplished viola-player. As I had to go to school, he arranged the rehearsals for Wednesdays and Saturdays so as to give me a chance to recuperate by resting next morning. We played chiefly classical quartets, but my teacher also took an interest in contemporary works: he used to play Franck at a time when provincial opinion still found that composer's work "too noisy" and thought that "the angels in heaven ought to play more sweetly—and more quietly too!" In 1905 we studied Debussy's Quartet, which was such a revelation to me that I hastened to buy the score of *Pelléas*. Opportunities of hearing symphony concerts were few and far between. There were, of course, the concerts conducted by Gabriel Marie at Marseille, but my parents did not approve of my going on long journeys, and only took me when there was some good chamber recital, such as those given by the Cortot-Thibaud-Casals Trio, or else when a virtuoso was going to play one of the concertos I had been studying. I remember hearing in this way Pablo de Sarasate, that truly great violinist, give dazzling interpretations of a Saint-Saëns concerto and of a few of his own entertaining compositions; Eugène Ysaÿe, the prince of violinists, whose playing held both depth and sobriety; Jacques Thibaud, sensitive and elegant; Jan Kubelik, a brilliantly dexterous virtuoso. Music was becoming a more and more imperious necessity for me, as my parents now realized. They thought I might become a virtuoso, and though they would certainly have preferred me to go into my father's business, they put no obstacles in the way of my aspirations; throughout my childhood and thereafter they gave me support, both material and moral.

Some cousins of my father, Annette Naquet Laroque and Esther Bloch Laroque, often came to spend their holidays in Aix. At Passover they would come back to their house in the Cours Mirabeau. They loved to revisit the scenes of their youth, and their drawing-room was always full of people: their old friends and relations were always dropping in, to join in animated conversation only interrupted about four o'clock when a herd of goats would stop before the outer door. My cousins would buy a little milk and drink it with the addition of a few drops of black coffee. Gabrielle, Esther Bloch Laroque's daughter, had married the philosopher Xavier Léon, who edited the *Revue de Métaphysique et de Morale* and was writing a book on Fichte. Both of them loved music, and never failed to ask me to play. They insisted, as did Bruguier, that my parents should send me to the Conservatoire, saying that what I needed was to feel the spur of emulation. My parents agreed, but said that I should first take my baccalaureate. From that time on, however, they got into the way of taking short holidays in order to accompany me to Paris and give me the opportunity of having a few lessons with Alfred Brun, the teacher in the elementary classes at the Conservatoire. His severity made me all the more appreciative of my own teacher's gentleness and patience. I also studied under Firmin Touche during a brief stay with the Xavier Léons at Dieppe in the summer of 1905. This was the first time I had ever stayed at the seaside, and it filled me with delight, as did the lovely Normandy countryside, whose contours seemed so soft after the harsh outlines of our Provençal hills.

In spite of my tender years, I held very pronounced musical opinions. The Concerts Symphoniques of Dieppe, conducted by Monteux, filled me with enthusiasm, but I could not stand the blare of the Casino Orchestra. I also made my dear parents walk out of the concert hall at Dieppe in the middle of the first act of *Samson et Dalila*. They willingly fell in with my wishes, though they had been looking forward to this opera as a great treat.

A few days after we got back to Aix, I went through the bar mitzvah, or initiation into the Jewish religion. What a great day that was! I had been getting ready for it for the previous two years, and knew just enough Hebrew to say my prayers. I have always regretted not having learned to read Hebrew fluently. As my "godmother," my grandmother gave me the traditional watch, and though too weak to attend the religious ceremony, she was able to sit at her bedroom window and from there take part in the family party held in the grounds of L'Enclos. Three days later, like a lamp whose oil was used up, she passed peacefully away, without suffering.

In October, Bruguier advised me to start studying harmony. In the whole of Aix only Lieutenant Hambourg, the conductor of the band of the 61st Regiment, was qualified to teach me. He was a splendid teacher, but dreadfully impatient, and as I could not always understand Reber and

Dubois's excellent treatise on harmony, he often had occasion to be angry with me—so much so that Mother was afraid his irritation might upset me, and pulled frightful faces at me behind his back. This would set me off into fits of untimely laughter, which I had much ado to conceal. I finished the study of chords as best I could, and attempted a few exercises in writing on a bass or developing set themes, but these bored me more than anything I had ever had to do before. I had started composing, turning out with great facility rather clumsy works, one of which was a Sonata in E minor for piano and violin. I was quite unable to grasp the connection between the study of harmony and the music I wrote, for in the latter I made use of harmonic sequences absolutely different from those I was making such efforts to learn.

The Laroques and the Xavier Léons, who were staying in the vicinity of Aix for a few weeks that summer, would often send word to say they were coming to see us. At once we would send out for a goat and shut up our dogs, which always terrified the two elderly cousins. The Léons were very hospitable, and had many visitors from Paris, whom they would often bring along too. In this way, there stepped down one day from the carriage that drove smartly up, Chartier, better known as the philosopher Alain. He asked to hear my music, and I played him a few settings I had composed for poems by Heine. I had been learning a little German that summer, and had tried to set the original words to music. Alain seemed to like my songs, and all that afternoon kept humming the refrain: *"Röslein, Röslein rot, Röslein auf der Heiden."* Xavier Léon suggested that he should show my music to Rabaud, then conductor of the Opéra, whom he knew very well. Rabaud did exactly what I now do myself whenever young composers submit their works to me; while recognizing that I had talent, he advised me to begin by learning my trade, offering to follow my efforts with interest. This was no vain promise.

According to Bruguier, it was high time that I had a better violin. He let me have a divinely proportioned Ruggieri he had picked up in Florence: we called it "Florentin." The back of the instrument was remarkable for the sumptuous glitter of the varnish; it was not a very powerful instrument, but at least it had an exquisite fullness and sweetness of tone. When Bruguier brought me my violin, I was playing with a diabolo and at once put down my toy to try the instrument, but as soon as my teacher had gone, took it up again and threw it so clumsily that it fell on the violin. In despair, I screamed: *"Maman! Maman!* I've broken Florentin!" We rushed off to Bruguier, who said he thought the crack was harmless and advised us to have it repaired by the instrument-maker Deroux at Paris. My parents had just paid fifteen hundred francs for my violin, which might now have been damaged beyond repair, but they did not punish me, and once again showed only indulgence toward me. They were not weak, however, and while my father, whom I saw less often owing to his work, seldom scolded me, my mother was firm, even strict as far as work was concerned, and I owe to her all the habits of discipline which have stood me in good stead all my life.

Milhaud and his parents, L'Enclos, 1911

Léo Bruguier,
Milhaud's teacher from 1899 to 1909

Emil Hertzka,
Milhaud's publisher, Cannes, 1927

Raymond Deiss,
Milhaud's publisher,
and his canary

LÉO AND ARMAND

MY ADOLESCENCE was lit by the glow of two wonderful friendships.

Four generations of doctors had handed on a practice from father-in-law to son-in-law in our doctor's family. Dr. Latil, who had become a widower shortly after the birth of his sixth child, now lived with his sister, who devoted herself to bringing up her nephews in their splendid Louis XVI *hôtel* with its monumental doorway. Their profound religious faith enabled them to bear with equanimity the manifold blows of fate. Léo, the fourth son, attended the Catholic school and also studied music under Bruguier. We became firm friends. He worshipped music and admired my early efforts with passionate conviction; he made me share his admiration for Maurice de Guérin, and we loved to discover contemporary poets together. I think Léo would probably have become a country priest. The infinite tenderness in his gaze betrayed a tendency to melancholy and a tormented sense of anxiety. He kept a diary that was one long lamentation in which spiritual weariness and painfully intense religious feeling, dominated ever by a deep spirit of sacrifice and absolute resignation, were interwoven with a passionate love of nature, of flowers, and of the exquisite blue lines of the horizon at Aix. He was a dreamer, in love with solitary brooding, but he accepted my presence. We often went for walks together; he would always take the same direction, toward the Étang de Berre, west of the town, where the softly curving hills merge into the immensity of the plain, on the edge of which stood Cézanne's property, Jas de Bouffan, with its famous row of poplars gently suffused with the colors of the setting sun. We never wearied of walking along between the fields of wheat, blue-green in spring, bordered with almond trees in bloom, dwarf oaks, and pines, through exquisite landscapes, some of which, like the Château de l'Horloge, evoked historical memories: according to Chateaubriand, it was in this solid, roomy farmhouse that Napoleon spent the night on his return from Elba. Sometimes we went as far as Malvalat, the Latils' estate near Granettes, a village that took its name from the painter Granet, who lived there; one of his pictures, representing the death of his wife, hangs on a wall of its little chapel.

It was on the other side of Aix, toward the Mont Sainte-Victoire and the wild plateau of the Colline des Pauvres, made famous by Cézanne's paintings, that my other friend, Armand Lunel, loved to go. Like Léo, he had a passionate love for the countryside around Aix, the *muscade* country as he called it, in honor of its rare qualities. Fearless of the burning sun, we strode across the scorched, arid, wizened hills, a scene to which a touch of solemnity was added by two cypress trees; climbed rocks where the cicadas noisily shrill beneath the torrid pines; clambered up to the lofty eyries of the glorious villages looking down upon the valley of the Durance, that dried-up stream whose stony bed divides the Bouches-du-Rhône from the Basses-Alpes. I had long known Armand, but his extreme shyness had kept us apart. I was in the "*seconde*" [approximately the last year or two before college] when I heard that the age-limit for entry to the Conservatoire was eighteen. As it was wiser to take the examination a year in advance, I decided to get my *bachot* out of the way as soon as possible; during the long vacation of 1908 I worked at the syllabus, and took my Classics baccalaureate in October. That meant I now joined the Philosophy set, where I met Armand Lunel again, and he overcame his shyness and his love of solitude to befriend me. He wanted to be a writer; his brilliant brain and intellectual curiosity would not let him neglect the minutest detail of the subjects in which he was interested; he loved to browse in archives, and devoted hours to the study of all sorts of historical documents. We discovered Maeterlinck's plays, and his verse, the *Serres chaudes;* we loved the poet's rather morbid, dream-thralled imagination, and as I was still strongly under the influence of Debussy, and *Pelléas* was still the favorite nourishment for my spirit, it was under these signs that, while we were still at school, our collaboration began. Armand wrote vague, excessively lyrical, and slightly extravagant prose poems, which I endeavored to set to music. Whenever he came to see me, he would roar out his poems, while I thumped out on the piano sequences of chords I tried to make as wild as I could.

At night before I fell asleep I would shut my eyes and imagine I heard music so amazingly untrammeled I could never have transcribed it. How shall I put it? To me it was a tremendous mystery in which my soul delighted, as in a refuge wherein, deep down in the recesses of my subconscious mind, my musical language was slowly taking form.

As SOON as we had taken our Philosophy examination, Armand and I set out for Paris. M. and Mme Lunel and my parents tearfully accompanied us as far as the station at Marseille, whence an express train was about to carry us off toward our new destinies: Armand was to try to get into the École Normale Supérieure in order to win the material position that would enable him to become a writer, while I was to attempt the competitive examination for entry to the Conservatoire.

I went to live in a boarding-house run by a delightful family at No. 2 boulevard des Italiens. I have always loved movement, and noise has never disturbed me; indeed, quite the contrary; so it was a real joy for me to gaze down from my window at the crowded boulevard, the tangled mass of cabs, whose drivers wore shiny top-hats of waxed cloth, and the horse-drawn double-decker buses.

Bruguier had advised me to continue my violin studies with Berthelier, who, like himself, attached as much importance to an expressive and sober style as to technical dexterity. He was totally blind, and only the untiring devotion of his wife, who went with him everywhere, enabled him to go on teaching. She sat through all his classes and played the piano ac-

24

companiment to the concertos executed by his pupils. Her musical talent and rare kindness endeared her to us all.

Having been cut off from concerts all through my childhood, I now made up for lost time and became an assiduous concert-goer. I heard Beethoven's sonatas played by Ysaÿe and Pugno; Povla Frijsh interpreting with an ineffable lightness of touch the melodies of Schubert; Olénine d'Alheim, accompanied by Cortot, singing songs by Mussorgsky with her head thrown back in an impressively grandiose and austere style. This music moved me so deeply that I rushed off and bought the score of *Boris Godunov*. I also went to the concerts at the Salon d'Automne, at which Ravel's *Gaspard de la nuit* was given its first performance, and the concerts of the Schola Cantorum when new works by Déodat de Séverac, Vincent d'Indy, and Charles Bordes were given, usually interpreted by Blanche Selva.

As a protest against the ultraconservative policy of the Société Nationale, which had just turned down the *Poèmes hindous* by Maurice Delage, a disciple of Maurice Ravel, the latter founded, in association with Florent Schmitt, Charles Koechlin, Louis Aubert, Roger Ducasse, Inghelbrecht, and Léon Moreau, a new concert society, the S.M.I., under the presidency of Gabriel Fauré. Their programs consisted almost exclusively of first performances of works characteristic of trends in European music at that date. I was a regular listener. I had got into the habit of spending Sunday evenings with my cousins the Naquet Laroques, whose daughter Cécile was a very gifted musician. After dinner the cellist Félix Delgrange, my fellow student at the Conservatoire, and my cousin Eric Allatini, who played the viola and the violin as an amateur, would drop in for the evening and we would play together. I also tried to form a string quartet from among my fellow students in the violin classes;

25

but as they were more anxious to develop their techniques than to extend their musical culture, I had to approach the students in the harmony class, Louis Fourestier, Victor Larbey, and Sauveplane, in order to realize my project. We used to meet at my lodgings every Tuesday.

When it was announced that *The Ring* was to be given in its entirety at the Opéra under the direction of Weingartner, I took a subscriber's ticket for the whole cycle. On this occasion I, who always climbed up to the gallery, took an orchestra seat in order to enjoy the spectacle properly. I had already heard fragments of Wagner at Marseille; I was interested by his lyricism and his tumultuous orchestration, and his reputation as a revolutionary disturbed me and made me feel closer to him. I shall never forget those four performances: the audience rapt in the depths of the music, silent and attentive as if in church, suddenly bursting into wildly enthusiastic applause at the end of each act, and I myself bored to tears. Unable as I was to share in the general emotion, I felt lonely, as if abandoned by the wayside. My cousin Eric Allatini, a fervent Wagnerian, took me to hear *Tristan*; I never dared tell him how deadly boring I found that "sonorous love-philter." When the Bayreuth copyright expired and *Parsifal* was given at the Opéra, I went to hear it: this work, for which everyone had been impatiently waiting, sickened me by its pretentious vulgarity. I did not realize that what I felt was merely the reaction of a Latin mind, unable to swallow the philosophico-musical jargon and the shoddy mixture of harmony and mysticism in what was an essentially pompous art. I felt that even the leitmotivs were a childish device, like so many thematic Baedekers, flattering the audience's self-esteem by the feeling that they always "knew where they were." I also deplored the influence of this music on ours. Yet I was not so

26

foolish as to underestimate its importance, and when Wagner's operas were published by Durand at five francs a copy, I bought them all; I don't remember ever having been tempted to play them. But *Pelléas* and *Boris Godunov* always stood by my bedside.

When I first saw a performance of the Ballets Russes, which had just made its debut in Paris, I was carried away with enthusiasm. At one bound, Diaghilev suddenly took the position of innovator which was to be his until the end of his career; he was not content to put on classical ballets like *Les Sylphides* or the *Spectre de la Rose* to show off the exceptional talents of certain of his dancers, Nijinsky and Karsavina, or specifically Russian ballets such as the *Prince Igor Suite*, *Scheherazade*, or *Cleopatra*, which seemed so vivid, savage, and new to us; he also had the merit of discovering and revealing the work of the greatest musician of the century, Igor Stravinsky.

I lived very close to the Opéra-Comique, but I went there only when there was something good to see—in other words, very seldom. Once I had been invited to go to see *Werther*, and I had squirmed in my seat to the end of the performance, not daring to leave the theater for fear of offending my hosts. But when they played Bloch's *Macbeth* (libretto by Fleg), whose virile qualities I found particularly pleasing, I went to the six performances. I also attended the dress rehearsal of Ravel's *L'Heure espagnole*. I found the subtle elegance of this music seductive, but felt some regret at not finding the same depth of feeling in Ravel as in Debussy. From that time on, therefore, I was hostile to Ravel, and so I have remained, though I freely confess my attitude was not always justified.

Every Thursday I went to call on Armand Lunel at the Lycée Henri IV. He was doing his "*Rhétorique Supérieure*" under Alain. On Sundays he would come and spend part of the day with me at my pension on the boulevard des Italiens. He always arrived early. Sometimes he would amuse himself by writing a poem, which I would set to music, and which my landlady, Mme Montel, who had a charming voice, would sing at sight. Armand and I assiduously visited all the current exhibitions of paintings. At Bernheim's, Félix Fénéon, Mallarmé's friend, showed amateurs the latest canvases by Bonnard, Rousseau, Van Dongen, Signac, and others. One day we went to Vollard's, and he gave us a very cold reception until he realized we were from Aix; then he at once became very amiable and showed us all his Cézannes, which he kept upstairs. Most of them represented some scene closely associated with the memory of one of our walks.

Aix kept breaking through into our Parisian existence; my mother wrote me every day, relating all that was going on around her; Father wrote less often, more briefly but no less affectionately. Léo poured forth his soul in his letters as in his diary. He was studying for his *licences* in Letters and in Law, and was following with passionate interest the lectures by Blondel, who was crippled by neuritis and lectured at home, dominating his incessant pain in order to carry his pupils with him into the pure empyrean of metaphysical speculation. Ever a lover of solitude, Léo shunned the company of his fellow students, whom he nicknamed the Bandar-log after the name given by Kipling to the troops of monkeys in the *Jungle Book*.

Armand and I spent all our holidays in Aix, and I saw as much of Léo as I could. We had a friend, whom we visited often, in Céline Lagouarde, a photographer and most brilliant pianist. How many times did we play together Lekeu's sonata, which filled us with such enthusiasm in those days!

28

She had some acquaintance with Francis Jammes, of whom she had made superb portraits; she showed us some of his poems, which I set to music. During the summer, Léo and I loved to go to Les Saintes-Maries de la Mer, a little village in the Camargue, with low lime-washed cottages; it had a fine romanesque church, a fortified building erected by soldier monks, with the yellow stonework all crumbling away under the combined effect of the sun and the mistral. We loved to scramble up into the belfry and look out over the surrounding plain, with its spacious horizons where the mirage often made the eye confound solid land and marsh. We even spent one night there; dawn was so steeped in mystery that it seemed to be heralding the birth of creation. We took Armand up into our tower, but he was more active than we and had no desire to indulge in endless contemplation: he preferred to drag us off with a horse and buggy to Aigues-Mortes, a beautiful little town whose encircling walls gave it an austere grandeur. The road wound through marshes where only *enganes* and red behen and a few rare trees with gnarled trunks contrived to grow.

Every day during my stay in Aix I was composing. Not having enough experience yet to elaborate purely musical work, I sought inspiration in literary ideas. In this way I wrote *Pièces pour quatuor*, inspired by a passage from St. Thérèse; a quintet called *Le Pauvre Pêcheur*; a trio that bore an epigraph of two lines by Francis Jammes; a ballet based on *Les Malheurs de Sophie*; and an opera on a libretto by Eric Allatini, *Les Saintes-Maries de la mer*. The first two acts related the story of the village stranded between sky and sea, where Marthe, St. Marie-Jacobé, and St. Marie-Salomé, together with their servant Sarah, landed after crossing the sea in a frail bark. The two Maries became the patron saints of the village. Their relics are enshrined high up in a little chapel under the roof of the church. The gypsies adopted Sarah as their saint, though she was never canonized by the church. The third and last act of my opera evoked the holiday of May 25, when the gypsies of Catalonia, Piedmont, and Provence go on pilgrimage to Les Saintes-Maries. I have several times witnessed this festival, when the gypsies encumber the village and all the roads leading to it with their caravans; they spend the night in prayer before a casket containing the relics of Sarah in the crypt under the church, which was built on the site of an altar to the ancient pagan deity Mithras. On the following day, the Archbishop of Aix, who is also Bishop of Arles and Embrun, heads a procession bearing the shrines and statues of the saints to the sea; he blesses the sea, and the procession winds its way back to the church, chanting a very ancient canticle that is repeated over and over again. I used this melody in my score. I did the orchestration for the whole opera, which meant more than six hundred pages of music; but I burned them, together with all my youthful compositions, when, some time later, I started to compose music that, as my teacher Gédalge put it, was "neither literature nor painting." From this holocaust the only thing I rescued was the *Cantique de Camargue*, of which I was especially fond and which I used again in my *Poème* for piano and orchestra. I have not destroyed this piece, but it will never be published by me.

During the summer of 1911 I composed a Sonata for violin and piano, my first work worthy of being preserved. That same year I passed my violin examination, and then had to attend classes in chamber music and orchestral playing. In these I made the acquaintance of Yvonne Giraud, a charming and very gifted violinist who had a very extensive musical culture; like me, she dreaded the chamber-music classes, in which only works we already knew from A to Z were studied. We shared the same desk in the orchestral class; our teacher, Paul Dukas, was a bad conductor and incapable of directing a rehearsal. None of the students respected him, but Yvonne and I had such an admiration for his work that we overlooked his clumsiness. We were shocked by the behavior of the hooligans. Paul Dukas was much surprised when I asked him to autograph my copy of his *Ariane*; this is what he wrote: "To Darius Milhaud, with best wishes for his future, Paul Dukas, Paris, 1911." I always sent him copies of all my printed music, and he invariably took the trouble of answering by letter, with very apt criticism.

Ever since my arrival in Paris I had been assiduously attending Xavier Leroux's harmony classes; often his place was taken by Raymond Pech, a former winner of the Prix de Rome. In spite of the kindness of both my instructors, the subject bored me just as much as at Aix, and I made no progress. My classmates knew how to insert little harmonic refinements, six-four chords in the "appropriate places," but I was quite incapable of doing so. The themes to which I was required to supply a bass or a harmonic development often seemed deadly dull to me, and I thought the exercises themselves anti-musical. Yet I went on composing and was making some progress. I decided to ask Xavier Leroux to grant me an interview, to show him my sonata. I shall never forget the expression of consternation on his face: how could I, who was so weak in harmony, ever dream of composing? What on earth could such a poor harmonist produce? Xavier Leroux refused to see me, citing all his manifold activities and the rehearsals for his opera *Théodora*, in which his wife, Mme Héglon, was to create the principal role. A few days later I renewed my request, and he let me play my sonata after the end of a class. At the very first bars his face lighted up; then he started to sing and play the violin part at the top of the

31

keyboard. At the end of the first movement he said to me: "What are you doing here? You are trying to learn a conventional musical language when you already have one of your own. Leave the class! Resign!" This appeared to me to be such a drastic step that I asked Pech for his opinion. After seeing my music, he confirmed Leroux's words with even greater vehemence. Nevertheless, before resigning from the harmony class, I went to see Rabaud, who fully corroborated what both my teachers had said, and advised me to go to Gédalge. He gave me a letter of introduction, which I sent off at once. The reply was frightening: "Monsieur, I will expect you at noon on Thursday, to see what you know." I knew nothing.

On the Thursday, with a beating heart, and carrying a briefcase bulging with manuscripts under my arm, I went to see him. Wearing a beret, and with a napkin round his neck, he was eating a chop. "Play me something," said he, without interrupting his eating. I played the first movement of my sonata. "Why have you used D sharp seventeen times on the first page? You don't know how to construct a melody. What do you want to do, learn your trade or win prizes?" "To know my trade," said I without a moment's hesitation. "Right! Then I'll take you in my counterpoint class." Gédalge disapproved of the type of exercise adopted by the authorities at the Conservatoire: the development of a theme, a hybrid exercise that looked like a fugue and yet was not one, and had very little to do with counterpoint. This was Caussade's forte, and his mass-trained pupils carried off all the prizes. My work was now corrected by Gédalge's assistants, Eugène Cools and Alice Pelliot. I did my counterpoint and all the studies on Bach's chorales, exercises that combine counterpoint and harmony, and, once the pupil is able to produce extended chorales, carry over into the sphere of composition. I made friends with some charming young men attending Gédalge's classes: Jacques Ibert, Henri Cliquet, who set Laforgue's poems to music and could read anything we asked him to, Arthur Honegger, who came up from Le Havre three times a week to study the violin with Capet, and Jean Wiéner, whom I had met at Aix. Wiéner proposed that we take composition lessions with Gédalge; these were extraordinarily interesting. Then our master organized, for us and one or two classmates, an orchestration class, which he made enthrallingly interesting and for which he refused all payment on the grounds that he had enjoyed himself too much.

In December 1910 I received an enthusiastic letter from Léo concerning *La Brebis égarée*, a play by Francis Jammes that had just been published in the *Revue Hebdomadaire*; I got a copy, and immediately conceived the idea of turning it into an opera. I asked Céline Lagouarde to get Jammes's permission for me, and no sooner had it been granted than I set to work. A few months later, in Aix, Céline told us of the last time she had seen Jammes, and of how he had talked much of Claudel and of the latter's conversion. She showed us *La Connaissance de l'Est*, which Jammes had brought to the station for her when she left. Every poem in it was a veritable miniature drama, charged with lyrical emotion. I borrowed the book and started to write settings for one or two of the poems it contained; Claudel's prose-poetry added something strong and passionate to my nature.

As my musicianly talent developed, I found the study of the violin increasingly tedious; it was as if I was being robbed of time that otherwise I could have devoted to composition. I was awarded no prize at the *concours* of 1912, and the idea of spending a third year on the study of the violin now seemed unbearable. This worried my mother, for she loved

33

success and wanted me to begin by going through with whatever I had undertaken. I countered her arguments and, very tactfully but firmly, announced my intention of abandoning my career as a violinist in order to be a composer. My father, realizing that my choice was irrevocable, gave me complete freedom to do what I wished; my cousins, the Xavier Léons, with whom we were staying for a few days after that unfortunate contest, sided with me.

That year at L'Enclos I finished my first string quartet. When I played it over with the Bruguier Quartet, only my beloved teacher understood what I was trying to say. His wife could not help blurting out: "It sounds just like Arab music!" and Ségalas, the carpenter violinist, declared with his heavy Marseille accent: "Good God! This is hot stuff!"

5

THE VISIT TO FRANCIS JAMMES

I WANTED to show Jammes the first act of *La Brebis égarée*, which I had now completed; Léo also wanted to show him a poem he had written. We planned to go and see him together, and as Act II of my opera was laid in Burgos, we decided to visit Spain on our way, in order that I might steep myself in the atmosphere of that austere and passionate land before going on with my work.

We stopped first at Barcelona; we were enchanted by the tree-shaded walks of La Rambla, thronged day and night by noisy and excited crowds; the peacefulness of the neighboring quarters was all the more impressive by contrast. Within these peaceful precincts stands the Cathedral, familiarly set down among the old houses as if for their protection, and its cloister, in which we saw three geese under a catalpa tree. We saw a bull-fight at Saragossa; a grand sight, the crowd, clad only in the darkest colors, silently participating in the spectacle as in some ritual whose every move was known in advance. While Léo meditated in the Church of Our Lady of Pilar, I talked to a few old men sitting outside their doors. They told me that the siege of their city by Napoleon's troops had been related to them so often that they had conceived the liveliest dislike for the French. We were

35

disappointed by Madrid, which we christened "Old Ugly," but not by the pictures in the Prado, through which the soul of Spain was revealed to us. Léo and I were great admirers of Barrès, not only because of his lofty ideas but also because some of his books dealt with scenes we loved, La Camargue or Spain, so we were looking forward to visiting Toledo. We were not disappointed. On a moonlight night swept with great black clouds as in some engraving by Gustave Doré, we sped across the bridge over the Tagus in a coach driven by four mules, and so galloped into Toledo. Next morning at daybreak we were awakened by the sounds in the street—the hoofs of mules and donkeys laden with milk, vegetables, or earthenware pots, the queer guttural cries with which the peasants spoke to their animals. This visit was sheer delight for us; everywhere we found the living presence of El Greco, at the museum, in the church, or in the country on the other side of the Tagus, looking back at this matchless city clasped in the yellow meanderings of its river.

We traveled third-class, in the company of worthy, warm-hearted peasants who never failed to offer us some of their meal of *tortillas*, a kind of cold omelet. The cars were constantly surveyed by the eagle eye of one of the *carabineros*, who, with their rifles slung from their shoulders and wearing patent leather hats, were continually on the move from one compartment to another. It was stiflingly hot as we crossed the orange-tinted uplands of Aragon, absolutely devoid of vegetation. Dust penetrated thickly into the train. At Burgos we found the atmosphere we had come in search of, the very same as that described by Jammes in his second act. We also noticed immediately how his sharp eye had recorded the most insignificant details to transmute them into poetry. As I strolled along the Plaza del Espolón under the acacias, whose foliage was lit from below by electric bulbs, I was able to watch the crowd listening to the military band, see the little coffins for children hanging next to some dried cod at the grocer's, and gaze at the little chapel of the Carthusian monastery of Miraflores, where a monk was tending daisies that grew so thick it was as if he were walking on a sky full of stars.

Before going on to Orthez, we stopped off in the Basque country to see Céline Lagouarde, who was spending her holidays in Cambo with one of her friends, Mme Inchauspé, a young widow with two magnificent little girls, Mimi, a dark child whose hair was cut short in a Joan of Arc crop, and Chopé, who had long golden curls and an amazingly solemn expression in the depth of her dark-blue eyes. Léo loved children, and throughout a ride we took together in a landau, he held little Chopé on his knees, a huddled, silent figure utterly indifferent to the scenes through which we were passing: the quaint little Basque villages with their neat, clean cottages, and the ritual wall for the game of pelota on every village square. Twenty years later I found myself once more in Bayonne, and went on as far as Cambo to see Mme Inchauspé, but was unable to find her house again. I had heard that little Chopé had died a year or two before. I laid some flowers on her grave in memory of that lovely drive and in memory of Léo.

Finally we reached our destination: Orthez. We arrived late in the afternoon. It was market day; the peasants in their Béarn berets were driving homeward, sometimes with little calves in the back of their buggy, just as in dear Jammes's poems. How glad and proud we were to find a note from the poet awaiting us at the Belle Hôtesse hotel, inviting us to spend the evening with him! He lived in an old house set in the midst of a garden, and gave us a very warm welcome. He introduced us to his aged mother, who had china-blue eyes and a cracked singsong voice, and his wife, Ginette, who had the rather emphatic speaking tones of people from Picardy. She was a musician, and sang for us in a clear, unpretentious voice the melodies that Raymond Bonheur had composed for Jammes's early poems. I played the ones I had written for *La Connaissance de l'Est*. Jammes was surprised to hear I had tackled such a formidable task as to provide a setting for a text so rich in meaning, and asked me to tell him all about it. Then he asked Léo to read some of his verse. Léo sat down near an occasional table. Dimly in the lamplight we could discern on the walls local landscapes painted by Jammes's boyhood friend Lacoste, a Brazilian Morpho butterfly in a little glass case, and a small Louis XVI clock in the form of a black boy, a wedding present from Gide, on the mantelpiece. In his muted, melodious voice, whose charm was compact of both sensitivity and lassitude, Léo read his poem, which was an utterly faithful expression of his inner-most nature, with its two constant themes of tenderness and sadness. Jammes was deeply moved by this sweet lament, and promised Léo he would help to get it published in the *Cahiers de l'Amitié de France*, a little review of which we were all very fond and in which Jammes grouped round him a number of young Catholic writers, including Mauriac, Vallery-Radot, André Lafond, and Eusèbe de Brémond d'Ars. We had got into the way of referring to these young men as "the chicks," while we called those gravitating around Claudel, Gide, and Jammes "the union."

During the next few days we walked and rode. We went as far afield as Lagor and the banks of the torrent. Jammes explained to us the art of fishing, and made us marvel at his knowledge of botany. When we got back to the house, he would carry us off to his tiny study and read us his verse—those poems which had so profoundly influenced our youth—

in his resonant voice, with its strong Pyrenean accent rolling the final syllables over his tongue and drawing out the resonance of each individual word.

When Jammes asked to hear my music, I refused to play it on his piano, which was practically unusable; so he begged his aged Huguenot cousins, the Lajuzan ladies, to offer us their hospitality. They had an upright piano, also very old, but in better condition than his. They very graciously consented to receive us, and offered us warm tea and very dry *petits fours* in an 1830 drawing-room cluttered up with bookcases, little tables covered with English doilies with blue ribbons, curtains of heavy lace net, armchairs covered in Utrecht velvet, and the inevitable aspidistra. The piano, on which stood a bronze ornament and two Gallet vases, was covered in heavy draperies. With nineteen-year-old enthusiasm I played the whole of the first act of *La Brebis égarée* without stopping—it lasts one hour and twenty minutes! At the top of my voice I sang all the parts and thumped with all my might on the old ladies' piano. They, being unfamiliar with the kind of music a student at the Conservatoire might be expected to write, probably thought they were at the mercy of a lunatic. Jammes was not at all disappointed by this hurricane of sound, nor was his wife. I believe they grasped the general lines of my work, the lovely words of which had echoed so deeply in my young musician's soul.

Next day we set out for home. On our way to the station, Jammes bought us in the market a masterpiece of popular toy-making: dark-violet paper vases with handles of cardboard that could be folded at will. We also carried away with us copies of his poems and an autographed photograph each. On Léo's he had written: "To the friend of my friend Darius Milhaud," and on mine: "To the friend of my friend Léo Latil."

39

6

NO. 5 RUE GAILLARD

BEFORE LEAVING Paris in July 1912, I persuaded my parents to let me set up a little apartment of my own. We found an ideal spot, No. 5 rue Gaillard. Although it was right in the center of the city, not far from the Church of the Trinité, this street was purely provincial in character. Hardly a carriage passed along it; pigeons fluttered up and down, and there were even hens strutting around in it; electricity had not yet reached there. It was a charming little apartment. I had it papered green and put divans covered in green velvet in the drawing-room and dining-room for when my father and mother came to Paris. As for myself, I contented myself for the moment with a big iron bed and a kitchen table and chairs, for I meant to get rid of this makeshift furniture and gradually replace it by carefully chosen antiques. Armand Lunel and I were crazy about antiques; everywhere we went we gave free rein to our passion. Antique-hunting for us had a genuine poetic exaltation about it. At Aix not a day passed but found us waiting for some dealer to return from an expedition, and we ourselves visited private individuals in quest of some treasure. We used to buy Second Empire at a time when this was still looked down upon by amateurs, who thought Charles X and Louis-

40

Philippe too modern. In Paris every Sunday saw us at the Flea Market at Saint-Ouen. There we would have a lunch of mussels and chips; then we would pile up all our finds in a cab and take them to my place. In this way my little apartment was soon adorned with Directoire furniture and colored prints of the First Empire.

We also collected rare books, but I confined myself to Claudel, Jammes, and Gide, my three favorite authors. I sold all my Victor Hugos to buy Claudel's *Cinq Grandes Odes*, published at forty francs in a limited edition by the Bibliothèque de l'Occident. The bookshop called L'Art Indépendant still existed at that time at the rear of a courtyard in the rue Saint-Lazare, but the old bookseller was now only interested in theosophy. He had in his stock rare books that were fetching high prices in the trade, but he let me have them at the ordinary prices, and in this way I acquired *La Ville* and *Paludes*. I also got a second-hand copy of *Les Cahiers d'André Walter* with the following strange dedication: "To Rodolphe Darzens, Poet of intimate worship and gloomy piety."

This book, like *La Porte étroite*, influenced me profoundly. I set to music some of the extracts from Alissa's diary, letters and snatches of dialogue, and fashioned them into a sort of long intimate song-cycle. Armand, Yvonne, and I had adopted a "paludian" manner of speech; Gide entered into our everyday lives. Armand and I wrote "paludian" letters to each other, and Yvonne and I kept up a correspondence steeped in the character of Angèle. We also had a great admiration for Claudel, and in a fine frenzy Armand would declaim whole passages of him to me.

Armand was always lighthearted and at ease with me, but though he was not unhappy at the École Normale, his timidity gave him the reputation of being standoffish among his

41

comrades. The prospect of the annual ball filled him with dismay. "You can't even go to bed," he told me; "they use the dormitories as cloakrooms!" To avoid this dreaded function, he proposed that we should go off on various little expeditions. We went to Chartres, to Rouen, and in the third year even as far as Holland. We reached Amsterdam on a Saturday morning, and the lovely old city enchanted us. We had time to visit the harbor with its shop signs written in every language under the sun, including Chinese; the Jewish quarter near the station; the beautiful synagogue attended by the descendants of the old refugees from Spain and Portugal, belonging to the Sephardic sect; the canals with their dark waters. Next day we visited the museums of Harlem—only the later Franz Hals found favor in our sight—and in the evening caught the train at The Hague just in time to get back to our work. Armand wrote a short account of our little journey and called it *La Géographie des Pays-Bas.* In it his compact style and personality were expressed more fully than ever before.

During my stay at Orthez, Jammes had pressed me to go to see his old friend Lacoste and he had written to him to say that I would call. He looked rather like Jammes himself; he had a long beard and lively eyes, but his smile was much gentler. He showed me his pictures with great affability and kindness. They nearly all depicted the scene from the windows of his apartment; the Lycée Pasteur and the boulevard Pasteur in the snow, or steeped in summer sunlight, or toned down by the golden leaves of autumn. Yet through all his paintings one could sense the longing for the light of his native Béarn. His wife, Jeanne, was a charming person; we soon became friends. She was a great reader, and introduced me to Saint-Léger Léger's [St.-J. Perse's] *Éloges* and Valéry's *Soirée avec Monsieur Teste*, both of which she loved. She was an excellent musician, a professional even, and often sang my songs, accompanied by one of her friends, a composer and a pupil of Gabriel Fauré. She introduced me to this friend, Jeanne Herscher, who immediately invited me to her house in Passy. She lived on the top floor of a new building erected by her architect husband, which contained a very large concert hall. On my way there I often visited the cemetery of Passy to pause a moment before the curious grave of Marie Bashkirtsev, "Our Lady of the Sleeping-car," as Barrès called her. Léo had sent me her *Journal*. I always gazed in astonishment at this "ever unsatisfied girl's" tomb, in which her whole studio had been faithfully reproduced down to the pouf cushions, hanging draperies, writing-desk, and even her easel.

On his own suggestion, Jammes had written to Claudel about me. I received a letter from Frankfurt am Main, where he was consul, to say he would be coming to see me soon. This was a bombshell. At the idea that the writer I revered more than any other was coming to see me, I was beside myself with excitement. Perhaps I was unconsciously aware that this meeting would decide what my life's work was going to be! I knew very little about him, except from Jammes, who had said he was high-strung, as restless as a force of nature, wore a Chinese robe with a consul-general's hat, hated the scent of vanilla, and was always prepared to pack up for some post in far-distant lands. "He's like a ship with steam up," concluded Jammes.

Between Claudel and me, understanding was immediate, mutual confidence absolute. We did not waste a single moment! I sang *Les Poèmes de la Connaissance de l'Est*, for which I had endeavored to find music as virile as I could make it. "How manly that is!" he cried, and at once started to speak of the translation of the *Oresteia* which he had begun in China

43

to assist Rosario's widow in her tragic loneliness: she had contracted leprosy, and he procured a printing-press for her. He had entrusted to her the limited edition of his *Agamemnon*: that was the reason why the first edition appeared in Fuchow. He talked of *Les Choëphores*, on which he was then engaged and concerning which he held very decided opinions about the kind of musical accompaniment required. He described scenes to me in which the text became so intensely lyrical that it called for musical expression; others in which only words could convey the fierce exaltation of the characters. I found his notions perfectly clear, and wholly consonant with what I wanted to do myself. What a happy day that was! It marked the first step not only in a faithful collaboration, but in a precious friendship too.

CHAPTER 7

THE UNION

DURING THE winter of 1913 Jammes came to spend a few days in Paris. He never liked to stay for long, despite the efforts of his friends to induce him to remain and the many receptions held in his honor. He was so kind as to get me an invitation to most of them; there was an air of a family party about them all, for whether at Mme Ernest Chausson's or Mme Alphonse Daudet's, or in the house of any other of Jammes's friends, it was always the same faces one saw, all eager to see him again. During these receptions Jammes would read his own poems, and Mme Lacoste sang some of my songs while I accompanied them. Jammes used to stay with the Arthur Fontaines, and it was there that I met one of their old friends, Saint-Léger Léger, known by his pseudonym, St.-J. Perse. While he was still at a boarding-school in the southwest of France, Jammes often invited him to spend the holidays at his home in Orthez. It was not only their poetic gifts that they had in common, for Jammes's ancestors too had inhabited the West Indies, as the Creole echoes so frequently heard in his verse attest. That same week Léo's poem appeared in the *Cahiers de l'Amitié de France*. I wrote to him at once: "Now you are one of the chicks!" to which he replied: "You are getting into the 'Union'!"

Céline Lagouarde was exhibiting some photographs at the Cercle de la Photographie, rue Volney; she took advantage of the opportunity this offered to come to Paris. She was slightly acquainted with Ravel, and took me to see him. The great kindness he showed me throughout his life was made manifest at that very first meeting; no sooner had he heard my violin sonata than he suggested I should submit it to the S.M.I. Léon Moreau, whom I met at dinner at my cousins' the Bloch Laroques, told me the news that my work had been accepted, and that all I had to do now was to choose two performers. After dinner he took me to his publisher, Costallat's, where Jane Bathori was rehearsing his new opera *Myrialde*, of which she was to give the first performance in the provinces. I had admired her a few weeks previously singing *Les Chansons de Bilitis* to her own accompaniment at the piano. I was unaware, however, that she was capable of reading any manuscript at sight, and when at her request I showed her my music, I committed the *faux pas* of singing it myself. She did not bear any malice, and when I met her again a few years later she said to me: "I'm sure you must have improved, come and see me!" This time *she* sang; ever after that, she was for me an exceptionally good interpreter and friend.

I don't think that Gide liked *Alissa* (the suite I had based on his *La Porte étroite*) very much. After hearing it, he said to me in his singsong voice: "Thank you for making me feel my prose was so beautiful." The appreciation was for his prose, not my music. Eighteen years later, in 1931, I rewrote *Alissa* completely. I was very much attached to my old style, though I had now left it far behind. The first version lasted more than an hour, so I cut it down by half; I rewrote

46

the music without altering the prosody, merely making the vocal line more melodic; I only varied the harmonies to avoid certain sequences that had dated overmuch, and emphasized the lines of the piano part by the addition of a little more counterpoint. It was of this version of *Alissa* that Bathori so often gave a characteristically sensitive and intelligent rendering. Indeed, for twenty years she was its sole interpreter.

I asked Yvonne Giraud and Georgette Guller to play my sonata at the S.M.I. Mme Berthelier had recommended Georgette to me. She was one of Philipp's pupils and had a depth of tone and brilliance of execution that occasionally reached the sublime. My two interpreters would come to my apartment for rehearsals, and then we would go on to a concert together. Before escorting them back to their pension in the avenue de Villiers, we would go for a ride in a cab in the Bois de Boulogne. They liked these little excursions so much that they invited some of their fellow boarders to accompany us. As the rules in their pension were very strict and the girls were not allowed out alone with young men, I used to hide at the back of the cab when I brought them home. The cab would only drive off after I had heard them call to me as they passed the concierge's lodge: "Good night, madame, and thank you."

A few months after the performance of my sonata, I received a special delivery from the selection committee of the S.M.I. to say that, owing to a cancellation, my First Quartet would be given on the next program. I played in it, with Robert Soëtens, Robert Siohan, and Félix Delgrange. After the concert, at the Salle Pleyel, while I was putting my instrument away and gazing at the old programs adorning the walls of the foyer, bearing witness to so many glorious performances and famous visits—one of them even referred

to a concert given by Chopin and Mendelssohn—I was jerked
out of my reverie by a gentleman with a white mustache and
goatee who said to me: "I am Jacques Durand, I should like
to publish your quartet. Come to see me tomorrow." Next
day I signed my first contract.

My cousins the Xavier Léons entertained philosophers
twice a month—all the philosophers in Paris, and foreign
visitors too. I tried to persuade Armand Lunel to come along,
but without much success, so great was his dislike of anything
remotely resembling a social function, though he was very
fond of Xavier and Gabrielle, more for their love of antiques,
for the possession of which they had competed with Armand
during their stays in Aix, than for the *Revue de Métaphysique
et de Morale*. It was at their place that I met Jacques-Émile
Blanche. He had a very keen taste for music, and often
played pianoforte duets with his sisters-in-law Yoyo and
Catherine Lemoine. He asked me to play my works at his
house for Princesse Edmond de Polignac. I brought along
Yvonne for the sonata. The Princess turned the pages. From
that time on, she often invited me to the musical evenings she
gave at her house. I was very fond of Jacques-Emile Blanche
and his wife, Rose. I liked his studio because "everybody that
was somebody" had had his or her portrait done there.
You saw Barrès and Debussy next to Bergson or Nijinsky:
no sooner had anyone made a name for himself in Paris than
Blanche got to know him and painted his portrait. He had an
amazing memory and could relate the most wonderfully
scathing anecdotes. His intellectual curiosity was aroused by
all the latest developments in music, painting, and literature,
and his powers of understanding were usually most acute.

That winter there was a revival of *Pelléas*; I went to nearly
all the performances; I also heard Debussy's *Rondes de
printemps* conducted by the composer himself at one of the

concerts organized by Durand to introduce some of the orchestral works published by him. I witnessed a very interesting dance recital given by a Russian dancer, Trouhanova, at which Florent Schmitt conducted *La Tragédie de Salomé*, Vincent d'Indy *Istar*, Paul Dukas the first performance of *La Péri*, and Ravel *Valses nobles et sentimentales*, under the title, for choreographic purposes, of *Adélaïde, ou le Langage des fleurs*. Louis Aubert had played these same waltzes a week or two before under very curious circumstances: the selection committee of the S.M.I. had decided to mystify the audience by not giving any composer's names on the program. Everyone was handed a program and a pencil and was asked to identify the composer of each piece. What a dangerous game! The results were unbelievable. Some of Ravel's friends and admirers, who were really very familiar with his music, did not recognize his style and mercilessly ridiculed *Valses nobles et sentimentales*. During one of Léo's flying visits to Paris, we went to see a performance of Wilde's *Salomé*; the décors by Bakst, and the unusual interpretation and strange accents of De Max and Ida Rubinstein, made it a most vivid spectacle and were perfectly suited to Wilde's prose and his æsthetic ideas.

A few days later I read in the *Figaro* that Lugné-Poë had announced a performance of *La Brebis égarée* with my music. Indignantly I rushed off to demand an explanation of him. Jammes had spoken of my music to him, and he had thought I would extract from it some incidental music and interludes for his performance of the play. I objected vehemently. The idea of chopping up my music into separate pieces seemed a betrayal of all it meant to me. Moreover, even if I had been willing to accept such a proposal, I should have demanded a full orchestra. This incident tickled Jammes, who said to one of his friends: "What could you expect Milhaud to do? He

wanted an orchestra, and Lugné offered him a fife and drum!"
On the other hand, I had produced a *Suite symphonique*
from my opera and had orchestrated it in class. It consisted
of an overture, the former overture of *La Brebis*, which I had
suppressed and replaced by a prelude, a slow movement
based on the somber themes of Act II; and a finale made up
of rapid extracts from the scene in which Paul evokes the
memories of his schooldays.

The pianist Robert Schmitz, with the help of his wife, who
handled all the business arrangements, had formed a chorus
and orchestra for presenting contemporary works, which he
performed with great enthusiasm. He provided me with the
opportunity of hearing my music when he conducted this
symphonic suite. I had no unpleasant surprise, but was reassured at the very first rehearsal: my orchestra sounded
exactly as I had wanted it to sound. *Les Évocations* by
Roussel was included in the same program, and I was able
to see for myself the modesty and youthful spirit of that
composer. I was enchanted by his work, which tended to
move away from the impressionism that, ever since Debussy,
had led French music into a veritable impasse. What interested me most at this time was the music of Magnard,
which seemed to me to have harsh and rustic qualities, a
sort of harmonic sobriety, providing an antidote against
these impressionistic tendencies. At the Opéra-Comique I
had heard *Bérénice*, which in spite of its lack of refinement
in the instrumentation, or perhaps for that very reason, I
had found impressive. I loved the deep feeling in the music,
and those long expressive melodies which Magnard gives
to the piccolo. Nevertheless, I failed to understand why
he had written in the preface to *Bérénice* that, while not having the genius required for a dramatic style properly so
called, he had adopted the Wagnerian leitmotiv. Magnard

seemed to me to be such worlds apart from Wagner! I also liked his four symphonies because of their straightforward character; their forthright scherzos are genuine French homespun. The character of the man himself pleased me, for he was independent enough to dispense with a publisher, having his works produced by an incorporated guild of printers.

It was at this period that I got to know Georges Auric, whom I met sometimes in the corridors of the Conservatoire. He made me marvel at the extent of his culture and his extraordinarily penetrating intelligence and uninhibited ease of composition. Whenever he came to see me, he would pull out of his briefcase manuscripts in which freshness and precocity were combined with a voluntary maturity already firmly under control, without, however, impairing the free play of a sensibility that was both carefree and humorous. These are the qualities that have gone to the making of his personality, in which tenderness unites with the scathing lucidity that characterizes the brilliant and straightforward works he has continued to produce. About 1910 or 1911 we would often be joined by Honegger when Auric was playing *Chandelles romaines* or *Gaspard et Zoë* on the piano at the rue Gaillard.

Honegger and I had started studying fugue in Widor's composition class. That charming teacher, a most brilliant conversationalist, would utter cries of alarm at every dissonance he came across in my works; as he listened he would exclaim: "The worst of it is that you get used to them!" How far away seemed the justifiably severe criticisms that Gédalge used to make! When the latter heard that I had passed in fugue, he ironically asked me how I had managed it. Wiéner and I were still taking private lessons with him, and I brought him my *Poème* for piano and orchestra (based on the theme of the canticle of La Camargue), which I had just completed. No sooner had he run through it than he sat down and wrote two letters that he asked me to post; one was to Gabriel Pierné, suggesting that he should conduct my work, and the other to Lazare Lévy, asking him to play it. This instance will serve to illustrate my master's outstanding generosity and devotion. Gabriel Pierné and Lazare Lévy both consented, and my *Poème* was given in 1915 at the Concerts Colonne-Lamoureux.

I saw Claudel again during the rehearsals for *L'Otage* which was being produced by Lugné-Poë at the Théâtre de l'Œuvre. He enthusiastically described to me the experimental work being done at the theater of Hellerau and persuaded me to go there in September for the performances of *L'Annonce faite à Marie*. He also talked of a satirical drama on which he was working and for which he would require a musical score: "But you are too serious-minded," he said to me, suddenly taking his leave.

Milhaud orchestrating
Les Choëphores, *1916*

Milhaud and Jean Cocteau,
London, *1921*

ARNOLD'S AMERICAN NOVELTY JAZZ BAND

L'Homme et son désir (*décor by Audrey Parr*), *Ballets Suédois, Paris, 1921*

Le Boeuf sur le toit (*décor by Raoul Dufy*), *Paris, 1920*

8

HELLERAU

I FOLLOWED Claudel's advice and went to Hellerau. I proceeded by easy stages. At Geneva I called on Ernest Bloch, who played me his *Poèmes juifs*, which have a powerful Biblical sweep about them. Jammes had written: "I have told Henri Duparc you will call on him. Do try to do so." He was moving the very day on which I was passing through Montreux, but he was kind enough to invite me to have tea with him in a little pastry-shop. He introduced me to Ernest Ansermet, then a young conductor who had just given up his post as a teacher of mathematics in order to devote himself wholly to music.

I made a brief halt at Munich, with its parks and green lawns, and blue-painted streetcars. I had always been impressed by what Barrès had to say about Venice during its decadence, and about Tiepolo in particular, but I had never had the opportunity of seeing several of his paintings at once. As I strolled through the streets of Munich, I came across, in one particular gallery, a retrospective exhibition of his works which thrilled me. On the other hand I could not stomach the paintings of Böcklin, who represented modern German art at that time, and had no inkling that they would have such influence on the young painters of 1930. I loathed

53

Nuremberg, which reminded me too much of pasteboard stage sets for *Die Meistersinger*. Hellerau was six miles from Dresden. To get there you traveled in a streetcar across a great plain dotted with a few clumps of pines, a sandy plain where tiny little wild pansies grew.

It was quite an ordinary village, only important for its experimental theater, which also provided a center for the activities of Jaques-Dalcroze. The theater had been built by Wolf Dohrn, an architect of Polish origin; the highly stylized scenery consisted of huge architectural cubes covered in blue cloth which could be built up in steps and arranged in tiers of varying height, so that performances could proceed on several planes at once. Strips of blue cloth hung from the ceiling, which, according to whether they were placed nearer together or farther apart, represented trees, houses, a wall, and so on. The lighting came from perpendicular rows of lamps on either side of the stage, which threw the light so that it appeared to come from the actual substance of the walls of the theater. In the hall the walls consisted of a series of screens that could be opened or closed at will, altering the acoustics according to their position. Salzman, a Russian producer, operated all the complicated permutations of the switchboard controlling the lighting. His wife was a dancer and had studied with certain religious sects in Afghanistan and in this way had learned to develop amazing hypnotic powers of endurance.

Claudel had always advocated vertical scenery, on the grounds that when you read a book you held it vertically in front of you, not horizontally. Thus the æsthetics of the theater of Hellerau exactly corresponded with his ideas. Later on I realized that in spite of the interest of such experiments, they led to a dryness and monotony of theatrical presentation that threw open the door to the most dubious form of expressionism. Some scenes in *L'Annonce* took place on two planes at once: the human and the divine. When Violaine broke off her engagement, she was playing on the upper plane, whereas her mother was seated down below in front of the fire, which was suggested by a reddish glow through a pile of blue cubes. When Violaine ascended to heaven at the end of the play, her brilliantly lit silhouette stood out against a great shining cross behind the draperies representing the firmament. Light played a very important part at Hellerau, and conferred a wonderful sense of mystery on the performances.

Claudel enjoyed considerable prestige in Germany. His works were displayed in the Hellerau bookshop, some of them translated into German. The King of Saxony attended the performance of his play, as well as many of the Czech friends whom he had made in Prague. After the play we lingered for a long time in conversation under an arbor of flowers. The writer Miloz Marten, who inspired the Czechoslovakia that was to be and was killed in 1918 fighting for the freedom of his country, was there, together with Zdenka Braunerova, Elémir Bourges's sister-in-law, who was also an ardent patriot. She was godmother to little Reine Claudel, who had been born in Prague. She used to draw, and had done a lot of vignettes for the colophons of Claudel's books.

First of all they had put me up in a vegetarian pension for girls which Claudel called "the gazelles' enclosure," but my youthful appetite was too keen for me to be satisfied with a diet consisting of nuts and raw tomatoes washed down with tea, and I took a room in a baker's where the fare was more substantial. I divided my time between work and rehearsals. I had started to write my music for *Agamemnon*, and I worked at it lying in the fields. Claudel had clearly indicated where he wanted my music to intervene in the play. He had

55

observed that in Æschylus's style, especially in certain choruses or dialogues, there were sudden transitions to a lyrical utterance of such a pitch that it absolutely demanded the support of choir and orchestra. He would not have any music until Clytemnestra came out of the palace with her bloodstained ax in her hand and encountered the Chorus of Old Men. It was from their violent altercation that the music sprang. I tried to avoid the usual type of incidental music, a form of expression I detested at that time. There is nothing more false than the intrusion of a musical phrase while the actors go on speaking their lines without a pause, for melody and speech exist on absolutely incompatible planes. To bring out this excess of lyrical content, what is wanted is a transition from speech to song. In my score the strophes sung by Clytemnestra (dramatic soprano) alternated with the antistrophes sung by the Chorus of Old Men (male choir) against the background of a normal symphony orchestra. I wrote variations on a fixed theme, which recurred unchanged at the heart of each new strophe, in the same key as at the beginning, and as a fanfare for the entry of Ægisthus after he has been proclaimed king. When he imposed silence on the crowd, the music came to an end, and the actors spoke their lines to the end of the play.

Æschylus wrote a satirical drama of which only the title has been preserved; Claudel had brooded over the syllables of this title, and so had come to write *Protée*, a work in which the most truculent fooling is mingled with the most exquisite poetry. He gave it to me to read before I left Hellerau, and I was able to tell him that, though he thought I was too "serious-minded," this mixture of buffoonery and real emotion raised problems that I found enthrallingly interesting.

56

I STARTED to write my music for Claudel's *Protée* in a delightful house owned by the Xavier Léons in Seine-et-Marne; it had formerly belonged to Madame Sans-Gêne. I had a very pleasant room, and I loved to contemplate the landscape spread out before my eyes: lawns and woodlands and the green flowers of two enormous American tulip trees.

Claudel always worked amid a positive whirl of plans, most of which came to nothing or else turned out quite differently from what had been intended; this was the reason why I came to compose three different versions of *Protée*. The first called for very little music: a little *a cappella* choir to suggest the different levels of sound produced by the bleating of a flock of sheep; a fanfare for unaccompanied brass to illustrate the feeding of the seals; a *pianissimo* nocturne to be played during the nocturnal bacchanalia (for the latter I used a piece I had written for piano and violin: *Le Printemps*, which I now scored for string quartet and oboe); and a finale *A la gloire du vin de Bourgogne* for male choir and full orchestra.

In 1916 Gémier planned to give some performances of *Protée* in a circus and asked me to prepare a version for an orchestra of about fifteen, which would play above the

57

theater like a circus band. Gémier was obliged to abandon his project. Then in 1919 Gheusi tried to put on a very luxurious production of *Protée* at the Théâtre du Vaudeville, with scenery by José María Sert. He asked me to expand my music and score it for full orchestra. Under these new circumstances I composed overtures to each act, a prelude and fugue to precede the meal of the seals, and a finale for Act I designed to accompany a film depicting the successive metamorphoses of Proteus. I rescored the parts already written. Gheusi's theatrical ventures were short-lived, however, and came to an end just when rehearsals were due to begin.

Wearied by all these changes, I made another *Suite symphonique* out of my *Protée* music. It is in this form that the work is now given in concerts and has been recorded.

In the absence of professional performances, *Protée* was staged by students on various occasions. It was played in Dutch at an important ceremony at the University of Groningen. Claudel and I were invited to attend, but he was at his post in Washington, and I suggested that his son Pierre should accompany me in his place. We were received at the station of Groningen by student representatives clad in their traditional university gowns. They escorted our four-horse carriage to the theater. The performance was a lighthearted and impromptu affair. In Geneva, as the students had only a limited number of instrumentalists at their disposal, I asked Jean Binet, an excellent musician from the French-speaking part of Switzerland, to adapt my music to their requirements. Finally, in Paris, the play was presented by the students of the Sorbonne with scenery by Jean Effel and—a piano.

The society of La Libre Esthétique, whose president was Octave Maus, organized many outstanding artistic events in Brussels. It was responsible for the first exhibition of impressionistic painting in Belgium; Gide lectured there on

"Criticism" and on "Literary Influence"; Vincent d'Indy, Chausson, and Magnard conducted concerts there. In 1914, for the first time, La Libre Esthétique engaged a musician belonging to my generation; they asked me to play my First Sonata with Georgette Guller. I was immediately struck with the hospitality of the Belgians and with their respect for music. I stayed with a painter, Anna Bock. It was at this time that I completed my Sonata for piano and two violins, my earliest chamber-music work that I did not later repudiate. Other older compositions, such as my Piano Suite, though published, no longer satisfy me, and I do not like them to be played.

Jeanne Herscher was a great friend of the composer Charles Koechlin. I often met him at her house. I loved his music, his harmonic experiments, and the marvelous range of his mind. On his way to the Var, he stopped for a few days at Aix. He was traveling with some hives of bees that he intended for his estate and had registered them with the luggage, which terrified the porters, especially when he had to change trains. He arrived at L'Enclos swathed in a great shepherd's cloak, with half a watermelon under his arm. We talked together about music, discussing *Le Sacre du printemps*, which we had hailed with such enthusiasm at its first performance a year before. We not only admired its violent rhythms, its harmonic discords and polytonality, all of which had been foreshadowed in *Petrouchka*, but, on quite a different plane, the novelty of the work. In it the ballet was getting away from picturesque externals toward a dramatic and barbaric goal. Many musicians were quite unable to accept this rift with the past. Despite his admiration for Stravinsky, Debussy was anxious about the way in which he was developing. Schmitt declared that "all that was left to him was to tear up his music." (What a pity he did not do so!) The

59

younger generation, on the contrary, felt encouraged by this work, in spite of its profoundly Russian character, which kept it alien to our own aspirations.

Georgette Guller followed Koechlin at L'Enclos. Every day we went for long walks together. We would often be joined by Léo, who spent most of his evenings at L'Enclos. He would read his poems, while Georgette would play Chopin, whom she interpreted marvelously; I would sing the settings I had just written for Léo's latest poems: *La Tourterelle, Ma Douleur et sa compagne;* then we would go and sit by the pool, with its myriad reflections of stars on nights when there was no moon, and listen in silence to the frantic warbling of the nightingales.

In July, Léo asked me to go with him to see Jammes. A day or two later I left him at Orthez so that he and Jammes might attend the Eucharistic Congress at Lourdes, where the Papal Legate was to say the Pontifical Mass, and I went back to Aix to complete the second act of *La Brebis égarée* and write the third. I felt somehow that I ought to hurry. I wrote the last scene at one sitting and finished it on July 28. Unfortunately my presentiment had been only too justified: on August 2, 1914, a gendarme came to stick the white mobilization poster on the walls of L'Enclos. It meant war! Caught in the Landes, where he had gone with Jammes and his wife, Léo hurriedly returned, traveling by troop trains. On the way he lost his luggage, containing the latest volume of his diary; the efforts he and Jammes made to recover it were in vain.

This was the first omen of grief to come, as was the sound of the tocsin at the Mairie, incessantly hammering out the announcement of war. I shall never forget its hurried tolling, mingling with the shrill notes of the cicadas.

10

THE WAR

WHEN THE German thrust toward Paris had reached its farthest point, just before the Battle of the Marne, many of my friends and relatives came and took refuge in Aix. Among them were my Aunt Lily and her two children, Étienne and Madeleine. Two of their neighbors in the country, Jeanne Thomassin and her mother, had come to join them. Jeanne was a former actress who had played with great success in the early plays of Tristan Bernard, and had made several tours in Russia, where she had distinguished herself. This gay, amusing, affected, emphatic woman, who was never seen without her mother or her dog, a horrible little pug, improvised a theatrical atmosphere around her wherever she went. She was an excellent teacher, and had taken an interest in my cousin Madeleine, who had been studying with her to be an actress ever since the age of six. Madeleine was also very gifted musically, and we played together all the music that came to hand, from Beethoven to *Le Sacre du printemps*. Although she was only twelve, Madeleine maintained a prodigious activity: she did all the housework for her mother, including the cooking if the need arose; she used to bring me delicious caramels cooked over a candle-flame; the remainder of her time was spent on her bicycle in the company of her brother, who worshipped her. These two children had such a profound understanding of each other that I always felt they were leagued together against all the rest of the family. Whenever I used to go to see them at Vaucresson before the war, their whispers and conspiratorial airs ceased only when the whole family set out for the inevitable traditional walk to "see the view" from the Bois de Villepreux, where they went to admire the sunset— *en famille* and in silence.

While I waited to receive notice calling me up, I remained in Aix and resumed work. I orchestrated *La Brebis égarée* and started on my Second String Quartet. Léo was stationed at Briançon in the Chasseurs Alpins. He looked on the war as a mission, a solution to his personal problems, and got himself sent to the front as soon as he could. Gradually the first bad news filtered through to us: Albéric Magnard shot by the Germans and his house burned down; my cousin Daniel Palm killed before Lunéville—his parents were notified the very day their youngest daughter, Suzanne, was repatriated from Germany, where she had been spending her vacation perfecting her German. When Étienne was called up with the 1915 class, Madeleine and I went with him in the streetcar as far as Pont de l'Arc, the first stop after Aix. We came back on foot along the little river, dark with shadows and lined with richly hued trees. It was the first autumn I had spent in Aix since 1908.

I was rejected for military service on medical grounds, and went back to Paris in December. Apart from Henri Cliquet, who was in the auxiliary services acting as gardener at the Hospital of Versailles, and Honegger, who had been mobilized for only a few weeks in Switzerland, all my friends from the Conservatoire were at the front. Every year the Conservatoire awarded the Lepaulle Prize for composition.

I won it with my Sonata for two violins and piano. That is
the only time in my life I have ever won an award. On my
way to the Conservatoire I would stop every day at the
window of my cousin Madeleine's room, to chat with her
for a moment—she and her mother were temporarily lodged
in a ground-floor apartment almost opposite my place. I
also got into the habit of going across to keep her company
during air raids by zeppelins.

As I wanted to engage in some form of war work, I
joined the Foyer Franco-Belge. This organization, whose
headquarters were at the Galerie Druet in the rue Royale,
was partly supported by funds collected in America by Mrs.
Edith Wharton. Its aims were to assist refugees by giving
them money and work. Gide played an active part in it and
put me in the section run by Charles Du Bos. Charlie was so
overworked that he rarely left his office before midnight;
he conducted every investigation like a psychological in-
quiry, hoping in this way to ensure the fairest possible
distribution of the funds. Some of the poor refugees had
difficulty in adjusting themselves to the idea of their mis-
fortune: "Ah, monsieur," one of them said to Gide, "we
were so proud at Waterloo!" I often went home on foot with
Charlie, and we engaged in endless conversations. He asked
me to organize a series of concerts to raise funds for the
good work. I leaped at the opportunity. Jeanne Herscher
lent us her music-room, and with the assistance of many
artists I gave a number of Foyer Franco-Belge concerts.
Gide called at my house several times, and I persuaded him
to read me his notes on Chopin, which were still unpublished
at that time. I was highly impressed by them; few men have
felt so clearly as he that Chopin was first and foremost a
tender and sensitive musician, and not the forlorn and morbid
romantic he was so often made out to be. Gide discerned the

63

authentic purity and nobility of Chopin's music and realized that the unfortunate reputation of *morbidezza* under which he labored was owing to performers who took liberties with tempos and rubatos, thus absurdly exaggerating the musical expression instead of strictly observing the time indicated. I told Gide of my intention to write a cantata on *Le Retour de l'enfant prodigue*, using only the passages of dialogue, and he gave me his permission.

Cipa Godebski, the brother of Misia Edwards, who worked at the Foyer, invited me to go and see him. He and his wife, Ida, were at home regularly on Sunday evenings. Ravel often went there. Viñes used to play Spanish music and works by Debussy. You might also meet there Satie, whose music was still somewhat unfamiliar to me; Gallimard, closely attended by some of his contributors to the *Nouvelle Revue Française*; and Fargue, who would turn up just when everyone else was going. The Engel Bathoris also entertained a few friends on Sundays for musical evenings, and I deserted the Godebskis to join them. What unforgettable times we spent together! Old Engel sang *L'Horizon chimérique*, we read through Ravel's choral music and all the latest published scores. In this way I came to play Debussy's Sonata for viola, flute, and harp, with Manouvrier and Jeanne Dalliez. When Durand heard about this, he asked us to give the first performance at his house. During one of the rehearsals he sent me to Debussy's house to ask for advice on one or two points. This was the first and only opportunity I ever had of meeting him. With what emotion I entered the room where the musician worked who held such an important place in my heart! He was already afflicted by the disease that was to carry him off; his face was deathly pale and his hands affected by a slight tremor. He sat down at the piano and played me his sonata twice. Through excessive modesty and discretion, though I had already written *Les Choëphores*, I made no mention of my own compositions.

During the summer of 1915 I took a short leave to go to see my parents. On my way back I broke the journey to call on Claudel's father-in-law, the architect of the church of Fourvière at Lyon, M. de Sainte-Marie-Perrin, with whom Claudel was staying for a few days before going back to his post of commercial attaché to the Embassy in Rome. All Mme Claudel's numerous family loved to congregate in that great château at Hostel en Valromay in the Ain. There were lots of children; in the evenings their cries gave place to the low-pitched murmur of the parents' conversation, which came to me along the terrace like a muted echo of the noises of the afternoon. Before going back to Paris I called on Jeanne Herscher, who owned an old priory near Vézelay. There I found Mme Claudel's brother and his wife, the daughter of René Bazin. Mme Sainte-Marie-Perrin was a poetess and writer who had written a very remarkable study of Claudel in which she showed proof of a profound understanding of his work. She translated some of Tagore's poems for me to put to music. Delightful as it would have been to linger there in the vicinity of Givry with its lovely dark streams, and the pink Burgundian roads, and the fascinating evenings when poetry was followed by music, I had to get back to Paris and work.

I had undertaken a thoroughgoing study of the problem of polytonality. I had noted—and interpreted as a sign for myself—that a little duet of Bach written in canon at the fifth really gave one the impression of two separate keys succeeding one another, and then becoming superimposed and contrasted, though of course the harmonic texture remained tonal. The contemporary composers, Stravinsky or Koechlin, made use of chords containing several tonalities, often handled contrapuntally or used as a pedal point. I set to work to examine every possible combination of two keys superimposed and to study the chords thus produced. I also studied the effect of inverting them. I tried every imaginable permutation by varying the mode of the tonalities making up these chords. Then I did the same thing for three keys. What I could not understand was why, though the harmony books dealt with chords and their inversions and the laws governing their sequences, the same thing could not be done for poly-tonality. I grew familiar with some of these chords. They satisfied my ear more than the normal ones, for a polytonal chord is more subtly sweet and more violently potent. I built up the music for *Les Choëphores* on the basis of my re-search, and added to my manuscript the subtitle: "Harmonic Variations." For each strophe and antistrophe, indeed, I established in most cases a definite line of harmonic research, applying to sequences of chords the technique used for varia-tions. The essential part of the music, however, remained the general melodic line. Even when I studied chords contain-ing twelve notes, I used them only to sustain a diatonic melody, remembering Gédalge's advice: "Just write eight bars that can be sung without accompaniment."

The score of *Les Choëphores* was constructed in the follow-ing way: a Funereal Vociferation for choir and orchestra to accompany the entry of the Choephori bearing libations to Agamemnon's tomb; a chorus *a cappella* entitled "Libation," my first attempt to write a chorus in two simultaneous keys, with the lines of chords in the male voices set over against the women's voices, and with both forming a background for a soprano solo; an "Incantation" sung by Electra (soprano), Orestes (baritone), and chorus before Agamemnon's tomb; and then "Presages" and "Exhortations," two scenes so vio-lent in character that they created a problem that I solved by having the words spoken in time with the music by one woman narrator, while the choruses uttered words or disjointed phrases, the rhythm but not the pitch of which was indicated. To support all these various speech elements I used percussion instruments having no definite pitch—quite ordinary instruments listed in all the treatises on orchestration. Finally, I ended with a "Hymn to Justice" for choir and orchestra, and a spoken "Conclusion" for voices and percussion.

On September 27, 1915, as I was going across the Place de Villiers, I felt an exceedingly acute physical pang, which lasted several seconds. I immediately thought of Léo and feared that some disaster had befallen him. Later I was to learn that I had felt this pain at the very moment of his death. It was at the height of an offensive in Champagne; he had been wounded, but though no longer able to handle a rifle, he refused to be evacuated, so that he might take part in the attack with his comrades. He was mown down by the German machine guns at the head of his company while encouraging his men. His family sent me a copy of his will; he had left me his diary. He had deposited it, together with my letters, in an old wooden chest, an eighteenth-century sailor's trunk; I added the letters I had received from him. Subsequently Dr. Latil had a selection of his letters and extracts from his diary published by Plon. This supreme testimony of his pure Christian faith and spirit of self-sacrifice was singled out for mention by Barrès on account of the nobility of its thought. While I was in Brazil I had a hundred copies of Léo's poems privately printed. A few months after his death, I wrote my Third String Quartet, dedicated to his memory. This consists of two very slow movements, in the second of which I introduced a soprano voice singing a page from Léo's diary, ending: "What is this longing for death, and which death does it mean?" This sentence had haunted my imagination ever since I had read it. I have refused to publish this quartet so long as I am alive, but the firm of Durand is under contract to publish it within six months after my death.

I left the Foyer Franco-Belge to work at the Maison de la Presse, which grouped together the propaganda services directed by Philippe Berthelot, and therefore came under the Ministry of Foreign Affairs. I was sworn into the army, and attached to the army photographic service. I made friends with a number of young diplomatists. We used to meet occasionally at a restaurant in the Place Gaillon. We had delightful meals, enlivened by the spicy anecdotes of Paul Morand and René Chalupt, the musician poet, and by Saint-Léger Léger's tales of the West Indies, to all of which Henri Hoppenot and I listened in silence. I had just finished my *Poèmes juifs*, settings for some anonymous poems I had come across in a review, and I was seriously thinking of composing music for the *Eumenides* in Claudel's translation. I mentioned it to him one day when I met him at the Maison de la Presse. He complained of having too much to do at Rome; he needed a secretary, and proposed that I should get Berthelot to send me there on detachment. Before this scheme could materialize, however, he was appointed Minister to Brazil. He renewed his request, and the idea of going with him so far away, joined to the great longing for solitude I had had since Léo's death, made me decide to accept.

At the end of December my parents and my friend Yvonne Giraud accompanied the great man and his "secretary" to the Gare d'Orsay.

CHAPTER

11

BRAZIL

I SHALL never forget the effect that the sight of neutral Spain produced on me. What a startling contrast to France, where in the streets you now met only aged civilians and old horses rejected for military service, spavined old hacks formerly used for farmwork. No sooner had you crossed the frontier at Irun than you saw crowds of young men and mettlesome horses, and, apart from those of the customs officers and gendarmes, not a single uniform. Portugal, on the other hand, had begun to feel the effects of war, and the convoy escorting our English steamer, the *Amazon*, out of territorial waters was conveying the first Portuguese military contingents to France.

The crossing took eighteen days. At night, on the completely blacked-out upper deck, I felt caught midway between the starry firmament and the sea. From that vantage point I witnessed the transition from northern to southern skies at the equator: the Great Bear still glittered on the horizon as the Southern Cross, closely attended by the twinkling glow of the two stars in the constellation of the Centaur, rose to meet it.

We reached Rio on February 1, 1917, a blazing hot day like midsummer. Claudel found quarters for me with him at the French Legation, magnificently situated in the Rua Pay-sandú, a street bordered with royal palms from the isle of Réunion, sometimes more than two hundred feet in height and crowned with swaying fronds over twenty feet long. Throughout these two years Claudel's activity was a constant source of marvel to me: he would get up at six in the morning and go to Mass; then he would work until ten a.m. After that he devoted his time entirely to his diplomatic duties until five p.m., when he would go off by himself for a walk. I would sometimes see him striding along the sea-front, nervously rubbing his hands together and so absorbed in his thoughts that he failed to see me. I would never accost him. Sometimes he took me with him for his walk along the shore, but it was usually on Sundays that we went out together. As soon as dinner was over, he would retire to his own room and go to bed early. His thoughts were always centered on the Bible. Every day he would write commentaries on verses from both Testaments. He let me read some of them, impressively lofty in their inspiration. At that time he was much preoccupied with the topic of water, which looms so large in mystical thought, and he would choose verses from Genesis naming water in all its manifold forms: sea, lake, cloud, rain, spring, river, moisture, dew, mist, well—and write commentaries on them. Claudel the Minister was no less amazing than Claudel the writer: he had a very catholic conception of his diplomatic function, and took a passionate interest in all economic and financial problems, for which he invariably found some ingenious solution. He only entrusted copying or code work to his secretaries, personally drafting all telegrams and dispatches.

Rio had a potent charm. It is difficult to describe that lovely bay, ringed with fantastically shaped mountains covered with a light shading of forest or crowned with solitary red-brown pinnacles of rock, sometimes topped with lines of palm trees that stand out like ostrich feathers in the murky light of the tropics against a sky shrouded in pearly gray cloud. I would often stroll in the center of the city where—a refreshing contrast with the broad Avenida Rio Branco—the cool, shady streets were too narrow for wheeled traffic. In the most colorful of them all, the Rua Ouvidor, antique-shops crowded with furniture from the Imperial period stood next to displays of luscious fruit, where I tasted delicious *refrescos* of mango or coconut. Not far away, on the hill, the little Gloria church, eighteenth-century baroque in style, like most of the ecclesiastical architecture in Brazil, displayed its colors of pink, blue, and tender green, and its *azulejos*, among which were to be seen magnificent examples of wood carving. I would also sometimes go to Copocabana beach, facing the Atlantic. Along it stood a few houses, including one delightfully amusing one by the architect Virzi. In the evenings I often walked around the Tijuca. I loved to see the panorama of Rio gradually spread out before me, with the bay clearly outlined in glittering lights; or else I would take a boat to the other side of the bay, near Nichteroy, and lie on the deserted beach for a part of the night, with the moonlight so bright that I could easily read.

The Botanical Gardens of Rio are most impressive; on either side of a long central path lined with gigantic royal palms, various kinds of exotic trees—mangoes, giant bamboos, bread trees, cacao trees—and different types of coffee plants, sugar cane, and tea grew in rich profusion. This array of foods and beverages stood next to lyre-shaped latanias known as traveler's-trees because the petioles secrete a refreshing liquid. In a pond fringed with trees no less picturesque, water-lilies floated on their enormous leaves, and towering above all else rose extraordinary banyan trees with roots springing halfway up the trunks, as if carrying them on their shoulders. What hours I spent in this garden of wonders! But the lure of the forest was greater yet. It began even inside the city, for so luxuriant was the vegetation that it invaded the least patch of unoccupied land. Any site that was not built over fell victim immediately to an invading horde of plants, and the roads on the outskirts of Rio passed through enchanted forests. Claudel and I often took the Corcovado funicular as far as Paineras, where we followed a little track along a rivulet from whose banks we looked down on the mountainside drowned in a torrent of dense vegetation in which glittered the shiny, silvery leaves of the bilo-bilo. No sooner had the sun set than, as if operated by an invisible switch, all kinds of crickets, cooper-toads, which imitate the sound of a hammer banging on a plank of wood, and birds with dull, sharp, or staccato cries peopled the forest night with their different noises, which sometimes rose swiftly to a pitch of paroxysm.

In order to recruit our strength after the dank heat of Rio, we would sometimes go and spend the week-end in the mountains at Terezópolis. The inn there was run by a Frenchman called Norbert. We could do some riding there, but what we liked best was to go on foot into the heart of the forest, accompanied by two Negroes who hacked a way for us through the tangle of trees, giant ferns, and intertwining lianas. They would also keep up a great fire for us all through the night. We slept under a vault of foliage from which occasionally long trailing clusters of orchids hung down amid the lianas. The contrast was equally striking between the inhabitants of the city and of the forest, for in Rio, on the very fringe of the forest, lived descendants of the Nordic races who had gradually reverted to savagery and now inhabited miserable huts, surrounded by a horde of half-naked children and having a wretched field of maize or one or two banana trees for sole possessions.

A month or two after our arrival in Rio, Henri Hoppenot was appointed secretary to the Legation. Overjoyed, I went to the boat to meet him and his wife, Hélène. Already I felt how much their presence was going to mean to me. Henri Hoppenot was a young writer and a great admirer of Claudel. What a curious Legation that was, with two writers and a musician! During our long walks together, we got to know one another better, and our friendship deepened. We would carry our friends off for the week-end to Terezópolis or Petrópolis; the latter was the summer residence for diplomats, members of the Government, or wealthy *cariocas* —inhabitants of Rio—and was too artificial for our liking, but we were drawn thither by Audrey Parr, a delightful friend of dazzling beauty and irrepressible high spirits. She was the wife of the secretary to the British Legation, and had got to know Claudel in Rome. As she could draw, he used to get her to do sketches for all the illustrations that thronged his ever fertile imagination.

My first contact with Brazilian folklore was very sudden. I arrived in Rio right in the middle of the Carnival, and immediately sensed the mood of crazy gaiety that possessed the whole town. The Carnival in Rio is an important event, whose coming is most laboriously prepared in advance. Several months beforehand the newspapers carry announcements of the formation of Carnival clubs, together with the name of their presidents, secretaries, and members. These little groups meet daily in preparation for the festivities, and often spend large sums, occasionally all their savings, on fancy dress adorned with elaborate decorations of ostrich feathers. Six weeks before the Carnival is due to begin, groups of *cordões* perambulate the streets on Saturdays and

Sunday evenings, select a little square, and dance to the music of the *violaõ* (a kind of guitar) and a few percussion instruments like the *choucalha* (a kind of round copper container filled with iron filings and terminating in a rod to which a rotatory motion is given, thus producing a continuous rhythmical sound). One of the dancers' favorite amusements is to improvise words to a tune repeated over and over again. The singer has to keep on finding new words, and as soon as his imagination begins to flag, someone else takes his place. The monotony of this never ending chorus and its insistent rhythm end by producing a sort of hypnosis to which the dancers fall victim. I remember seeing a Negro completely carried away by the music, dancing frenziedly all by himself, holding in his hand a huge sherbet, which he would lick with his pink tongue in time with the music.

The crowds in the ballrooms were much more elegant. The Carnival-organizers decree one single shade for the ladies dresses; they must wear a different one every night. They go to the ball in all their finery, leaning on their husbands' arms. As most of the Negro dancers are servants, they borrow their masters' clothes and even sometimes their names and titles. One evening I heard "the President of the Senate" and "the British Ambassador" announced, and saw two Negro couples, dressed up to the nines, proudly come forward. For six weeks the whole populace is passionately given over to dancing and singing. There is always one song that wins more favor than the others, and thereby becomes the "Carnival song." Thus "*Pelo Telefono*," the Carnival song for 1917, was to be heard wherever one went, ground out by little orchestras in front of the cinemas in the Avenida, played by military bands and municipal orchestras, churned out by pianolas and phonographs, whistled and sung after a fashion in every house—and it haunted us all winter.

I was fascinated by the rhythms of this popular music. There was an imperceptible pause in the syncopation, a careless catch in the breath, a slight hiatus that I found very difficult to grasp. So I bought a lot of maxixes and tangos and tried to play them with their syncopated rhythms, which run from one hand to the other. At last my efforts were rewarded and I could both play and analyze this typically Brazilian subtlety. One of the best composers of this kind of music, Ernesto Nazareth, used to play the piano at the door of a cinema in the Avenida Rio Branco. His elusive, mournful, liquid way of playing also gave me deeper insight into the Brazilian soul.

Before I left Paris I had met André Messager, back from Brazil, who had recommended that I get to know the music of Glauco Velasquez. When I had done so, I was struck by its resemblance, both structurally and in inspiration, to that of Guillaume Lekeu. An uncanny likeness, as both composers died at the age of twenty-six! One Sunday a young pianist named Luciano Gallet took me to see an aged relative of Velasquez who lived on the enchanting island of Paquetá. Her delightful, rather tumbledown old house, surrounded by overgrown gardens, dated from the colonial period. I was shown the rough draft of a Trio by Velasquez, which I found to be complete. I edited it, and had it played at one of my lectures at the Lycée Français. The director of the Conservatoire, Henrique Oswald, often invited me to dine with him of a Sunday. He was married to a vivacious and witty Florentine lady who, with her children, kept up a constant flow of high spirits all the evening. At their house I met the conductor of the Symphony Orchestra of Rio, Francesco Braga, who had been taught by Massenet in Paris, as well as a young newly wedded couple of musicians, the Oswald Guerras. Oswald composed music steeped in the French

75

tradition, while his wife Nininha, who also composed, was above all an excellent pianist. Her father, Leão Velloso, a piano teacher, had encouraged her to play a great deal of contemporary music. He instilled a taste for it in all those around him—his daughter, his pupils, and even his dog, who answered to the name of Satie. I became friendly with the Vellosos and often went to see them. They introduced me to the music of Satie, which was imperfectly known to me at that time, and I ran over it with Nininha, who was extremely good at reading any contemporary music.

Every mail brought me piles of letters from my mother and my faithful friends. Bathori would keep me up to date with musical life in Paris. As soon as I received a copy of *En Blanc et Noir*, which had just been published by Durand, Leão Velloso and his daughter played it. I had organized concerts in aid of our war charities, and the Vellosos' unwearying devotion enabled me to give several recitals of chamber music in which I included the sonatas of Magnard and Debussy and my Second Sonata for piano and violin, which I had just completed.

In the course of a lecture tour that I undertook on behalf of the Red Cross and Prisoners of War Comforts Fund, I visited the state of Minas Gerais, which is rich in gold and diamond mines. Our train was boarded at Belo Horizonte by a very strange individual wearing a great cloak and a pistol belt, and with a wide-brimmed hat pulled down over his eyes. In the baggage car he registered eighty-eight pounds of rough diamonds. The gold mine of San Juan del Rey, considered at that time the deepest mine in the world, was run by Englishmen. It was situated near the pleasant little town of Ouro Preto, and when you saw the latter spread out over several hilltops and crowned with a picturesque church, it was difficult to imagine the infernal underground workings so near at hand. I visited the mine, going down 5,000 feet in the cage and another 6,000 feet in a kind of basket. Down below, there was an old mule that had not seen the light of day for many a year, tirelessly hauling trucks piled high with broken stone, which half-naked Negroes streaming with sweat hacked from the living rock. The whole scene had the grandiose beauty of an ancient bas-relief.

As soon as I arrived in Rio, I started work on *Les Euménides*. In the *Choëphores* I had used chords superimposed in masses; the nature of the musical thought in *Les Euménides* led me to adopt the same device. When I wrote the *Récit de la Pythie* for narrator and a few percussion instruments, I mentioned it to Ansermet, who at the time was conducting the rehearsals of the Ballets Russes, and he suggested he should get together the players required for this scene and have them play my music at the end of a rehearsal, in order to give me an opportunity of hearing what it sounded like. I gladly accepted. I have seldom been surprised by the sound of my orchestrations, but this time the performance surpassed my hopes; this resonance expressed for me an authentic intensity of dramatic feeling such as I had imagined. I composed and completed *L'Enfant prodigue*. I chose an orchestra of twenty-one players to accompany the voices of the singers (piccolo, flute, oboe, English horn, clarinet, bass clarinet, bassoon, horn, trumpet, trombone, timpani, harp, and percussion, and two quartets of strings placed one on either side of the conductor). What I wanted was to eliminate all nonessential links and to provide each instrument with an independent melodic line or tonality. In this case, polytonality is no longer a matter of chords, but of the encounter of lines. Owing to the intricate mingling of the instrumental parts, I could make only an arrangement for two pianos, which I hastened to play with Nininha. In composing this music, I

77

had recaptured the sounds I had dreamed of as a child when I closed my eyes for sleep and seemed to hear music I thought I should never be able to express. I was attracted by the unusual quality of small groups of instruments, and embarked on a series of *Petites Symphonies* for seven or eight different instruments. I was most eager to hear the effect of these experiments in tonal independence: Braga conducted the *Première Symphonie* at one of his concerts. The audience did not seem to object to the sound of my music, but ignorant or forgetful of the fact that in the days of Monteverdi the word "symphony" was sometimes used to denote a single page of instrumental music, it expected to hear a huge work played by a huge orchestra and was shocked by the brevity of my piece.

Various troupes succeeded one another in Rio that winter: Régina Badet and André Brûlé came, and Caruso sang at the Opera. There were also several concerts. Artur Rubinstein's recitals were a veritable triumph. At one of them, just when Artur was about to play the first measures of one of his pieces, an enthusiastic Negro rose to his feet in the upper gallery and made a seemingly interminable speech, at the conclusion of which he threw the pianist, who was amused and remained motionless, an enormous bouquet, which missed its target and fell in the orchestra pit. Rubinstein often visited the Legation. What grand times we had! Hardly had he finished telling, or rather miming, one of his stories when he sat down at the piano and played us his whole repertoire, as well as transcriptions of orchestral works. He played in the most masterly fashion the subtlest of scores, such as *L'Après-midi d'un faune* or *Le Sacre du printemps*, of which he managed to express the soul. Rubinstein was one of the first to make known in Europe and the United

States the music of Villa-Lobos, the composer who is now so famous, but who in those days was compelled to play the cello in a movie house to keep body and soul together.

Diaghilev's Ballets Russes also gave a series of performances in Rio that winter. The troupe came to spend the evening at the Legation. We were eager to hear the details of Cocteau's ballet *Parade*, for which Satie had written the music and which had just been given its first performance in Paris. Ansermet described to us the scenery and costumes by Picasso, and the accessories with which Satie had augmented the orchestra, such as a typewriter, a roulette wheel, and a siren. Dressed in their working-clothes, the dancers Chabelska, Idzikowski and Woizikowski now reproduced Massine's choreography in the tropics, and though it had scandalized the Parisian public, it delighted the French Minister and his friends, perched on piles of woolens in the grand ballroom of the Legation, which had been transformed since the beginning of the war into a sewing-room for war charities.

Nijinsky and his wife also came to see us. How handsome he looked, glancing up over his shoulder to talk to someone standing behind his chair! His head turned, but the head only, and with such a swift and precise movement that it was as if not a single muscle had moved. Claudel was so impressed by his dancing that he immediately conceived the subject of a ballet for him. In order to explain it to him more clearly, he took him off into the forest. Nijinsky liked the project, but his health prevented him from carrying it out. We did not know then how ill he really was, so hagridden with anxiety that he had surrounded himself with detectives. Shortly after our meeting, his reason gave way altogether. Nevertheless Claudel and I continued work on our projected ballet. This is

79

the subject of *L'Homme et son désir* as described by Claudel in the program note he wrote for its performance:

This little plastic drama was born of the Brazilian forest, in which we lived submerged, as it were, and which has almost the uniform consistency of one of the elements. How unearthly the moment when the night begins to be peopled with movements, strange cries, and furtive glimmers of light! It is precisely one such night that our Poem is intended to portray. We have not attempted to reproduce with photographic exactitude the impenetrable tangle of the *floresta*. We have simply draped it like a carpet of blue, purple, and green around a central pattern of sable over the four tiers of our stage. The latter is conceived vertically, held perpendicularly to the beholder's eye like a picture or book. If you like, it also resembles a page of music, on which every action is noted on its own particular staff. Along the topmost crest move the Hours, all in black, with golden head-dresses. Below them the Moon, escorted across the sky by a cloud, just like a great lady preceded by her serv-ant. Underneath, in the waters of the vast primeval swamp, the reflected images of the Moon and her serv-ant follow the regular progress of the heavenly pair. The action proper takes place on the intermediary plat-form between the sky and the waters below. And the principal character is Man, over whom the primitive forces have resumed their sway, and who has been robbed by Night and Sleep, of Name and Countenance. He enters, led by two identical veiled shapes, who spin him around like a child that is caught in the game of hide-and-seek and make him lose his way. One is Image and the other Desire, one Memory and the other Illusion.

Both sport with him for a moment and then vanish.

He remains standing, with arms outstretched; he sleeps in the blaze of the tropical moon like a drowned man in the depths of the waters. And all the beasts, all the sounds of the everlasting forest come to gaze at him, filling his ears with their music: the Bells and the Panpipes, the Strings and the Cymbals.

Man begins to stir in his dreaming. Now he begins to move and to dance. And his dance is the eternal dance of Desire, Longing, and Exile, the dance of captives and abandoned lovers, the same that sets those who are tortured by insomnia feverishly pacing their veranda all night long or makes animals in captivity hurl themselves again and again against the unyielding bars. Now it is a hand from behind him that pulls him back, now a perfume that saps all his strength away. Then the theme of his obsession becomes ever more frantic and violent, and one of the women returns and revolves around him as if fascinated. Is it a living woman, or a dead one? The sleeper snatches the corner of her veil as she turns and spins around him, unwinding herself until he himself is wrapped up like a chrysalis and she is almost naked. Then, joined to him still by one last strip of cloth, tenuous as the fabric of our dreaming, the woman covers his face with her hand and both move off toward the side of the stage. Of the Moon and her Follower only one last faint reflection remains below.

The Dark Hours have now passed by, and the first Daylight Hours begin to appear.

During the week-ends at Petrópolis, Audrey Parr and Cacique—the nickname she gave to Claudel—prepared the sketches of the scenery. He would suggest all the colors of the vast carpet that was to cover the four tiers and link them together by draping their walls; the appearance of the characters, which Audrey would cut out of cardboard and paint at once; and the dimensions of the steps on which the musicians were to stand. I was enchanted by this last notion. Already I could visualize several independent groups: on the third tier, to one side a vocal quartet, and on the other, oboe, trumpet, harp, and doublebass. On the second tier, on either side, the percussion. On one side of the first tier, the piccolo, the flute, the clarinet, and the bass clarinet; on the other, a string quartet. I wanted to preserve absolute independence, melodic, tonal, and rhythmic, for each of these groups. I realized my desire, and in order to facilitate the execution of my score, written for some instruments in common time, for others in triple time, and for others in six-eight, and so on, I inserted an arbitrary bar-line every four beats, adding accents to preserve the authentic rhythm. The percussion faithfully evoked for me the nocturnal sounds of the forest; I used it unaccompanied, though discreetly and never for more than thirty measures at a stretch, in the scene in which the elements tempt Man as he sleeps. The complexity of the score made a piano version practically impossible, but Nininha did not despair and finally managed to produce a version for piano duet; the individual notes were blurred, but it was possible to follow the thread of the music. She also made the piano-duet arrangement of my Fourth String Quartet, composed in Brazil, and my Fifth, composed later in Paris.

On the invasion of Belgium on August 2, 1914, Brazil was the only neutral to protest to Germany. Thereafter Senator Ruy Barbosa pleaded the cause of the Allies. He used to win the attention of crowds by his very lengthy speeches, given in a scarcely audible voice. After a number of diplomatic incidents, Brazil declared war on Germany.

Claudel undertook two journeys to study the various projects in which French interests were involved, and I went with him. We went to Santos on a French warship, the *Marseillaise*, which was then on an official visit to Rio. We went on to São Paulo, the coffee kingdom, by the new highway, whose bends and twists revealed landscapes of grandiose and impressive beauty. We passed through the states of Paraná and Santa Catarina, whose inhabitants are mostly Germans and have retained the customs and schools of their land of origin. At that time, both were in a state of ferment because of the contested ownership of a coniferous forest, which was in any case quite abandoned. The dispute had become so envenomed that it had become necessary for federal troops to intervene. This was the reason why we saw soldiers even in settlements lost in the depth of the forests, sometimes seated in front of their tents, playing the guitar, with a parrot perched on their shoulders.

We were traveling by special train. The commander of the *Marseillaise* and two hundred of his men had joined us on their way to Rio Grande do Sul to take over tugs chartered by the French government. One night there was an incident worthy of the Théâtre du Châtelet: a band of outlaws with drawn revolvers boarded the train and immobilized it by keeping the engineer covered while their confederates prevented the telegraph operator at the station from notifying the police. Claudel was called. Escorted by Commandant de Closmadeuc impeccably dressed and wearing tails, Claudel, in pajamas, calmly called for an explanation of the situation. All that the bandits asked him to do was to set down one of their number at the next station. To avoid provoking an incident, Claudel agreed to do so, and the train crew, still at the point of the pistol, moved the train on. The remainder of the night passed quietly. Next morning when we arrived at a little town, the representative of the military authorities, Colonel Virgilien de la Porcioncule, offered Claudel his government's apologies and discreetly refrained from telling him that he had enabled a rebel leader who was being actively pursued by the federal troops to make good his escape. With no ill feeling, he invited us to a drink in our honor at the station buffet, where there were assembled delegations of Syrians and Poles who wished to demonstrate their loyalty to the representative of France. The military band struck up the Brazilian national anthem, that of the state of Rio Grande, and finally the *Marseillaise*. The thunderous strains were suddenly interrupted by a fearful crash: the unaccustomed weight of the spectators had caused the floor to give way beneath us, while the tables, flung in every direction, hurled their piled-up crockery to the ground. After this day was over, our journey continued with no further tragicomic incident. At Pôrto Alegre, the last town we passed through, the shops belonging to Germans had been looted on the declaration of war. As we entered the plain, we could see, as far as the eye could reach, gauchos galloping after their cattle, deserts strewn with the bones of oxen and horses, and little ostriches, like gigantic hens, their plumage ruffled by their frantic running. What an amazing contrast with the pines of Santa Catarina!

After a few weeks in Rio, Claudel was obliged to set out on a fact-finding trip toward the Bolivian frontier. Once more I accompanied him. The train left São Paulo only three times a week and steamed through the forest for five consecutive days. We installed ourselves on a little seat in front of the locomotive, an ideal position during the heat of the day. Hordes of monkeys fled before our approach, as well as hundreds of parrots and clouds of innumerable Morpho butterflies fluttering so slowly that we could see the velvety black undersides of their broad enamel-blue wings. Throughout this region only the dozen yards or so required for the right of way bore any trace of human labor. We crossed the great River Tieté, so famed for its prodigiously extensive low falls, and the River Paraná, more than one mile wide and bordered by trackless forest wastes. Claudel and I felt as if nothing in this country had been changed since the first chapter of Genesis. The Indians lived in the woods, and were rarely seen except at the stops, when one or two occasionally emerged, wearing canvas trousers and shirts just like Portuguese peasants, though like their ancestors they still used their feet to shoot the arrows from their bows. When we reached our destination, we were invited to visit a model farm on the plain, which could only be reached on horseback. This lovely ride was only disturbed by herds of wild oxen or *caracus* (a kind of buffalo whose horns are used to make delightful walking-sticks), which galloped across the vista toward the unknown.

In August 1918, at the end of the southern winter, Spanish influenza made its appearance in Brazil, and rapidly reached epidemic proportions; four thousand deaths were recorded daily. The authorities were overwhelmed. In the hospitals the dead were removed from the beds before they were cold, in order to make way for the dying. The supply of coffins gave out, and you constantly saw cartloads of corpses that were thrown into common graves in the cemeteries. Nininha lost her mother, and she herself was dangerously ill. I did not see her again until the day I left. She was still in bed, pale and emaciated. I realized that she had had a narrow escape from death.

After November 11, 1918, gloom was succeeded by gaiety; the crowds poured into the streets to celebrate the return of peace at last. Claudel was sent to Washington to represent France on an interallied economic mission and took me with him. Afterward we would go on to France. I was very happy at the thought of going back to Paris and of seeing my parents and friends again, but my joy was tinged with a certain nostalgic regret: I had fallen deeply in love with Brazil.

12

A DIFFICULT VOYAGE

I T W A S not easy to find a boat going to New York. All the regular services were English, and had been suspended for the repatriation of troops. Claudel decided to take one of the German ships seized by the Brazilians and chartered to the French government. They offered him the *Leopoldina*, of the Hamburg-American Line, which, like most of the German vessels, had been sabotaged by her crew during internment and had had to undergo serious repairs.

There were not many passengers on board: a few government officials rejoining their posts, and six sailors going home to France. Our accommodations were therefore very comfortable. The officers and crew were all Brazilians.

The engines did not seem to be running very well, and we put into Bahia for a brief halt in order to have them overhauled. There are three hundred and sixty-five churches in this town, and one of them, situated on a hill a little way outside the town, is a famous resort of pilgrims, who throng the roads leading to it every Sunday. All along the way you see beggars, blind men, and paralytics exhibiting their crippled limbs, their stumps, and their sores, with mumbled prayers or loud cries to attract attention, pity, and alms. The church is very rapidly filled, and the congregation gathers outside the porch. All the Negresses in Bahia wear charms attached to the belt of their colored crinoline-like dresses. These charms are nearly always held together by a clasp in the shape of a hand, a piece of wood mounted in metal, a guava, or a bunch of grapes. Although they are Christians, most of the Negroes practice voodoo rites. Because these are forbidden, the ceremonies are held at night in the country. The secretary of the Consulate took me there one night. The worshippers sit on the ground around the leader or sorcerer, who selects an individual and puts him into a trance. When the subject falls, screaming and foaming at the mouth, the sorcerer dabbles his fingers in the saliva and touches the lips of all the adepts, who immediately become possessed and also fall into a trance. At this point the ceremony reaches its paroxysm, and we deemed it prudent to jump on our horses and ride back to the "city of three hundred and sixty-five churches."

Another breakdown of the engines enabled us to go ashore in Pernambuco. The sea was as translucent as an emerald. *Jamgadas*, or little fishing-craft, consisting merely of rafts on which the Negroes fix a chair, crisscrossed it in all directions. As we left, we were accompanied for a long way out to sea by the faint chimes, muffled by distance and the dense heat, of the bells of the city's innumerable convents and churches.

About two hundred miles out of Pernambuco the engines failed completely. The sabotage must have been more thorough and more complicated than had been thought, for even the wireless was not working. What was to be done? The weather was magnificent and the sea perfectly calm. All we had to do was wait patiently in the midst of the sea. The vessel was transformed into a luxury hotel. Claudel translated the Psalms (I wrote musical settings for some of them a few weeks later in New York); I was composing *Les*

88

Euménides; the officers remained on deck all day long, and the seamen fished. One day, contrary to all expectations, the ship began to move slightly. Miracle of miracles! We were in the Gulf Stream! An attempt was made to get the engines going again, but they ran for only a few moments. The current pulled us along at two knots, and a day or two later Barbados hove into sight. We wanted to get to the French West Indies, where the Messageries Maritimes had fairly large ship-repairing yards, so we only stayed a few hours in Bridgetown—just time enough to visit the market, where the Negresses gabbled English, and to go for a stroll in the countryside among the sugar-mills and taste some pretty little fruit, which caused such indigestion that we hastened back on board. At every step in Barbados, English influence is evident, in the cottages and grass lawn-tennis courts; but at Fort-de-France we found ourselves back in the atmosphere of a typical French *sous-préfecture* on the Grand' Place, where a statue of the Empress Josephine stood amid innumerable palm trees and the inevitable green park seats. On a closer examination, we found that the engine stood in need of lengthy and extensive repairs. Having received orders from Paris, Claudel decided we would take the *Pérou*, which was leaving for Saint-Nazaire and would call at Puerto Rico, where we could easily get a boat for New York. Until our departure, the Governor took us all over the island in his little Ford. We were struck by the silence of the West Indian forests, less luxuriant than their Brazilian counterparts; not a single bird seemed astir in them. We were told that the reptiles destroyed them and that an attempt had been made, a few years before, to remedy this by importing a whole ship-load of mongooses, which are enemies of snakes and eat their eggs; but apparently a truce was gradually established between the two inveterate foes, for the forests had fallen

89

silent again, and teemed with snakes. We had to give up an excursion to Mont Pelé owing to bad weather. We spent the night at Saint-Pierre, where the incessant sound of the rain was only interrupted by the furtive and continual rattle of a tropical insect called the "kid of the woods." Next morning we were again confined to our quarters in the hotel by a downpour so violent that it noisily tore away the topmost fronds of the palms. In the West Indies the manifestations of nature, including catastrophes, reach gigantic proportions, and as you travel around, you are constantly coming across traces of them. "Here," they will tell you, "is where the church steeple was destroyed by a hurricane," or "This is where a village was submerged by a tidal wave." Not to mention Saint-Pierre itself, twice destroyed by a volcanic eruption.

As soon as the *Pérou* had come alongside, we went on board. It was Christmas, our first since the armistice. To celebrate the victory, the officers organized a ball and invited all the society of Fort-de-France. The Martiniquais came in force: government officials, Creole families, wealthy Negro planters wearing long frock coats and accompanied by their daughters, lightly made up, and clad in bright-colored evening gowns. As they danced, they all mingled together and joyfully rediscovered the habits of peacetime, the climate of happiness. In the Bal Doudou, where a young officer took me a few days later, the atmosphere was the same: the typical bal-musette orchestra, the guests' dance, quadrilles, beguines, the women in their printed cotton dresses, gold necklaces, and all the grace and charm of a solemn occasion.

The *Pérou* was taking a contingent of young soldiers from Guadeloupe home to be demobilized. Lying on the decks in the after part of the ship, they sang all night long enchantingly lovely melodies (some of these I later used in the vocal quartet *Le Brick*, based on a poem by René Chalupt). Our stay in Puerto Rico interested me because of the continual contrast between United States influence and the traces of Spanish colonization (the modern port has shower baths for the stevedores, while the old town is surrounded by Spanish turrets and ancient ramparts). In the club opposite the hotel, strictly reserved to Spaniards, I could see from my room dark-skinned, bright-eyed women wearing shawls and mantillas, dancing the tango with slim young men with side-whiskers, while on the main square the American military band played marches by Sousa and fox-trots. While I was there, I heard dances by a Cuban composer Romeo, in which he seemed to be playing with Bach-like allegro themes and sharp syncopated rhythms of popular music combined with the emphatic grinding rhythm of the *guícharo*. I bought one of these in the market, and introduced it later in one or two of my orchestrations; it is a percussion instrument made of a long gourd on which a series of very close grooves have been traced. To play it, these grooves are violently rubbed with a piece of iron mounted on a handle.

Two days after leaving Puerto Rico and its dank heat, we ran into our first snowstorm at sea. We arrived in New York, with its forest of skyscrapers, at the beginning of January. The voyage had lasted fifty-five days.

Like all other cities after the war, New York was in the throes of a housing shortage. Claudel was provided with a divan in one of the drawing-rooms of the Hotel Lafayette, while I slept on a plank laid across a bathtub. It was the last few days before the introduction of Prohibition, and the city was in a ferment. On all sides you could hear speeches in favor of Prohibition. Even vaudeville audiences were asked to write their opinion on slips of paper and drop them in urns at the exits. It was a genuine national issue.

This was the first winter for me since 1916. Thanks to my mother's far-sightedness in sending me my fur coat and warm underclothes, I was able to face the cold and have a good look around New York. I went about on the upper deck of the buses, especially downtown.

During a soirée given by M. de Coppet, I met once more the Flonzaley Quartet, whom I had got to know in Switzerland through Céline Lagouarde. They told me that they had played my quartet several times during their tours. I believe they were the first to perform my works in the United States. They played a quartet by an aged American composer, born in Alsace of German stock, Charles Martin Loeffler, and later they introduced me to him. A few days after, I went to see Marion Bauer, the composer and musicographer, who introduced me to a charming young man, Charles Griffes, who composed sensitive works, slightly tinged with the influence of Debussy and Ravel. I met him again several times and showed him my music. He thought that the publishing firm of Schirmer might be interested in *Love Poems* by Tagore, which I had set to music both in the English words and in the French translation by Elisabeth Sainte-Marie-Perrin. He put me in touch with the head of the firm, who agreed to publish them.

Claudel was delighted to see Copeau again in New York, where he had set up his theater during the war. In the meantime Jane Bathori directed the Vieux-Colombier. She had put on several musical shows, the latest of which, Paul Méral's *Dit des jeux du monde*, had scandalized the public by the novelty of its presentation. It was not at all surprising that they should be shocked by the masks made by Guy-Pierre Fauconnet to confer on the characters a new kind of unity and grandeur, or by Honegger's score, but I could not understand the fatuousness of audiences who were so sure of never being in the wrong that they always mistook youthful daring for wanton extravagance.

I little thought that soon I too, and for a long time, was going to experience the ill will of the public.

CHAPTER

13

PARIS

I RETURNED to a Paris jubilant with the victory celebrations. But it was as a stranger that I took possession of my old apartment again, for my eyes still retained too much of the murky light reflected from Brazilian skies, my ears were still too full of the sumptuous sounds of the forest and the subtle rhythms of the tango. I took out of my trunk all sorts of knickknacks that I had bought in South America: nutshells engraved and painted by the Indians, clay whistles in the shape of birds, Morpho butterflies, heavily ornamented toothpick-holders, and specimens of Portuguese colonial silverware. I placed on the mantelpiece of my room all these silent witnesses to the lovely voyage I had made.

Fortunately I was soon caught up in the artistic movement that developed around me and tore me away from these memories. The nightmare of the war as it faded had given birth to a new era. Everything was changing, both in literature, with Apollinaire, Cendrars, Cocteau, and Max Jacob, and in painting; exhibitions followed close on one another; the Cubists were beginning to make names for themselves, and pictures by Marcel Duchamp, Braque, and Léger were hung beside those of Derain and Matisse. In music, activity was no less intense. Reacting against the impressionism of the post-Debussy composers, what musicians asked for now was a clearer, sturdier, more precise type of art that should yet not have lost its qualities of human sympathy and sensitivity. Louis Durey and Poulenc had been added to the musicians I had known before the war. I met Poulenc at René Chalupt's while he was still in the army. He played us his *Mouvements perpétuels* and sang the *Bestiaire*, which he had just completed. I thought that day of a saying of d'Indy concerning the development of music: "French music will become what the next musician of genius wants it to be." After all the vapors of impressionism, would not this simple, clear art renewing the tradition of Mozart and Scarlatti represent the next phase in the development of our music? At all events, I remember feeling that day that Poulenc would achieve greatness and would attain to a place in music's history. He reminded me that he had met me one day in the country at the house of some friends in 1915, when he was fifteen, and that we had played tennis together. I was still at the Conservatoire at the time. Shortly after this, young Francis had written to me for an autograph or to ask me about some musical question, I don't remember which, and I had answered with the affectionate solicitude of an elderly man addressing a young musician. We have often had a good laugh at this first contact of ours. The fresh charm of Poulenc's music was the most endearing feature of that period. Having been mobilized with the 1919 class, however, he had not had the opportunity to practice his technique adequately. Wisely, he was not content with his immediate successes, and placed himself in the hands of Charles Koechlin, in order to learn his trade. That admirable teacher, whose treatises on harmony and counterpoint are monuments of learning and pedagogical method, was the sole continuer of the tradition of Gédalge. I have always felt that it was a deplorable injustice that he

95

should not have been appointed to be Conservatoire after the latter's death.

There were many concerts that winter. A young conductor, Vladimir Golschmann, presented a series of new works at the Salle des Agriculteurs. Delgrange abandoned the cello to devote himself wholly to the cause of the new art; he organized concerts in a little hall in Montparnasse, the Salle Huyghens; the backless benches were uncomfortable, and the atmosphere was unbreathable because of the fumes of the stove, but all that was elegant in Parisian society, as well as the artists and devotees of the new music, rubbed shoulders there. Jane Bathori and Ricardo Viñes, the faithful pioneers, the (female) Capelle Quartet, the pianists Juliette Meerovitch and Marcelle Meyer, and the actor Pierre Bertin, who also sang, lent us their devoted help and disinterested services. There was also a very important center of intellectual activity, placed under the ægis of Shakespeare and of contemporary literature, in the two neighboring bookshops of Adrienne Monnier and Sylvia Beach in the rue de l'Odéon. There you might often meet Joyce and other authors and poets, both French and foreign. Valéry and Fargue used to read their verse there, Balguerie gave the first performance of *Socrate*, with Satie playing the piano, and Bathori did my *Alissa* for the first time.

I had met Satie again at a reception given by the Comte de Beaumont in honor of the Queen of Romania, at which he had been accompanying a few of his songs. At once he told me he had often heard me practicing during the summer of 1916; whenever he went to call on some friends of his who lived opposite me, he had heard me through my open windows tirelessly repeating over and over again the same phrases on the piano. He had been greatly interested by this, for he did not know at the time who was the tenant of the apartment

96

from which these little fragments of music proceeded. In the course of the winter, Cocteau published a book that created a great stir: *Le Coq et l'arlequin*. In this little treatise on æsthetics, he attacked the so-called serious music—the kind one listens to with one's head in one's hands—and the "Russian pedal," which is the influence of Mussorgsky and Rimsky-Korsakov and impressionism in the manner of Debussy. He exalted the barbarian feeling of Stravinsky's *Le Sacre du printemps*, the purity of *Socrate*, and the astringent art of Auric; he called for a decisively French type of music. Always given to generalization the critics lost no time in hailing Cocteau as the prophet, theoretician, and animator of postwar music.

After a concert at the Salle Huyghens, at which Bertin sang Louis Durey's *Images à Crusoë* on words by Saint-Léger Léger, and the Capelle Quartet played my Fourth Quartet, the critic Henri Collet published in *Comœdia* a chronicle entitled "Five Russians and Six Frenchmen." Quite arbitrarily he had chosen six names: Auric, Durey, Honegger, Poulenc, Tailleferre, and my own, merely because we knew one another, were good friends, and had figured on the same programs; quite irrespective of our different temperaments and wholly dissimilar characters. Auric and Poulenc were partisans of Cocteau's ideas, Honegger derived from the German romantics, and I from Mediterranean lyricism. I fundamentally disapproved of joint declarations of æsthetic doctrines and felt them to be a drag, an unreasonable limitation on the imagination of the artist, who must for each new work find different, often contradictory means of expression; but it was useless to protest. Collet's article excited such world-wide interest that the "Group of Six" was launched, and willy-nilly I formed part of it.

This being so, we decided to give some "Concerts des

Six." The first was devoted to our works; the second to foreign music. The latter program consisted of works by Lord Berners, Casella, Lourié, who was then People's Commissar for the Fine Arts in Soviet Russia, and Schönberg and Bartók, whose latest works we had been unable to hear owing to the war. Satie was our mascot. He was very popular among us. He was so fond of young people that he said to me one day: "I wish I knew what sort of music will be written by the children who are four-year-olds now." The purity of his art, his horror of all concessions, his contempt for money, and his ruthless attitude toward the critics were a marvelous example for us all.

The formation of the Group of Six helped to draw the bonds of friendship closer among us. For two years we met regularly at my place every Saturday evening. Paul Morand would make the cocktails, and then we would go to a little restaurant at the top of the rue Blanche. The dining-room of the Petit Bessonneau was so diminutive that the Saturday customers filled it completely. They gave free rein to their high spirits. We were not all composers, for our numbers also included performers: Marcelle Meyer, Juliette Meerovitch, Andrée Vaurabourg, the Russian singer Koubitzky; and painters: Marie Laurencin, Irène Lagut, Valentine Gross, Jean Hugo's fiancée, Guy-Pierre Fauconnet; and writers: Lucien Daudet, and Raymond Radiguet, a young poet who was brought to us by Cocteau. After dinner, lured by the steam-driven merry-go-rounds, the mysterious booths, the Daughter of Mars, the shooting-galleries, the games of chance, the menageries, the din of the mechanical organs with their perforated rolls seeming to grind out simultaneously and implacably all the blaring tunes from the music halls and revues, we would visit the Fair of Montmartre, or occasionally the Cirque Médrano to see the Fratellinis in their sketches, so steeped in poetry and imagination that they were worthy of the *commedia dell' arte*. We finished the evening at my house. The poets would read their poems, and we would play our latest compositions. Some of them, such as Auric's *Adieu New York*, Poulenc's *Cocardes*, and my *Bœuf sur le toit* were continually being played. We even used to insist on Poulenc's playing *Cocardes* every Saturday evening, as he did most readily. Out of these meetings, in which a spirit of carefree gaiety reigned, many a fruitful collaboration was to be born; they also determined the character of several works strongly marked by the influence of the music hall.

Belgium was the first foreign country to devote a concert to our works. This was done under the auspices of Mme Vandervelde, the wife of the Minister of Fine Arts. Satie, who had just withdrawn from the Socialist Party to join the Communists, asked me to inform her that "Erik Satie, of the Soviet of Arcueil, kissed her feet." Our program began with an Introduction by Cocteau. Then Auric and I played *Parade* as a pianoforte duet, as well as my Second Sonata for violin and piano (for at that time I still played the violin), and Germaine Tailleferre, her *Jeux de plein air* for two pianos. During the concert I noticed a young man following from the score all the music we played. He introduced himself; he played the piano, and knew all about our movement. His name was Paul Collaer.

Delgrange decided to extend the range of his activities to include conducting concerts of contemporary music. He performed *Petrouchka*, *Parade*, and my music for *Les Choëphores*. Owing to the small funds at his disposal, he found some difficulty in staging my work. The devoted Bathori came to the rescue by recruiting and rehearsing singers. She took the main singing role (soprano solo) and that of

99

Narrator. The *Exhortation* scene for spoken chorus and percussion called for seventeen additional instrumentalists, which was far more than the resources of Delgrange's budget could stand. He therefore engaged professionals at union rates only for the drums, and asked Cocteau, Auric, Lucien Daudet, Poulenc, and Honegger to play the others. The concert was given on June 19, 1919. The *Exhortation* scene was tremendously effective, and was encored.

I postponed my departure for Aix in order to see the Victory Parade. On the night preceding July 14 the scene in the streets was unforgettable. There was dancing at every street corner, to the strains of little bal-musette orchestras. On the 14th at dawn, Honegger, Vaurabourg, Durey, Fauconnet, and I made our way toward the Étoile. We managed to clamber up on a seat from which we had a view over the heads of the crowd. There were people everywhere; every tree, every roof, every balcony had its cluster of human faces, and from all sides the crowds continued to arrive in an uninterrupted stream. The parade began at eight o'clock. Now at last the victory that had been paid for so dearly was felt to be something tangible, visible, making our hearts swell with boundless hope. All the great Allied leaders, whom we only knew by their photographs or the newsreels in the cinemas, were now before us in flesh and blood: Marshal Foch, Marshal Joffre, Field Marshal Douglas Haig, and General Pershing preceded the French regiments, each with the flag it had covered in glory, the English, who had grouped their flags like a sea of banners, the Americans marching to the rhythm of their *Over There*, the Belgians, the Serbians. Everything at that time seemed to us to be big with promise for the new era of peace.

During the holidays my friends the Hoppenots came to spend a few days at L'Enclos; to our great joy, they have always had the habit of dropping in on us, on their way from one distant post to another. At the same time Cocteau and Louis Durey were making a short stay at the Hôtel Sextius in Aix. Jean kept us in fits of laughter with his descriptions of the peculiarities of that delightful hotel. The manager was also an antique-dealer, and accumulated most of his acquisitions in his patrons' rooms, but whenever he found a buyer for them, he would take them away without notice, and if some Louis XV chest-of-drawers had been sold, the unfortunate hotel guests were likely to find all their things scattered on the floor in the middle of the room. The hotel organized operatic performances in the grounds, which created a fearful din: to the infernal caterwauling of the undermanned orchestra, supported by a piano, would be added toward midnight the sound of Werther's pistol-shot. I toyed with a musical setting for one of Jean's poems: *L'Hymne au soleil*. (It proved a failure, and I destroyed it.) We all wanted to hear it, but it was no easy matter to recruit musicians in Aix. I appealed to the town band for the brass, and hired a big drum and several other percussion instruments. We all sat on the terrace. Jean read his poem; a few of our friends, Hélène Hoppenot, and Louis Durey provided the percussion, and the Marquise de Grimaldi Régusse, who unexpectedly turned up, was roped in to play the triangle. The result was a frightful cacophony, and the experiment did nothing to improve my reputation among those amateurs of music accustomed to hearing marches by Ganne and fantasias on airs from operettas played by the town band.

Still haunted by my memories of Brazil, I assembled a few popular melodies, tangos, maxixes, sambas, and even a Portuguese fado, and transcribed them with a rondo-like theme recurring between each two of them. I called this fantasia *Le Bœuf sur le toit*, the title of a Brazilian popular song. I thought that the character of this music might make it suitable for an accompaniment to one of Charlie Chaplin's films. At that time, the silent films were accompanied by fragments of classical music rendered by large or small orchestras or even a single piano, according to the financial means available. Cocteau disapproved of my idea, and proposed that he should use it for a show, which he would undertake to put on. Cocteau has a genuis for improvisation. Hardly has he conceived the idea of a project when he immediately carries it out. To begin with, we needed some form of financial backing. Jean took the plan of the Comédie des Champs-Élysées to the Comte de Beaumont, who undertook to reserve in advance, at a high price, the boxes and the first rows of orchestra seats. A few days later, as if at the wave of a magic wand, the whole theater was sold out, and the Shah of Persia even paid ten thousand francs for a front seat from which he could not see a thing, but was himself in full view of everyone. The expenses of the show being covered, all that remained to be done was to set to work.

Cocteau produced a pantomime scenario that could be adapted to my music. He imagined a scene in a bar in America during Prohibition. The various characters were highly typical: a Boxer, a Negro Dwarf, a Lady of Fashion, a Redheaded Woman dressed as a man, a Bookmaker, a Gentleman in evening clothes. The Barman, with a face like that of Antinoüs, offers everyone cocktails. After a few incidents and various dances, a Policeman enters, whereupon the scene is immediately transformed into a milk-bar. The clients play a rustic scene and dance a pastorale as they sip glasses of milk. The Barman switches on a big fan, which decapitates the Policeman. The Redheaded Woman executes a dance with the Policeman's head, ending by standing on her hands like the Salome in Rouen Cathedral. One by one the customers drift away, and the Barman presents an enormous bill to the resuscitated Policeman.

Jean had engaged the clowns from the Cirque Médrano and the Fratellinis to play the various parts. They followed implicitly all the extremely precise orders he gave them as producer. Albert Fratellini, being an acrobat, could even dance on his hands around the Policeman's head. In contrast with the lively tempo of the music, Jean made all the movements slow, as in a slow-motion film. This conferred an unreal, almost dreamlike atmosphere on the show. The huge masks lent peculiar distinction to all the gestures, and made hands and feet unperceived. Guy-Pierre Fauconnet designed them, as well as the costumes. We got together one Sunday at my place to arrange the entrances and dances in accordance with my score, as well as for Fauconnet to draw the characters as Jean described them to him. We worked so late that I offered to put Fauconnet up for the night, but he preferred to go home to Montparnasse after arranging another rendez-vous with us. He did not turn up. Anxiously, Jean rushed to his house and learned that the poor fellow had died trying to light a fire; he was, unknown to us, extremely ill, having, apparently, an enlarged heart. In him we lost a very dear friend. This was the first loss our little group was to sustain. Later we were to lose Meerovitch, Radiguet, Emmanuel Faÿ, Nininha Guerra. . . .

Raoul Dufy agreed to take over the work on the scenery for Le Bœuf, keeping our friend's masks and designs for the costumes. During rehearsals Lucien Daudet was devotedly helpful. His mother, Mme Alphonse Daudet, who kept up with all the latest literary and artistic movements, received us most kindly. One evening she even prepared a delicate surprise for her guests: she engaged two Hawaiian musicians for Prince Firouze, who was the Persian Minister for Foreign Affairs at the time, and was so crazy about Hawaiian music that he always took some musicians with him when he went to a restaurant, while for Jean and me she had served for desert a little house of caramel, surrounded by an ox, the whole garnished with vanilla ice cream.

We announced three performances of *Le Bœuf*. Cocteau was so nervous that he was afraid no one would come after the first, which was not open to the public. He persuaded Lucien Daudet to send three hundred *pneumatiques* (special delivery letters) each entitling the bearer to "a small box." There was an indescribable crush at the doors, which only the skillful handling and diplomacy of Lucien Daudet, who consented to take charge of the situation, managed to keep in hand.

The program included *Trois Petites Pièces montées*, especially written by Erik Satie for our show, Auric's *Fox-Trot*, and Poulenc's *Cocardes*, sung by Koubitzky, accompanied by violin, trumpet, clarinet, trombone, and big drum. Golschmann conducted our orchestra of twenty-five instruments. This isolated demonstration was taken by both critics and public as a declaration of æsthetic faith. The lighthearted show, presented under the ægis of Erik Satie and treated by the newspapers as a practical joke, was regarded by the public as symbolizing the music-hall and circus system of æsthetics, and for the critics it represented the so-called postwar music. Forgetting that I had written *Les Choëphores*, both public and critics agreed that I was a clown and a strolling musician—I, who hated comedy and in composing *Le Bœuf sur le toit* had only aspired to create a merry, unpretentious divertissement in memory of the Brazilian rhythms that had so captured my imagination and never—no, never!—made me laugh.

CHAPTER

14

SCANDALS

I SHOWED Gabriel Pierné the *Suite symphonique* I had written, based on the incidental music for *Protée*, and at the same time Honegger brought him an *Interlude* he had composed for a play by Max Jacob called *La Mort de Sainte Alméenne*. Pierné decided to perform both our works at the Concerts Colonne on October 24, 1920. They were grouped together in a program under the heading of "Polytonality"; in my opinion this was a mistake, for the development of music should take the form of a natural growth and not follow the imposition of a system. The audience is always in a skeptical frame of mind at the first performance of a new work, and this descriptive heading, with its air of saying "You will see what you will see," did nothing to improve matters. In fact, it was I who was to see. Pierné rehearsed our works so carefully that in order to have more time for them he included only pieces from the repertoire in the program of the concert that preceded ours.

My parents came to Paris for the occasion and we shared an orchestra box. I had never for one moment dreamed that my music could possibly be provocative, yet the audience was already restive before the end of the overture, expressing its feelings by cries of "Take it away!" and animal noises, whereupon counter-demonstrations of bravos and applause broke out, all of which did nothing to help win a hearing for the music. I began to have fears for the fugue, in which the insistent use of the brass might cause some bewilderment. It was written for three trumpets and three trombones, and was accompanied by a *continuo* for doublebasses and four bassoons, like a pedal point. I was not mistaken; with the fugue an indescribable tumult broke out, a real battle, in the course of which Monsieur Franck, the organist from the Temple de la Victoire, had his face slapped by Durey. One couldn't hear the orchestra; the din grew worse; the police intervened. The balconies were cleared by the municipal guard. I had the satisfaction of seeing Monsieur Brancour, the critic of *Le Ménestrel*, thrown out by two policemen. Before starting the third piece, Pierné made a speech, in which he said: "If I include a work in the program for the Concerts Colonne, it means I think it is worthy to appear there. It is your right not to approve of it, and to express your opinion accordingly, but only *after* it has been played." This speech was succeeded by a brief respite, and a start was made on the *Pastorale*. The audience was too excited, however, to calm down completely; after a short while the uproar broke out again, and the noise covered the sound of the orchestra right to the end of the piece. From the next box I caught a reassuring glance from my cousin Madeleine; she left her seat to come and sit beside me till the demonstration was over. My parents were horrified; not that they had the slightest doubt concerning my work, but because of their fears for my future. As for me, I was extremely proud: this genuine, spontaneous, violent reaction filled me with boundless confidence. It is the indifference of the public that is depressing; enthusiasm or vehement protests prove that your work is *alive*.

The history of music is littered with the débris of such

scandals: Wagner had to exercise extraordinary cunning to get the Ninth Symphony accepted in Leipzig; Berlioz had all the difficulty in the world in persuading the orchestra of the Conservatoire to play the "*Eroica*," and his own music was never appreciated during his lifetime. Not to speak of *Carmen*, or *Pelléas*. Is not the *Sacre*, which had been given such a stormy reception not long before, now listened to in a religious silence? All this reassured me, but I wondered anxiously what Pierné thought. He set my fears at rest immediately. "If that is the way it is, I'll play your work again on my next program," said he, and was as good as his word. There was another uproar, but it was less spontaneous this time. I had gone up into the galleries with Claudel, Audrey Parr, Madeleine, and a few other friends to study people's reactions. The newspapers had made such a splash about the "Scandal at the Concerts Colonne" that large numbers of people had only come out of curiosity and to demonstrate. Much later I learned that Pierné's courageous attitude had earned him the unanimous disapproval of the musicians at the Institut, and delayed his own election to that august body. The *Ménestrel* reproduced a letter written to him from Algiers by Saint-Saëns. From it I took the following extract, which I had framed and hung on the wall of my studio in Aix: "I am grieved to see that you are opening the doors to all sorts of bedlam aberrations and trying to force them down the public's throat when it protests. Several instruments playing in different keys have never produced music, only a babel!"

The next year Golschmann conducted my *Cinq Études* for piano and orchestra, with Marcelle Meyer as soloist. In this work I had employed a musical language based on a long tradition; each *Étude* dealt with a different problem of harmony and construction. (In the *Art of the Fugue* and the

Musical Offering, Bach used much more complicated com-
binations.) I adopted the language of polytonality, and in
this way obtained a more subtle sweetness and a greater
intensity of violence. The third *Étude*, "Fugues," consists of
four simultaneous fugues, one for the wind instruments in
A, one for the brass in D flat, one for the strings in F, while
the one for the piano is in two parts based on the notes
common to all three keys, and states the theme and answer
of the fugue while the orchestral fugues provide the *diverti-
mentos* and vice versa. The fourth *Étude*, both violent and
dramatic in its content, is constructed crabwise; that is, the
piece is divided into two, the second being an exact replica
of the first, but reversed. From the mid-point it runs back-
ward to the beginning. The audience was bewildered by this
device and lost no time in showing it: the hall became rowdy.
Marcelle Meyer took no notice, but went on playing, wringing out the violent harmonies with all the force of her finely
tempered technique. My old friend Engel walked out of the
Salle Gaveau in disgust. The attendant, a mulatto who had
known me for years, was worried about my physical·safety
and went to get a policeman to sit beside me. I was not disturbed by this new outburst, for I was determined to go
ahead with my research, whatever the public might think of
me.

Diaghilev's Ballets Russes had opened the season tri-
umphantly with *Le Sacre du printemps*. The critics, who had
at first had considerable difficulty in getting accustomed to
this work, now listened to it with fervent enthusiasm and
lauded its composer, though they hoped he would not
change his manner again. Diaghilev, who was strongly influenced by the theories advanced by Cocteau in *Le Coq et
l'arlequin*, was distinctly attracted by the amusingly direct
art personified by Poulenc and Auric; on the other hand, he

was not very fond of my music. Nevertheless, to please José María Sert, who was a great admirer of Claudel's, he asked me to play *L'Homme et son désir*. The performance took place in Misia Edwards's drawing-room. (She was to marry Sert a few weeks later.) She was a great friend of Diaghilev, and lent him devoted assistance in putting on his shows. He placed great confidence in her judgment, which was trenchant. Like Diaghilev himself, she was always on the alert for the novelty of the day, or rather of the latest minute, and if she liked a work, she would take it up. Otherwise—Satie used to say: "If you keep a magnificent pedigree cat, you should hide little birds from it!" and, acting on this principle, he kept the music of *Parade* (which he had nevertheless dedicated to her) a secret from her until the day of its first performance. It was therefore amid an atmosphere heavy with skepticism and unspoken reservation that I played my score. The icy silence that followed it was broken by a conversation in Russian between Diaghilev and Massine. I soon realized that my symbolic and dramatic ballet no longer corresponded with the needs of the day.

That winter another troupe of dancers, the Ballets Suédois, gave a series of performances at the Théâtre des Champs-Élysées. A Swedish Mæcenas named Rolf de Maré devoted all his leisure to it and provided its financial backing. These dancers had not the virtuosity of the Russians, but their sincerity and love of the art were very captivating. At first their repertoire consisted of Swedish works and folk dances, but on the advice of their conductor Inghelbrecht they extended it to include Albéniz's *Iberia*, Ravel's *Le Tombeau de Couperin* and Inghelbrecht's *El Greco*. The choreography was by Jean Borlin.

Honegger had composed a very lovely ballet called *Horace victorieux*, and Fauconnet had prepared designs for the scenery, costumes, and masks. To honor the memory of his dead friend, the composer submitted this work to de Maré, but the latter preferred to commission a new ballet from him to be called *Skating Rink*, with scenery by Fernand Léger. Yet when I submitted to him my *L'Homme et son désir*, he agreed to put it on in spite of the singers, the orchestra of soloists, and the large number of percussion instruments required. Through his generosity our Brazilian collaboration came to fruition. Audrey Parr designed the costumes on the basis of suggestions by Claudel. The latter had just been appointed Ambassador to Japan, and as the heir to the Imperial throne, Prince Hirohito, was passing through Paris at the time, often had to escort him. He would suddenly appear on the stage of the Théâtre des Champs-Élysées wearing a morning coat and top hat and interrupt the rehearsal at the most unexpected moments to suggest some new steps to Borlin.

Apart from Honegger's music, Inghelbrecht had no great love for the works of Les Six. My relations with him were far from cordial; indeed, once when I asked him in the nicest possible way to alter a nuance slightly, he retorted very gruffly: "You have no business here!" In spite of this incident, however, I had no fear, for I knew his artistic integrity and was sure he would conduct my music flawlessly. I was right, too. There was a young flautist in the orchestra, Roger Désormière, who stuck up for me unceasingly. He lived opposite me and often came to take me out with his motorcycle and sidecar, visiting the country around Paris, which he knew intimately.

The first performance of *L'Homme et son désir* took place on June 26, 1921. I was anxious about the passages for unaccompanied percussion, but they did not provoke any hostile demonstration, for they were short, and the music that followed immediately soothed the audience's irritation, and the vocal quartet acted as a sedative. On each occasion the reaction of the public was different, ranging from restiveness to solemn attention. De Maré paid no heed to these fluctuating responses and kept my ballet in the repertoire.

He had asked Auric to write a score on a subject proposed by Cocteau, but was unable to carry out his intention for lack of time. So Cocteau decided to put on a show by Les Six. We all agreed to take part except Durey. The décors for *Les Mariés de la Tour Eiffel* were by Irène Lagut, and the costumes were the first revelation of the talent of Jean Hugo, who advanced from strength to strength thereafter. The dancers wore masks and painted costumes; they had a sort of *trompe-l'œil* effect that was really very charming. Cocteau and Pierre Bertin read through cardboard loudspeakers placed on either side of the stage the running commentary that accompanied the ballet between the various pieces of music. The plot was very simple: a young newly married couple, accompanied by their relatives and an old friend, a general, have come to have their wedding banquet on the first-floor terrace of the Eiffel Tower. During the banquet the general mimes a speech. A wedding-group photograph is taken, but every time the fateful words: "Watch the bird!" are uttered, some unexpected apparition interrupts the proceedings. First of all it is the "Bathing Beauty from Trouville," then "Telegrams"—for the Eiffel Tower has been the handmaiden of the post office ever since its aerial was erected—and finally a lion that devours the general. This is only the beginning of the misfortunes that befall this unlucky wedding party, for it ends by being 'massacred' as in a coconut shy at the fair by the 'Child of the Future.' We were all interested and amused at taking part in such an extraordinary mixture of different ingredients, the fanciful nature of which would not have been disowned by the Dadaist movement, then at its height. Auric composed a brilliant *Overture* and a series of enchanting ritornelles; Poulenc *La Danse de la Baigneuse de Trouville* and *Le Discours du Général*; Tailleferre *La Valse des Dépêches*; Honegger *La Marche funèbre du Général*, and I *La Marche nuptiale* and *La Fugue du massacre de la noce*. Apart from Poulenc's polka, whose deliberate drollery was a great success, and the pieces by Auric, the whole work was rather feeble. Only Honegger's contribution was taken seriously, and when they began to play it, a well-known critic exclaimed: "Ah! Some real music at last!" without recognizing the Waltz from *Faust*, which Arthur had used in the bass in order to give his composition the required authentic touch of satire.

The Opéra-Comique decided to put on *La Brebis égarée* in November 1923. I have often been reproached for authorizing performances of this youthful work, but I do not disown it and will never be against its being played. In spite of the prosody, which derives undoubtedly from that of *Pelléas*, and the themes representing the various aspects of the work, which enabled me to use the so-called "cyclic" method of treatment, as well as the excessive use of chords of the ninth and the doubling of parts in the orchestra, I think that my score reflects a certain lyrical spirit, highly personal to me, which found expression in this work to a much greater extent than in any other of my youthful compositions. The revivals of *La Brebis* in Germany for the one hundred and fiftieth anniversary of the Berlin Opera, and on the Paris and Belgian radio on the occasion of Francis Jammes's death, did nothing to make me revise my opinion.

The production of *La Brebis* at the Opéra-Comique was most elaborately planned. I had asked Jammes's old friend Lacoste to collaborate, and he produced carefully painted little *trompe-l'œil* tableaux, in which the accessories were reduced to a minimum in order to facilitate changes of scenery—this was essential, for there were twenty different scenes. The play was very cleverly staged by Albert Carré, who introduced a second curtain, smaller than the main one, and operated by three narrators, who sang the description of the various changes of scene. The narrators played the part of a Greek chorus, though descriptive rather than dramatic. They were dressed in the fashions of 1910, with garlands of flowers like those you see on the picture postcards of the period. This was the first occasion on which an opera had been performed using 1912 costumes, but I had insisted that it should owe its character to the period when it was written, even if that period was one of excruciatingly bad taste.

Although the opera was flawlessly produced, it roused violent demonstrations of feeling, for which I believe that the colloquial language of the text was more responsible than the music. For instance, when Pierre, who is about to abduct Françoise, nervously consults a railway timetable, his understandable agitation raised a laugh. Yet it was little touches like that which created the characteristic atmosphere of the play and, better than lyrical outbursts, expressed the ideas of love, moral indigence, repentance, and forgiveness. The incidents followed the familiar pattern of whistles and cat-calls succeeded by untimely applause. The outcry led to counterdemonstrations in my favor, and gradually degenerated into complete disorder, with everyone shouting violent insults at one another. Albert Wolff continued to conduct the orchestra with fervor and courage. During the third performance he scathingly addressed the audience as follows: "If you don't like this, come back tomorrow night—we're playing *Mignon*." That evening I was sitting in the gallery— I like to mingle with the people in the cheaper seats during performances of my works—and the students were all for me, calling the jeerers in the boxes and orchestra seats "dirty bourgeois." Next to me, a young man wearing an enormous *lavallière* kept vigorously applauding. Unable to stand any longer my impassive attitude, he turned to me and said: "Why don't you clap—shout—cheer? You ought to come back every time they play this opera! I'm here every time to defend it!" During the intermission I introduced myself to my youthful admirer, and thereafter never omitted to invite him to my first nights. Shocked by the attitude of the public, Albert Carré went so far as to place on every seat a copy of the sarcastic reviews that had greeted the first performance of *Pelléas*, together with the one phrase: "Be careful!" I was deeply touched by this gesture, but it only irritated the audience, and my work was withdrawn after the fourth performance.

In 1920–1 I undertook to write some articles of musical criticism for the *Courrier Musical*. It was a pleasant task to assume the defense of contemporary music, which was being assailed from all sides, and to express freely my own opinions. I also felt that it was an opportunity to explain one or two points of view and to dissipate certain misunderstandings. In this connection I was given a demonstration of the perfidious nature of some of my colleagues. Émile Vuillermoz, who pontificated in *L'Excelsior*, never let an opportunity pass of attacking my supposed anti-Debussy views. I requested an interview with him in order to undeceive him. I have never attached any importance to criticisms of my own work, but this was a question of my attitude to a musician whom I held in veneration. I took along all my articles to prove he was wrong. I even took the trouble of underlining in blue pencil all the references to Debussy. Vuillermoz pretended to be delighted, but went on to deplore my attitude toward Ravel and Florent Schmitt, whereupon I gave him my reasons. He thanked me for having enlightened him on all these points. A few days later he did not fail to treat me once more as a thankless "anti-Debussyite"—which led me to suspect that the politics of music held many a mysterious secret.

The Sunday concerts were a sort of musical Salon Carré, an exhibition of the masters of the past. I loved classical music, but protested in my articles against the excessive number of Beethoven-Wagner and Wagner-Beethoven programs. It was very tiresome. Every Sunday, the Fifth, the Third, a *Leonore* Overture. And Wagner every Sunday. Apart from one or two of his overtures, his works should never be performed in the concert hall. When the Concerts Pasdeloup announced yet another Wagner Festival, I headed my article simply: "Down with Wagner!" which provoked a veritable scandal. I received protesting letters, insults, and even anonymous letters. Wagner was worshipped like the golden calf. And I hated his music more with every day that passed, for it represented a type of art that I detested; yet I could never have guessed that it would one day become the standard-bearer of Nazi philosophy until the hour when its high priests would be swallowed up in a new *Götterdämmerung*.

Since that time I have often attended admirable performances of Wagner's works in Germany, but have been unable to revise my opinion. My Latin mind refuses to swallow this music, which Debussy used to call "tetralogical tin plate"; as, however, our criticisms are wasted and we shall always have to put up with festivals of this kind, I am prepared to shout: "Long live Beethoven!" even after the hundred-thousandth performance of the Fifth, but—oh, yes, certainly—always ready to cry: "Down with Wagner!"

15

MY FIRST ENCOUNTER WITH JAZZ

IN JUNE 1920 Claudel, who was then Minister to Denmark and High Commissioner for the Schleswig-Holstein plebiscite, came to Paris for a few days, and invited me to motor back with him to Copenhagen. I gladly accepted. We waited just long enough for me to get the necessary papers and then set out. We had with us Copeau's daughter, little Marie-Hélène, who was going to spend her vacation with her grandmother in Denmark. We were favored by the weather and had a very pleasant journey despite the fact that it was rather hurried because Claudel had to attend an official dinner on the occasion of the plebiscite that had just been held. So we sped across Belgium and Holland and through the empty harbors of a Germany in the deadly grip of inflation, across the Great Belt and the Little Belt, and over the plains of Denmark. One hour after our arrival at the Legation, Claudel, hatless and wearing the Grand Cordon of the Order of Danbrog, chewing leaves he idly plucked from the bushes as we went by, set out on foot for the Royal Palace.

I loved Copenhagen, with its sixteenth-century quays, its beautifully laid-out ancient palaces rubbing elbows with huge colorful modern brick buildings reddened by the sun. The

A PAINTING BY JACQUES-EMILE BLANCHE

(CLOCKWISE): *Germaine Tailleferre, Milhaud, Arthur Honegger, Jean Wiéner, Marcelle Meyer, Francis Poulenc,
Jean Cocteau, George Auric*

Milhaud, Heinrich Burkard, and Béla Bartók, Baden-Baden, 1928

Paul Hindemith and Milhaud, Paris, 1928

museum amazed me by its important collection of sculptures by Carpeaux of the famous personalities of the Second Empire. Claudel took me to Elsinore. As we gazed at the portrait of the royal family, whose members had wedded so many sovereigns, Claudel confided in me that he would like to see a performance of *Hamlet* in a décor like that in the picture, with its padded furniture and satin cushions. As we went back to Copenhagen, the car seemed to be floating through a sea of cyclists lured out into the countryside by the long bright evenings. I took advantage of my free time to make a start on my first two *Études* for piano and orchestra and a dance suite for the piano, inspired by South American rhythms and not based on folk music, entitled *Saudades do Brasil*. Each piece bore the name of one of the districts of Rio.

I was to join Cocteau in London for some performances of *Le Bœuf sur le toit*. I went by way of Esbjerg. We soon realized that the charming young man who acted as our manager had only the vaguest ideas of how our show should be organized; instead of acrobatic dancers, he had engaged some weird-looking youths who looked as if they had come straight out of Whitechapel. The rehearsals were held at the Baroness d'Erlanger's house, Lord Byron's former town house in Piccadilly. Our dubious-looking actors came every day to study their dance movements among the priceless furniture of a richly appointed drawing-room. The bar was represented by a splendid Coromandel screen laid across two chairs. *Le Bœuf* was to hold the bill for two weeks at the Coliseum, London's biggest music hall. This seemed rather risky to us, but its audiences were apparently used to the most heterogeneous programs; the Ballets Russes had played there with great success. The rehearsals were difficult, with musicians unaccustomed to playing music like mine, and I often had to berate the lady horn-players. To mollify me, they would show me photos of their babies during the intermissions. I conducted the first performance, and all went well. *Le Bœuf* was sandwiched in between a number by Japanese acrobats and Ruth Draper's highly original sketches. In any case, this was not the last time *Le Bœuf* was given in a music hall. Mme Rasimi, the manager of the Ba-ta-clan, put it in one of her revues, famous for their displays of nudity and their comedians' broad humor. One night Cocteau heard one of the audience—a workman wearing a cloth cap—say to his wife: "It ain't that it makes you laugh; but it's different, see, so it makes you laugh!"

It was during this visit to London that I first began to take an interest in jazz. Billy Arnold and his band, straight from New York, were playing in a Hammersmith dance hall, where the system of taxi-girls and taxi-boys had been introduced. A dozen young men in evening dress and girls in blue dresses with lace collars sat around in a box, and for sixpence any timid young man or neurotic old maid could have one of them to dance with. For the same fee they could have another dance with the same or any other partner.

In his *Coq et l'arlequin* Cocteau had described the jazz accompaniment to the number by Gaby Deslys at the Casino de Paris in 1918 as a "cataclysm in sound." In the course of frequent visits to Hammersmith, where I sat close to the musicians, I tried to analyze and assimilate what I heard. What a long way we had traveled from the gypsies who before the war used to pour their insipid, mawkish strains intimately into one's ears, or the singers whose glides, in the most dubious taste, were upborne by the wobbling notes of the cimbalom, or the crudity of our bals-musette, with the unsubtle forthrightness of cornet, accordion, and clarinet!

The new music was extremely subtle in its use of timbre: the saxophone breaking in, squeezing out the juice of dreams, or the trumpet, dramatic or languorous by turns, the clarinet, frequently played in its upper register, the lyrical use of the trombone, glancing with its slide over quarter-tones in crescendos of volume and pitch, thus intensifying the feeling; and the whole, so various yet not disparate, held together by the piano and subtly punctuated by the complex rhythms of the percussion, a kind of inner beat, the vital pulse of the rhythmic life of the music. The constant use of syncopation in the melody was of such contrapuntal freedom that it gave the impression of unregulated improvisation, whereas in actual fact it was elaborately rehearsed daily, down to the last detail. I had the idea of using these timbres and rhythms in a work of chamber music, but first I had to penetrate more deeply into the arcana of this new musical form, whose technique still baffled me. The musicians who had already made use of jazz had confined themselves to what were more or less interpretations of dance music. Satie in the *Rag-Time du Paquebot* of *Parade* and Auric in the fox-trot *Adieu New York* had made use of an ordinary symphony orchestra, and Stravinsky had written his *Ragtime* for eleven solo instruments, including a cimbalom.

I had lost sight of Jean Wiéner since the war. Life had not been easy for him, and he was married and had a little daughter. Putting a bold face on things, he now earned his living by playing the piano in a night club. He came to me and suggested that we should transfer our Saturday evening meetings to the place where he worked. I was attracted by this idea and hurried off to see Cocteau, whom I greeted with the words: "I've got a bar for you!" The very next Saturday my apartment was abandoned in favor of the Bar Gaya in the rue Duphot. We were given a warm welcome by the owner, Moyses, who had even adorned the walls with little many-colored posters, each bearing one of our names. As the bar's customers invariably arrived later than we did, and left before us, there was always one part of the evening when we were all alone and free to make music to our hearts' content. Jean Wiéner played syncopated music with aerial grace and sensitivity, with an especially light rhythm. We loved to listen to his playing, and to that of his partner, Vance, the Negro, who was an admirable saxophonist and banjo-player. Without any transition these two would pass from fashionable ragtime and fox-trots to the most celebrated works of Bach. Besides, syncopated music calls for a rhythm as inexorably regular as that of Bach himself, which has the same basis.

In May 1921 Pierre Bertin put on an *avant-garde* show. The program included a play by Max Jacob, imbued with the spirit of chivalry, and Radiguet's charming one-act play *Le Pélican*, with music by Auric. I remember one very amusing scene in which Monsieur Pélican points out to his son that he ought to think of taking a pen name if he wanted to be a poet, to which the young man retorts that: "Pelican is no sillier than Corneille (crow) or Racine (root)." Together with these plays, a play by Cocteau called *Le Gendarme incompris* was given; it rather audaciously introduces a whole passage from Mallarmé. This is so apt in the new context that, as it was pronounced with the traditional comic accent of the stage policeman, no one ever suspected its origin. Poulenc had composed music so witty and pungent that I have always felt sorry he would not allow it to be played again. Gratton, the Negro, danced a shimmy composed by me and entitled *Caramel mou*. (Cocteau had written some words for it; it was scored for clarinet, saxophone, trumpet, trombone, and percussion.) But the chief event of the evening was un-

120

doubtedly Satie's extraordinary play *Le Piège de Méduse*, whose dialogue was full of his own inimitable wit. The unbridled fantasy of this play bordered on the absurd. In the role of Baron Méduse, Bertin wore a make-up that made him look like Satie himself; it was as if he had assumed the latter's actual bodily presence. The action was interrupted from time to time by a stuffed monkey, which came down from its pedestal to execute a little dance. Satie had written very short dance tunes scored for a small group of instruments; this was to be conducted by Golschmann, who, however, withdrew at the last minute as a result of a tiff.

Shows of this kind, so variegated in character, were excellent training for us, enabling us to experiment in all sorts of techniques and to strive constantly after new forms of expression.

16

"MUSIQUE D'AMEUBLEMENT" AND

CATALOGUE MUSIC

J UST AS one's field of vision embraces objects and forms, such as the pattern on the wallpaper, the cornice of the ceiling, or the frame of the mirror, which the eye sees but to which it pays no attention, though they are undoubtedly there, Satie thought that it would be amusing to have music that would not be listened to, *"musique d'ameublement,"* or background music that would vary like the furniture of the rooms in which it was played. Auric and Poulenc disapproved of this suggestion, but it tickled my fancy so much that I experimented with it, in co-operation with Satie, at a concert given in the Galerie Barbazange. During the program, Marcelle Meyer played music by Les Six, and Bertin presented a play by Max Jacob called *Un Figurant au théâtre de Nantes*, which required the services of a trombone. He also sang Stravinsky's *Berceuses du chat* to the accompaniment of three clarinets, so Satie and I scored our music for the instruments used in the course of these various items on the program. In order that the music might seem to come from all sides at once, we posted the clarinets in three different corners of the theater, the pianist in the fourth, and the trombone in a box on the balcony floor. A program note warned the audience that it was not to pay any more attention to the ritornellos that would be played during the intermissions than to the candelabra, the seats, or the balcony. Contrary to our expectations, however, as soon as the music started up, the audience began to stream back to their seats. It was no use for Satie to shout: "Go on talking! Walk about! Don't listen!" They listened without speaking. The whole effect was spoiled. Satie had not counted on the charm of his own music. This was our one and only public experiment with this sort of music. Nevertheless Satie wrote another *"ritournelle d'ameublement"* for Mrs. Eugene Meyer, of Washington, when she asked him, through me, to give her an autograph. But for this *Musique pour un cabinet préfectoral* to have its full meaning, she should have had it recorded and played over and over again, thus forming part of the furniture of her beautiful library in Crescent Place, adorning it for the ear in the same way as the still life by Manet adorned it for the eye. In any case, the future was to prove that Satie was right: nowadays, children and housewives fill their homes with unheeded music, reading and working to the sound of the radio. And in all public places, large stores and restaurants the customers are drenched in an unending flood of music. In America cafeterias are equipped with a sufficient number of machines for each client to be able, for the modest sum of five cents, to furnish his own solitude with music or supply a background for his conversation with his guest. Is this not *"musique d'ameublement,"* heard, but not listened to?

We frequently gave concerts in picture galleries. At Poiret's, Auric and I gave the first performance of Debussy's *Épigraphes antiques* for piano duet. At the Galerie la Boétie, Honegger played his violin sonatas with Vaurabourg, and the pianist André Salomon pieces by his friend Satie. Delgrange conducted my *Machines agricoles*.

I had written musical settings for descriptions of machinery taken from a catalogue that I had brought back from an exhibition of agricultural machinery which I had visited in company with Mme de B. and Mlle de S., who wanted to choose a reaper for their estate in the Bordeaux area. I had been so impressed by the beauty of these great multicolored metal insects, magnificent modern brothers to the plow and the scythe, that the idea came to me of celebrating them in music. I had put away in a drawer a number of catalogues, that I came across in 1919. I then composed a little suite for singer and seven solo instruments in the style of my little symphonies; the titles were "*La Faucheuse*" (reaper), "*La Lieuse*" (binder), "*La Déchaumeuse-Semeuse-Enfouisseuse*" (harrow, seeder, and burier), "*La Moissonneuse Espigadora*" (harvester), "*La Fouilleuse-Draineuse*" (subsoil and draining plow), "*La Faneuse*" (tedder). A few months later I used the same group of instruments for settings to some delightful poems by Lucien Daudet inspired by a florist's catalogue: *Catalogue de fleurs*.

Not a single critic understood what had impelled me to compose these works, or that they had been written in the same spirit as had in the past led composers to sing the praises of harvest-time, the grape harvest, or the "happy plowman," or Honegger to glorify a locomotive, and Fernand Léger to exalt machinery. Every time anyone wanted to prove my predilection for leg-pulling and eccentricity he cited *Les Machines agricoles*. I have never been able to fathom why sensible beings should imagine that any artist would spend his time working, with all the agonizing passion that goes into the process of creation, with the sole purpose of making fools of a few of them.

PAUL COLLAER AND JEAN WIÉNER

PAUL COLLAER, the young man we had met at the
concert we gave in Brussels, assumed the direction of all
the *avant-garde* musical functions in Belgium. About the
same period four young men—Alphonse Onnou, Laurent
Halleux, Germain Prévost, and Quinet—formed the Pro Arte
Quartet. By dint of talent and artistic integrity, they quickly
attained perfection. Their exceptionally wide repertoire was
carefully rehearsed, and they brought to a modern quartet,
which they would have an opportunity of performing only
once in public, the same earnest application they gave to one
of the classics. In order to earn their living, they played in
the orchestra at La Monnaie or in those dismal ensembles
whose function it is to besprinkle movie shows liberally with
music. These four lent Collaer their enthusiastic and devoted
support, and it was largely thanks to them that he was able
to carry his enterprise through. He was also assisted by a
charming singer, Evelyne Brelia, who interpreted our songs
with intelligence. She had married the cellist Quinet, whose
place was taken by Maas when he left the quartet to become
director of the Conservatoire in Charleroi. A few months
later he underwent a cruel ordeal: his wife was murdered,
no doubt by a lunatic, for no trace of her assassin was ever

found. Collaer's concerts were rechristened Les Concerts Pro Arte. They included chamber-music recitals among their aims, as well as works for small ensembles. Arthur Prévost, the viola-player's brother, undertook to conduct the orchestra. He was the bandmaster of the excellent regimental band of the *Guides*, from which he was able to recruit the woodwind and the brass for the orchestra. Moreover, Collaer was not obliged to pay them, which was a considerable relief for him in view of the comparatively slender financial resources at his disposal.

Paul Collaer carried on an impressive range of activities: he was an excellent pianist, admirable for sight-reading, and personally rehearsed all his soloists. He advised them, and if necessary won them over. He also looked after all the administrative side of the concerts: hiring the hall, printing programs and tickets, getting new subscribers. In the evenings, when a concert was over, he loved to refresh his spirit in the company of his fellow musicians at the café, but would rise hurriedly toward midnight in order to catch a train to Malines, where he lived. Next morning, in accordance with a long-established family tradition—all the members of his family were either teachers or headmasters of lycées—he would quietly walk, pipe in mouth, to the athenæum where he taught physics and chemistry. Thus Collaer divided his time between music and science, and in summer, in his wife's native Switzerland, he would go off into the mountains to pursue his investigations into "the influence of light on chlorophyll." As soon as he got home from school, while his wife prepared one of her succulent repasts, he would rush to the piano and enthusiastically play over scores, both classical and modern. He was also an ardent gardener, and would get up in the middle of the night to keep an eye on the temperature of the greenhouse in which he grew rare orchids. From his house on the banks of the canal on the outskirts of the town, you could just hear the peals of the carillon in the Cathedral, and the bay window of his drawing-room looked out on the heavy barges constantly going to and from Holland. I frequently stayed with him. I have heard my chamber-music works played in the Pro Arte concerts so often that I hardly think there is one that Collaer did not have performed. I took advantage of the concerts to spend a few days in Malines and work in that incomparably calm and friendly atmosphere.

A few years later Collaer tried to extend the range of his activities. There was in Brussels an organization giving symphony concerts known as Les Concerts Populaires, whose finances were guaranteed by M. Henri Lebœuf, to whom Brussels also owes the Hall of the Palais des Beaux Arts. Like most associations of its kind, it was not much inclined to welcome contemporary works, though the Belgian public, less skeptical than the French, always listens respectfully before passing judgment. Collaer, who loved a fight, set out to rejuvenate their programs, sometimes successfully. Through him I was engaged in 1924 to conduct my *Deuxième Suite symphonique*. He also persuaded Louis de Vocht to produce my *Choéphores* in Antwerp. Whenever the director of the La Monnaie Orchestra summoned me to play one of my works, Collaer always took time off to come with me to help me perform my music. He became enamored of ancient instruments and bought several of them. He trained a quartet of recorders and produced Purcell's *Fairy Queen*, Monteverdi's *Orfeo*, and Emilio del Cavalieri's *La Rappresentazione di anima e di corpo*. He wrote a very good book on Stravinsky and one on myself, containing very shrewd analyses of my work. But so many diverse activities ended in overtaxing his strength, and when he

127

was offered the post of artistic director in the Flemish broadcasting system, he gave up teaching in order to devote himself wholly to music.

When the Bar Gaya was transferred to new premises, its owner, Moyses, asked Cocteau and myself to allow him to use the name *Le Bœuf sur le toit*. The idea tickled our fancy, and we agreed. We had no inkling that this would cause so much confusion: from then on, it was supposed that we were the owners of this bar, an error that was all the more deeply rooted because we went there so often, and it was stated in program notes for concerts that I had called my ballet after a night club. Jean Wiéner played there regularly, together with Clément Doucet, an excellent pianist. To a remarkable extent they were complementary to each other; they performed all syncopated music with rare distinction. Their records are a valuable addition to the history of jazz during this period; they were the first to give concerts of this type of music in Europe, and went on many tours. Yet all this activity was not enough for Wiéner, who decided to organize a series of concerts at his own expense. He became our "artist Mæcenas."

For the first concert he engaged the Billy Arnold orchestra, which had gone from strength to strength since I had heard them in London. The public, accustomed to concerts of so-called serious music, was indignant at first that anyone should dare to play dance music or restaurant music in a hall that had been graced by the presence of so many distinguished virtuosos; but gradually it yielded to the lure—that is, the languorous charm of the blues and the exciting clamor of ragtime and the intoxicating freedom of the melodic lines. When the concert was over, the audience in the Salle des Agriculteurs seemed to have been overcome by vertigo: they had encountered an unknown force. Although the quality of the music was often questionable, at least it was firmly rooted in the soil from which folk music sprang. Through it the voice of America made itself heard, fresh, vital, compelling, as well as husky or melancholy; and sometimes peaceful, slightly sentimental, or imbued with a kind of desperate poetry.

Jean Wiéner decided to give a first Paris performance of Schönberg's *Pierrot Lunaire* and asked me to conduct it. The work consists of twenty-one pieces based on poems by the Belgian poet A. Giraud, written in a decadent style and rather dubious taste. In it Schönberg uses a kind of recitative halfway between speech and song, but on very precisely indicated notes. After continuous practice, our admirable Marya Freund succeeded in "speaking" the words without singing them, and "singing" them without falling over into speech. As we felt that it would be essential for the words of such a musical innovation to be clearly understood, she agreed to translate, or rather adapt, them. The simplest thing would obviously have been to substitute the original words for the German text, but this was out of the question because Schönberg's prosody was based on a translation into German. Marya therefore made a translation of this translation. In spite of its ultra-expressionistic character bordering on morbidity, this wholly atonal music, composed in 1913, was tremendously evocative. We had twenty-five rehearsals. The orchestra consisted of five players, one of whom played the violin or viola according to requirements, another the flute or piccolo, the third the clarinet or bass clarinet, the fourth the cello, and finally Jean Wiéner at the piano. *Pierrot Lunaire* was such a success that we repeated it twice in Paris, and Collaer engaged us for Brussels. After conducting this work so many times, all my nerves were on edge. I was exasperated by the recitative running over the whole range of the vocal register with the most unexpected leaps and intervals. After conducting it in London, therefore, I decided that this would be the last time. Yet the other day I listened with genuine pleasure to the recording made by Schönberg himself, and I find that in spite of the years that have come between, this music has kept an authentic freshness.

Other works by Schönberg were presented by the Concerts Wiéner, among them *Herzgewachse* on a poem by Maeterlinck. This was sung by Mathilde Veillé-Lavallée, who had a very shrill voice, while Poulenc played the celesta, Wiéner the harmonium, and I conducted the weird ensemble. In his love for contemporary music, Wiéner bore all the material responsibility for these concerts, and was so modest that he himself seldom appeared as a soloist. He engaged the Pro Arte Quartet to play the Czech composer Alois Hába's quarter-tone quartet. I had then, and still have, no prejudice against this kind of experiment, provided the works concerned are powerful, sincere, and moving, but this was not the case in this instance: we found it both boring and weak. Wiéner had several of my works performed. He had singers who had been rehearsed by Collaer in preparation for a concert in Brussels a few weeks later come from there to play my *Cantate du Retour de l'enfant prodigue*. He organized several Stravinsky festivals, too. He presented the *Symphonies pour instruments à vent* and *Mavra*. This *opéra bouffe*, which was created by the Ballets Russes at the Opéra in 1922, represented an important stage in Stravinsky's development. It marked the break with the period leading up to *Le Sacre* and *Noces* and with the period that was really a prolongation of the other, including works such as *Renard* or even *L'Histoire du soldat*. The atmosphere of France, in which Stravinsky had been living for so many years, as well as his admiration for Tchaikovsky, had perhaps induced him to substitute for his vividly colored, Oriental, Russian art, almost Asiatic in feeling with its complicated harmonies and barbaric rhythms that had the violence of a hurricane, a type of music that was spare, stripped of inessentials, economical in the means it employed, and imbued with a sense of proportion that by no means excluded grace or grandeur, but conveyed a feeling that was pure, quintessential, devoid of artifice. *Mavra* was the first step along this path, from which Stravinsky never strayed again; from then on, his works, while retaining a precisely defined style, adequate to their subject, and full of an individual flavor and richness, all took on a more austere character. Later, in his marvelous *Apollon Musagète*, *Perséphone*, *Symphonie des psaumes*, and even *Ode* for orchestra and the pellucid Sonata for two pianos, a serene tenderness, of a quality previously unknown in his work, was to make itself felt.

The public, which had taken ten years to swallow *Le Sacre*, was scandalized by the simplicity of *Mavra*. It could not bear the idea that Stravinsky should change his manner just when they had him neatly labeled as the composer of *Le Sacre*. The press showed a pitiful lack of comprehension; it screamed that Stravinsky no longer wrote like Stravinsky, that he was no longer capable of expressing himself, that his music was dull and insipid, that his melodies were "old-fashioned." Vuillermoz's article was so full of incomprehension that Stravinsky could not resist pasting it on the first page of his manuscript. A small number of musicians— Auric, Poulenc, Roland-Manuel, Rieti, Sauguet, and myself —were so deeply moved by this work that Jean Wiéner gave us another opportunity of hearing it. Courageous defenders such as he and Paul Collaer reward the efforts of composers, who so often have to contend with incomprehension and skepticism.

131

ROBERT SCHMITZ and his wife had been living in New York since 1918; they worked hard to spread the knowledge and appreciation of contemporary music, more especially of French music. They were good enough to put me in touch with their manager, Miss Bogue, a white-haired spinster who found for me a sufficient number of engagements to justify a trip to the United States. Some of these involved difficulties. I had been invited by certain conductors to appear as a pianist, and as I was no virtuoso, I had to compose *for myself* an easy work that would give the audience the impression that it was difficult. This was how I came to write the *Ballade* for piano and orchestra. In 1926 and again in 1941 a similar set of circumstances led me to compose *Le Carnaval d'Aix* and my Second Piano Concerto, some of the passages in which were beyond me. A few weeks before leaving France, I received a telegram from my manager telling me that I was to conduct a concert in Philadelphia. It stipulated that the program should be half modern and half classical. This was a new complication. I had no experience as a conductor beyond conducting my own works.

On arrival in Philadelphia, I learned that Stokowski had

appointed Enesco, Casella, and myself to take his place during his absence in Europe. Naturally, neither he nor my manager, Miss Bogue, nor Arthur Judson, the manager of the orchestra, had the slightest inkling that I would have the audacity to make my debut as a conductor with his orchestra. I was not too nervous, however; as I had to begin some time, it was all to the good that it should be with the finest symphony orchestra in the world. I think it was the prospect of this that turned my head and prevented me from realizing what an adventure I was rushing into. I chose a relatively easy program: a concerto by Philipp Emanuel Bach, Mendelssohn's "Italian" Symphony, the second suite from *L'Arlésienne*, *Parade*, Auric's *Nocturne des fâcheux*, Honegger's *Pastorale d'eté*, an overture of Poulenc's based on the finale of the Sonata for two pianos, which I had orchestrated, my *Sérénade*, and one or two *Saudades*. The contemporary works bothered me less than the others. I studied the scores very thoroughly, and the rehearsals did not go too badly. The orchestra must have found me awkward, but the men were very kind. My friends the Schmitzes came over from New York, terribly anxious. It was a dreadful shock for them to find me, half an hour before my concert was to begin, calmly seated at table eating my dessert. I endeavored to conduct with simplicity and precision, and this was my salvation. I even had the satisfaction of reading in one newspaper that I was a good conductor but a deplorable composer. But I still tremble when I think of my audacity, or rather my innocence at that time. Where ignorance is bliss—

I made my debut as a pianist under Dirk Foch, a Dutchman who conducted the New York City Symphony Orchestra. I played my *Ballade* and conducted my *Sérénade* on the same program. Miss Bogue had booked other engagements for me, of the most varied character. I gave a little talk on Satie and the music of Les Six from the pulpit of the Church of St. Joan of Arc, in the middle of the service, while Robert Schmitz illustrated my talk with extracts on the piano. The congregation was eager for instruction, and the day before, in similar circumstances, had heard a lecture on grapefruit-growing. I also went to Princeton University and Vassar College. At the latter, the audience, wholly composed of young ladies, intimidated me; I certainly had no idea that I should spend several years of my life teaching musical composition in a similar college. The wife of the publisher of the *Washington Post*, Mrs. Eugene Meyer, a great friend of Bibi Picabia and Germaine Survage, asked me to play some contemporary music at her home. She owned some very lovely modern paintings, as well as sculptures by Brancusi, whom she had induced to come to the United States for an exhibition of his works, and they had remained on excellent terms. A year or two later I met her again in Paris at a dinner in Brancusi's house, to which Satie and I had also been invited. We ate a delicious dinner cooked in the sculptor's great furnace.

At Boston I took part in a concert of my works given by a group of players from the Boston Symphony Orchestra and conducted by the flautist Laurent. I gave a lecture at Harvard, and the members of the Harvard Glee Club prepared a surprise for me by singing the *Psalm* I had composed for them at the request of their director, Dr. Archibald T. Davison, whom I had met in Paris on the occasion of a lunch given in his honor, and in honor of the members of the musical delegation from Harvard University, by Marshal Foch. The lunch took place at the Cercle Interallié, and the marshal had invited musicians of all generations, from members of the Institut to the so-called rebels. When the dessert was served, the young Americans had greeted the Marshal with some of their college yells and Indian war-cries. In Boston, Dr. Davison introduced me to some of his friends, who at once decided to offer me a party. This was right in the middle of Prohibition, and the tiniest authentic drink cost a small fortune. Whisky was served in teacups, which were filled underneath the table. Dr. Davison had chosen the Hotel Brunswick for the party, because it had an excellent jazz orchestra and he knew I would like to hear it. When I arrived in New York, I had told the newspapermen interviewing me that European music was considerably influenced by American music. "But whose music?" they asked me; "Macdowell's or Carpenter's?" "Neither the one nor the other," I answered, "I mean jazz." They were filled with consternation, for at that time most American musicians had not realized the importance of jazz as an art form and relegated it to the dance hall. The headlines given to my interviews prove the astonishment caused by my statements: "Milhaud admires jazz" or "Jazz dictates the future of European music." Of course, my opinions won me the sympathy of Negro music-lovers, who flocked to my concerts. The chairman of the Negro musicians' union even wrote me a touching letter of thanks. Little suspecting what complications this would cause, I immediately invited him to lunch: no restaurant would serve us, but at last Germaine Schmitz solved this delicate problem by asking the manager of the Hotel Lafayette to receive us. I was also called upon by Harry Burleigh, the famous arranger of Negro spirituals, who played me Negro folk tunes and hymns, which interested me keenly, for I wished to take advantage of my stay to find out all I could about Negro music. The jazz orchestra of the Hotel Brunswick was conducted by a young violinist called Reissmann, who got from his instrumentalists an extreme refinement of pianissimo tones, murmured notes, and glancing chords, whisperings from the muted brass, and barely formulated moans from the saxophone, which had a highly individual flavor. The regular rhythm was conveyed by the muffled beat of the percussion, and above it he spun the frail filigree of sound from the other instruments, to which the high notes of the violin lent an added poignancy. It made a great contrast to Paul Whiteman's lively orchestra, which I had heard a few days before in New York and which had the precision of an elegant, well-oiled machine, a sort of Rolls-Royce of dance music, but whose atmosphere remained entirely of this world.

I owe to Yvonne George my introduction to the pure tradition of New Orleans jazz. In the course of a little reception that followed a lecture I gave at the Alliance Française, she came up to me and said: "You look bored, come and have dinner with me, and afterwards I'll take you to Harlem when I've done my number." She lived in the Hotel Lafayette. In the next room to hers Isadora Duncan and her Russian poet Essenin used to quarrel and chase one another right out on the fire escape. Yvonne introduced me to Marcel Duchamp, an old friend of Satie and Picabia, whose paintings were closely associated with the beginnings of cubism and had played a dominant part in its development. After dinner I heard Yvonne George give her number. She was on Broadway, singing French songs of an intensely realistic character in a style that was both plain and charged with desperate feeling.

Harlem had not yet been discovered by the snobs and æsthetes: we were the only white folk there. The music I heard was absolutely different from anything I had ever heard before and was a revelation to me. Against the beat of the drums the melodic lines crisscrossed in a breathless pattern of broken and twisted rhythms. A Negress whose grating voice seemed to come from the depths of the centuries sang in front of the various tables. With despairing pathos and dramatic feeling she sang over and over again, to the point of exhaustion, the same refrain, to which the constantly changing melodic pattern of the orchestra wove a kaleidoscopic background. This authentic music had its roots in the darkest corners of the Negro soul, the vestigial traces of Africa, no doubt. Its effect on me was so overwhelming that I could not tear myself away. From then on I frequented other Negro theaters and dance halls. In some of their shows the singers were accompanied by a flute, a clarinet, two trumpets, a trombone, a complicated percussion section played by one man, a piano, and a string quintet. I was living in the French House of Columbia University, enjoying the charming hospitality of Mlle Blanche Prenez; the Schmitzes were my close neighbors. As I never missed the slightest opportunity of visiting Harlem, I persuaded my friends to accompany me, as well as Casella and Mengelberg, who were in New York at the time.

When I went back to France, I never wearied of playing over and over, on a little portable phonograph shaped like a camera, Black Swan records I had purchased in a little shop in Harlem. More than ever I was resolved to use jazz for a chamber work.

19

AUSTRIA — POLAND — HOLLAND — ITALY

As FRANCIS POULENC and I were eager to renew our contacts with the Austrian musicians from whom we had been separated by the war, we went on a journey to central Europe. Marya Freund went with us. Vienna had suffered a terrible food-shortage, from which it was only just recovering, and was still a prey to inflation and poverty; yet its artistic life continued. At the Redoutensaal, an enchanting little rococo theater, we saw a performance of *The Marriage of Figaro* and at the Opera Strauss's *Ariadne auf Naxos*. The libretto by Hofmannsthal, Strauss's collaborator-in-chief, was of the greatest interest. He had contrived a double plot, most skillfully worked out, of the adventures of Ariadne and of scenes from Italian comedy. We met Hofmannsthal at the house of Frau Mahler, the widow of the composer, who entertained all the intellectual and artistic élite of Vienna. This lady, whose beauty was equaled only by her kindness, wanted us to meet all her friends: Alban Berg, for whom we had the greatest admiration; Anton Webern, with some of whose grippingly interesting quartets the Pro Arte Quartet had regaled us a few weeks previously; Egon Wellesz, a very erudite composer and a specialist in Byzantine music, who showed us real friendship when, a week or two later, Poulenc fell seriously ill and had to be operated on for an abscess in the throat. I shall never forget how Wellesz brought him a jar of jam, which at that time represented a real sacrifice for a Viennese, especially if he had children.

Erika Wagner, who sang Schönberg's works in Germany, happened to be in Vienna at the same time as we, and Frau Mahler thought that it might be a good idea to organize a double performance of *Pierrot Lunaire* in the German and French versions. Schönberg agreed, and we used the same instrumentalists, including the pianist, Steuermann, an ardent devotee of Schönberg's work. It was a most exciting experience; Schönberg's conducting brought out the dramatic qualities of his work, making it harsher, wilder, more intense; my reading, on the other hand, emphasized the music's sensuous qualities, all the sweetness, subtlety, and translucency of it. Erika Wagner spoke the German words in a strident tone, with less respect for the notes as written than Marya Freund, who if anything erred on the side of observing them too closely. I realized on that occasion that the problem of recitative was insoluble.

After the performance of *Pierrot Lunaire* in such widely varying interpretations, Schönberg and I discussed our respective points of view, so different, yet equally justified. He invited us to call on him at Mödling, in the neighborhood of Vienna. We spent a wonderful afternoon together. At his request, I played my Second Suite. Francis played his *Promenades* for the piano, which he had just completed. Schönberg talked to us at length of his works, especially of the operas *Glückliche Hand* and *Erwartung*, whose scores I had just bought. He gave me a copy of his Five Orchestral Pieces, the score he had himself used for conducting the first performance, with all his penciled annotations. A princely gift! Then he took us into his dining-room to have tea. The room was decorated with haunting pictures painted by himself, all representing parts of faces in which only the eyes were visible.

Marya Freund, who was Polish, had organized concerts for us in Warsaw and her native town of Kalisz. There too we found traces of the war's ravages: poverty, cold, and famine. Our hosts, Marya's relatives, spent a fortune on keeping us warm. As all the pipes had burst because of the cold, we gave our recitals by candlelight, huddled in our overcoats.

In September 1922 I was invited, together with Roussel and Ravel, to attend the Festival of French Music organized at the Amsterdam Concertgebouw by Mengelberg. This was the first occasion on which a work of mine had been included in a program given under official auspices. Apart from my *Suite symphonique*, Ravel's *La Valse*, Roussel's *Pour une fête de printemps*, Fauré's *Requiem*, and Debussy's *Fantaisie* for piano and orchestra were played. Ravel enjoyed considerable prestige abroad, but I had a greater admiration for Roussel, whose development and unremitting research had led him to a complete mastery of his art, while he never lost the freshness of his imagination.

During my stay in Amsterdam, I often went out with Bob de Roos, a young composer whose acquaintance I had made in Paris when he called on me to show me his music, in which I immediately detected sterling qualities. Whenever Dutch reporters plied me with the inevitable question: "What do you think of Dutch music?" I used to answer (in this imitating Satie, who never let an opportunity pass of praising the young): "I won't talk to you about musicians who are already well known, but of Bob de Roos, in whom I have the greatest hopes.' When the questioners expressed astonishment at this unknown name, I would add: "He is only fourteen, but remember his name!" When, ten years later, his two symphonies were played, as well as his Studies for piano and orchestra and his music for *Ajax*, which classed him among the best Dutch composers, I wonder whether any one of these reporters thought of my prediction. I stayed with the curator of the Rijks Museum, Mr. Van Notten, who took me to see Van Gogh's sister, a very old lady inhabiting a modest little apartment, and so conventional that she did not have a single canvas by her brother on her walls. She possessed only a few of them, and they were relegated to the attic. I strolled a great deal around the silent streets of Amsterdam, austerely bordered by ancient houses and interrupted by slow-moving canals that hardly seemed to move at all. What a contrast with the modern districts where the white and airy buildings were triumphant examples of all that is best in modern architecture! It was a pleasure for me to go back to Amsterdam a year or two later when Mengelberg engaged me to play my *Ballade* and Monteux to perform my *Carnaval d'Aix*. It was also in Amsterdam that I heard Hindemith give the first performance of the Concerto for viola that I had written for him.

Poulenc and I had such good memories of our previous trip together that we were on the lookout for an opportunity to undertake another. The idea of going to Italy was attractive, but we needed a pretext. Casella tried to get us an engagement with the Santa Cecilia, the oldest chamber-music society in Rome, but the reputation enjoyed by the "Groupe des Six" was not calculated to appeal to the society's reactionary audiences. We therefore contented ourselves with a private concert in the house of Count Lovatelli as a justification for our journey.

In the course of my travels I have often visited towns as a

tourist does, hurrying from museum to church and from church to museum without wasting a single moment. In Rome, however, I had such a sense of being at home that my only ambition was to bask in the sunshine on the steps of the Piazza di Spagna, nibbling shiny black olives sprinkled with chopped garlic. But after we had spent a few days in idling, my cousins Marcelle and Renée Milhaud, who were staying with one of their aunts, persuaded us for our own delectation to explore the city in good earnest. We went everywhere: Tivoli, Frascati, the Villa d'Este—the last conjuring up for us the conversations between Lamartine and Mme de Girardin—accompanied by the murmur of those same cascades that Liszt, too, glorified in song. We often ate in little *trattorie* outside which, on market days, innumerable painted carts would call a halt, each with its hood folded back to enable the driver to rest before going on to Rome to unload his cargo of wine.

Claude Delvincourt, who held the Prix de Rome at that time, invited us to meet some of his colleagues. The immediate surroundings of the Villa Medici have an unutterable charm; you go in through a little square adorned with a broad-based fountain splashing into a pool. It is an ideal haven for the artists who, for three long years, are freed from material cares to work, meditate at leisure, and exchange ideas with their gifted colleagues. Just as my voyage to Brazil had given me that change of scene which is desirable for any young man or woman beginning to take stock of his or her own abilities, the Villa Medici serves to develop the imagination of these young artists, while at the same time giving them the opportunity of seeing new faces and a new country.

In Naples a disagreeable surprise awaited us at our hotel: there would be no room available for two whole days. Rather than sleep in the open, we decided to take a boat and sail to

Palermo. We arrived in Sicily early in the morning in dazzling sunlight, and endeavored to cram as many things into our visit as we could: the lovely old palaces, the Cathedral of Monreale on the outskirts of the town, and even the catacombs of the Carmelite Convent, in which the skeletons of prelates and bishops stand ceremoniously clad in their most sumptuous robes. This macabre sight is more Spanish than Sicilian in taste.

Once back in Naples, we went for long walks around the harbor area, in the working-class quarters, where the steep, narrow streets are festooned with lines of many-colored washing stretched from window to window like gaudy rainbows. One night we hired a queer sort of vehicle driven by what appeared to be half a driver—he had only one eye, one leg, and one arm—who leaped up to his seat on the box and took us to see all the puppet theaters in the Neapolitan suburbs. Everywhere we went, we saw the same medieval battle scenes, enacted before a noisy, exuberant audience that greeted every line with a roar and consisted solely of men and little boys, mostly wearing caps and no waistcoats, often no jackets either, and reveling in their untidiness. (In Naples, working-class women never go to the theater.) A year or two later, when I happened to be in Liége, I went to the Petit Théâtre Royal des Marionnettes in the rue de la Roture. This was the pompous way in which a little bistro in one of the most populous quarters of the city described itself. There you could drink "Gueuse" beer, foamy and bitter, in a little back room like a fairground booth, with narrow backless benches set too close together, on which was huddled a mass of noisy, ragged urchins, poverty-stricken old women, and a few idle drinkers. Twice a week for years these spectators had crowded to see the same spectacle showing the adventures of Sir Corydon at the court of Charlemagne. There were interminable battles between the infidels and the glorious warriors of the Emperor, conversations and conspiracies between officers, the arrival of a princess, who recited long poems in Walloon dialect which excited wild enthusiasm. During the battle scenes the action was accompanied by a single drum supported by the regular percussion supplied by the sound made by the legs of the puppets as they fought. What interested me most about these helmeted heroes in medieval armor or these princesses in hennins and dresses adorned with gold and brocade was that the puppets and their actions were the same as those I had seen in the little theater in Naples, the home of Pulcinella. Out of this primitive form of art had sprung the prettiest theater that could possibly be imagined, that of I Piccoli in Rome: an ideal theater in which every effect is obtained by means of machinery so complicated that the puppets are capable of miming an actor's every gesture and of dancing a ballet in perfect time and with absolutely accurate steps. The puppets represent all kind of things, animals or fairy chariots. All that seems unreal and impossible in an ordinary theater becomes easy and possible in this little theater, where the most extravagant fantasy has been let loose. The repertoire of I Piccoli is amazingly extensive. Its director, Podrecca, put on ballets and classical operas, or sketches by Casella and other modern composers in décors by contemporary painters.

Before leaving Naples we visited the museum, which contains some magnificent bronzes from Herculaneum and a "secret" collection of a rather special character, to which women are not admitted, and the Aquarium, where there are wonderful kinds of tiny fish, some as bright as golden nails, others elegantly adorned with wavy crinkled gills like the lace collars worn by seventeenth-century noblemen. We spent an unforgettable day at Pompeii, where one can still see traces of nearly all the everyday customs of that community so suddenly engulfed by death.

There is a local superstition to the effect that those who throw a coin into the Fountain of Trevi in Rome come back to Rome again. Like most tourists, I had of course performed the traditional rite, with a smile on my lips, but hope in my heart. Was it to those two or three sous that I owed the fact that I was engaged in 1924 to play my *Ballade* at a symphony concert at the Augusteo? Casella and Malipiero warned me immediately that the Roman public was not enamored of contemporary music, to which it always gave a stormy reception. The rehearsals went off very well, even cordially. The same was not true of the concert itself. At the very first measures the audience started to shout. They stopped while I was playing, but shortly afterward the tumult broke out again and lasted to the end of the piece. I bowed coldly and walked slowly off into the wings, where I found Molinari, who had fled so rapidly before the last note had properly died away that to me he had looked as if he were swimming out through the violins. Some of my friends in the Ambassador's box, and my host, Jacques Truelle, were already convinced there was going to be an anti-French demonstration. I was able to set their minds at rest in this respect and to assure them that the audience at the Augusteo was just as hostile to the works of contemporary Italian composers.

Vittorio Rieti invited me to his house to meet Mario Labroca and Renzo Massarani. They played me some of their music; a little *a cappella* chorus by Rieti called *Barabau* which I found so pleasing that I carried away a copy that I showed to Diaghilev on my return, when he asked me what I had heard in Rome. He immediately commissioned from Rieti a ballet to be based on this little choral work of the folk-

145

music type, steeped in malicious jollity. The ballet, for which Utrillo painted the scenery and Balanchine did the choreography, was an enormous success. After that, Rieti fell into the way of coming often to Paris for long stays, and took part in all our musical activities.

Although I did not bring back with me from these later travels any musical inspiration, they at least gave me the opportunity of forming bonds of friendship with Vittorio Rieti and the managing director of Universal-Edition in Vienna, Emil Hertzka, who was to be for me not only a devoted publisher, but also a faithful friend.

20

BALLETS

As soon as I came back from the United States, I got in touch with Fernand Léger and Blaise Cendrars, with whom I was to work on a new ballet for Rolf de Maré. Cendrars chose for his subject the creation of the world, going for his inspiration to African folklore, in which he was particularly deeply versed, having just published a Negro anthology. On this occasion I remained more closely in contact with my collaborators than for any other of my works. They were great frequenters of bals-musette, and often took me with them, thus revealing to me a side of Parisian life with which I had not previously been familiar. Wearing cloth caps and with mackintoshes slung from our shoulders, we would set out from the little restaurant in the rue de Belleville, famous for its tripe, where we had had dinner, and make our way to the rue de Lappe. From every café came the strains of the accordion, sometimes accompanied by the clarinet, the cornet, the trombone, or the violin. Men wearing caps and soft-colored shirts, with a bright-hued muffler wound round their throats, danced with their pleasant-faced girls, so well trained that they would never consent to dance with anyone else. Their "man" paid for the right to dance, handing the money to the lessee of the dance hall, who went about among the couples constantly repeating the words: *"Passons la monnaie!"* (Pay up please), dropping the coins into a broad pouch she wore slung round her shoulder. Sometimes the cries of customers calling for a drink—a *"fraisette"* or a *"rince-cochon"*—drowned the sound of the music. Here the scene was always gay and animated. On the boulevard Barbès or the Place des Alpes the atmosphere was quite different. Behind the Bastille, the *Auvergnats* of Paris danced the bourrée to the sound of the hurdy-gurdy, while in the rue Blomet the West Indians, with their womenfolk wearing printed cotton headdresses, met to dance the beguine, whose irregular rhythm conjured up the palm trees and savannas of their islands. During our explorations Léger, Cendrars, and I were working out the details of our ballet. Léger wanted to adapt primitive Negro art and paint the drop-curtain and the scenery with African divinities expressive of power and darkness. He was never satisfied that his sketches were terrifying enough. He showed me one for the curtain, black on a dark brown background, which he had rejected on the grounds that it was too bright and "pretty-pretty." He would have liked to use skins representing flowers, trees, and animals of all kinds, which would have been filled with gas and allowed to fly up into the air at the moment of creation, like so many balloons. This plan could not be adopted because it would have required a complicated apparatus for inflating them in each corner of the stage, and the sound of the gas would have drowned out the music. He had to be satisfied with drawing his inspiration from the animal costumes worn by African dancers during their religious rites. At last in *La Création du monde* I had the opportunity I had been waiting for to use those elements of jazz to which I had devoted so much study. I adopted the same orchestra as used in Harlem, seventeen solo instru-

Willem Mengelberg,
Milhaud,
Ernest Schelling,
and Ludwig Wüllner,
Amsterdam, 1923

Program of French première *of Schönberg's* Pierrot Lunaire

ADMINISTRATION DE CONCERTS A. DANDELOT (fondée en 1898) 83, Rue d'Amsterdam

3ème CONCERT JEAN WIÉNER

LUNDI 16 JANVIER 1922, à 9 heures, à la SALLE GAVEAU, 45, Rue La Boëtie

PIERROT LUNAIRE

d'ARNOLD SCHÖNBERG

MÉLODRAME EN 21 PARTIES POUR VOIX ET PETIT ORCHESTRE

1re Partie : 1. Ivresse de lune - 11. Colombine - 111. Pierrot dandy - 12. Une au lune - 5. Valse de Chopin - 41. Évocation - 511. L'ape malade
2me Partie : 511. Nuit - 13. Prière à Pierrot - 5. Vol - 41. Messe rouge - 5411. Chant du pendu - 5411. Décapitation - 5512. Les croix
3me Partie : 55. Nostalgie - 5551. Insolence - 5551. Parodie - 55515. Tache de lune - 515. Sérénade - 55. Le retour - 5551. Le vieux parfum

MARYA FREUND
JEAN WIÉNER
MM. FLEURY, DELACROIX, ROËLENS et FEUILLARD

SOUS LA DIRECTION DE

DARIUS MILHAUD

PIANO GAVEAU

AUCUN BILLET DE FAVEUR NE SERA DONNÉ

PLACES à 3, 4, 6, 10, 12, 15, 20 et 25 francs, à la SALLE GAVEAU, 45, Rue La Boëtie ; chez DURAND, 4, Place de la Madeleine ; au BUREAU MUSICAL, 30, Rue Tronchet et à l'Administration de Concerts A. DANDELOT, 83, Rue d'Amsterdam, Téléph. Gut 18-62

Milhaud and Francis Poulenc, 1922

Milhaud, Jean Cocteau, and Francis Poulenc, 1952

ments, and I made wholesale use of the jazz style to convey a purely classical feeling.

I wrote *La Création* in the new apartment I had just taken at 10 boulevard de Clichy. Paul Morand had changed houses at the same time as I, and as his apartment was very tiny, and we had so many friends in common, he proposed that we should combine forces and celebrate our housewarming at my place. I piled up my furniture in every corner, and still the congestion was terrible. Our friends thronged the staircase outside and even invaded the café of La Chope Pigalle on the ground floor. Through the open windows came the blaring of the *Limonaires*, shots from the shooting-galleries, and the growls of wild beasts from the menageries, for the *fête de Montmartre* had been in full swing since the beginning of June. We had arranged a surprise for our guests. Morand would have liked to bring a lion, but as the lion-tamer had told us that it would refuse to come down the stairs again, we had to be content with a Bird Theater. What a charming show it was! Tame canaries and sparrows perched on their master's fingers and shoulders and head, or flew round the room performing a thousand different tricks. Then they enacted a little sketch. One canary shot another bird with a tiny canon, and its victim lay still on the ground. They laid him on a little hearse drawn around the table by two birds, and to conclude the performance a canary magician revived him by stroking him with his wing, whereupon he flew off as fast as he could go.

A little while after this party I went to stay with my parents at Aix, to enjoy a month or two of solitude and work in the peace of L'Enclos. Désormière and Paul Collaer and his wife were to join me there in order that we might all go on to Sardinia together. I was fascinated by this country, which the travel bureau never mentioned and none of my friends had ever visited. Paul Collaer, that admirable organizer, had prepared our expedition a long time in advance, and he had been in touch with the Italian Touring Club for information on all the peculiarities of Sardinia. He had prepared an interesting itinerary based on market days and popular feast days and attached especial importance to the Feast of Fonni, among the most famous.

We took advantage of a short halt in Genoa to visit the *campo santo*, which startled us by the pompous ninetyish style of its funerary monuments, adorned with statues of the defunct wearing frock coats or dresses in the fashion of 1900. We saw the living replicas of these when that evening we attend a ridiculous performance of *Aïda* in which there was such a straining after effect that the dramatic feeling was swamped by a flood of sham lyricism. We embarked at Civita Vecchia, where Stendhal had once been French consul.

Sardinia is so well protected by its insularity that it has remained unspoiled, authentic, wild. If it had not been for the war, few of its inhabitants would ever have seen the Continent. In one little village the children ran after us shouting: "Cinesi! Cinesi!" (Chinamen!), for we were the first foreigners they had ever seen. Our only luggage consisted of the haversacks we carried on our backs, and this enabled us to travel by horseback as well as by bus. On market days the latter did not serve the most outlying villages. We also took the local trains, crammed with peasants. It was not unusual to find them lying in the corridors, helpless with malaria, which is endemic on the east coast.

The villagers wore extremely picturesque costumes with short skirts, resembling those worn by the Montenegrins, over their bare legs, waistcoats of tanned skins lined with lamb's wool and adorned with brilliant designs, and a kind of bonnet of black wool shaped like a stocking. The younger men wore dark-colored European-type suits. On Sundays they forgathered to dance local dances to the strains of the accordion and the *sampogna*, a kind of rustic oboe. The custom of serenading is still very popular in Sardinia, and it was not uncommon to hear in the early part of the night a song repeated over and over to the accompaniment of the guitar. The music would never come to an end if the "fair one" or the friend to whom it was addressed did not appear at the balcony and distribute thanks and little gifts to the musicians. I noted down several of these melodies, of Spanish or Saracen origin, little thinking that I should have the opportunity to use them soon.

It was a very attractive country. We visited a great number of villages perched on the heights and looking down over vast landscapes, often intersected by the prehistoric buildings known as *nouragues*. In the little towns, architectural details, balconies and window-gratings of forged iron, bore witness to the period of Spanish domination of the island. We stopped for a few days at Cagliari, the capital, and the well-stocked shops were a pleasant change after the harsh austerity of the villages. In the museum there is an antique collection of old Sardinian bronzes, most of which go back to the mists of antiquity, and twelfth-century fabrics with complicated friezes representing stylized birds and geometrical designs.

We took the train to go to the Feast of Fonni, and at every little station we would get out of the train to stretch our legs. Once we picked some of the fruit of the prickly pear, and as we did not know how to skin it, our fingers were full of little prickles that were very difficult to extract. We were so enchanted by the prospect of seeing the Feast of Fonni that we were full of high spirits; this interested our fellow travelers, who asked us where we were going.

"*Andiamo per la Festa di Fonni!*" we said, and as they did not seem to understand this, we explained in our halting Italian what the purpose of our journey was. Immediately our peasants shook their heads, and informed us that the Feast of Fonni, of which we had read a glowing description in our up-to-date guidebooks, had long since ceased to exist. The beauty of the surrounding landscape made up for our disappointment, and we went for some wonderful rides on horseback around Gennargentu, the highest mountain in Sardinia.

We had to think of getting back to our respective countries and jobs, however, and so we re-embarked at Porto Torres. A policeman asked us suspiciously what the significance of the color of our shirts might be, and what party Déso [1] and I belonged to. The poor Fascist would no doubt have been incapable of understanding that we had bought the shirts in the market at Aix because we liked their blue color and thought they were practical.

The Collaers had never been to Rome before. We tried to show them as much as we could in twenty-four hours, and then we parted. Before returning to Paris, Déso and I spent a day or two in Florence, which, in spite of the lovely surrounding country and the splendor of its buildings, seemed to me to be more of a museum than a town, and when we had thoroughly explored it I was not sorry to leave.

A few weeks afterward the Ballets Suédois gave the first performance of *La Création du monde*. Léger's contribution helped to make it an unforgettable spectacle. The critics decreed that my music was frivolous and more suitable for a restaurant or a dance hall than for the concert hall. Ten years later the selfsame critics were discussing the philosophy of

[1] This was the nickname we had given to Désormière.

152

jazz and learnedly demonstrating that *La Création* was the best of my works.

De Maré was to undertake a tour of the United States and wanted to put on an authentic American work, but did not know whom to approach. He was afraid of coming across some composer struggling along in the wake of Debussy, Ravel, or someone composing music *à la Brahms* or *à la Reger*. I had met Cole Porter several times at the house of the Princesse de Polignac. This elegant young American, who always wore a white carnation in the buttonhole of his faultless dinner jacket, sang in a low, husky voice songs having just the qualities that de Maré was looking for: I introduced them to each other. De Maré immediately asked him to treat a subject admirably suitable for his music: the arrival of a young Swede in New York. Charles Koechlin undertook to orchestrate his score, which was redolent of the pure spirit of Manhattan, with wistful blues alternating with throbbing ragtime rhythms. This odd partnership between the technician of counterpoint and fugue and the brilliant future "King of Broadway" was an outstanding success. Fernand Léger asked an American artist, Gerald Murphy, to paint the scenery, and the skyscrapers of Time Square were seen to rise on the stage of the Théâtre des Champs-Élysées.

Despite all the praiseworthy efforts by the Ballets Suédois and all the esteem in which they were held, the Ballets Russes achieved a greater technical perfection. On the instigation of Stravinsky, their indefatigable promoter, Diaghilev, even attempted an interesting experiment. Together they picked out one or two of the little operas that were no longer played, and Diaghilev decided to produce them. As most of the arias were linked together by passages of spoken dialogue, however, he decided to follow the precedent set by Berlioz in providing musical settings for the recitatives in *Der Freischütz*, and by Guiraud, who did the same thing for *Carmen*, and asked Satie, Auric, and Poulenc to compose some music for the spoken passages in three of Gounod's little operas: *Le Médecin malgré lui*, *La Colombe*, and *Philémon et Baucis*. He also proposed to produce Chabrier's *L'Éducation manquée*, but had not yet decided on a composer for its recitatives. Satie, who had had many arguments with Diaghilev about me, took the opportunity of mentioning my name. He pointed out that, bearing the stamp of Chabrier's style, my music would be less likely to incur his displeasure, and during the summer I received the following letter from Satie.

Saturday, July 21, 1923

My very dear friend,

I have been requested by Diaghilev to ask you to do him a favor: to complete *L'Éducation manquée* for him. I told our dear Director that you were the *only possible* one able to complete the work as it ought to be done, thanks to your so noble inspiration and your unerring craftsmanship.

I pulled his leg a little about his ostracism of you, and he seems to be better disposed toward you now.

What do you say?

Loyally, I cannot advise you. I must tell you that one thousand francs is the price mentioned, and that the work is only short, but . . . *most important*, and *deserves* to be followed by some form of *compensation*. Yes.

Judge for yourself.

PS. Poulenc has already done wonders for *La Colombe*. So I understand. Lucky fellow!

154

In view of the aversion that I felt Diaghilev entertained for me, I hesitated to accept this work, amusing, certainly, but which would be less interesting than an original composition, and would no doubt lead nowhere. Satie, who was devoted to me, did not lose hope of winning me over, and wrote to me again:

Sunday, July 28, 1923

My very dear friend,

Diaghilev is not here. I have just written to him and told him to write to you himself.

Your letter gave me very great pleasure. You are absolutely right. Once you get into the company, they will adore you, and Diaghilev will see for himself what a magnificent artist you are. I have told you already: he is coming round to better feelings toward you. Our friend Stravinsky was working him up a bit against you, if I may say so. Let's forget the past—and even the future too!

I am working on the *Docteur qui s'imagine l'être*, I'm not getting on at all.

Sunday, August 19, 1923

I am working like mad. . . . Yes. . . . It's a good joke (for me). . . . I am churning out Gounod like a house on fire. It's all very Reberish (and *all balls* if I may say so. . . . Yes).

Saturday, September 25, 1923

Dear friend,

Come back soon and let us have a talk together. . . . I am overjoyed to think that (at last!) Diaghilev has written to you. It's a victory over X. (I'd like to know who X is. Yes.)

155

I am working like a worker at work (a rare thing). I have just finished Act II of *Le Médecin malgré lui.* "Someone" (?) told Jean I was going to let it drop. Hm. . . . Could that "someone" have been—our friend Auric?

In the end my friend Satie's persistence wore down my resistance; I accepted the work, and found it engrossing. *L'Éducation manquée* is written for three singers; but as there are only arias for the baritone and the tenor, we wanted to give the soprano one. Mme Bretton-Chabrier and the publishing firm of Enoch gave me access to Chabrier's unpublished manuscripts, among which I discovered an enchanting melody that I could use without change. René Chalupt wrote words that fitted in with the dramatic situation, and the gap was filled. For the connecting passages between the scenes, I endeavored to stick close to Chabrier's style in order to ensure continuity in the musical development and in the orchestration. I believe I was moderately successful in this aim, for during rehearsals I heard Diaghilev asking in an undertone: "And what about this? Is this Chabrier?" He could not tell the true from the false.

The Hereditary Princess of Monaco had given her patronage to the troupe of the Ballets Russes, which thus had the further advantage of working at Monte Carlo, free from material cares. Diaghilev therefore always went there to prepare his plans for the new season. The operas were given such a cool reception at the Casino of Monte Carlo that he abandoned the idea of presenting them in Paris, with the exception of *L'Éducation manquée* (décors and costumes by Juan Gris). As nearly always happens, the public proved to be lacking in imagination and spurned the unexpected. It felt itself cheated, and clamored: "Bring on the ballets!" so noisily that *L'Éducation* had to be withdrawn from the program.

The Paris season of 1924 was a particularly brilliant one from the choreographic point of view, with Diaghilev's troupe vying with Massine's. The latter had left the Ballets Russes in order to strike out on his own, and the Comte de Beaumont, like the noble patrons of the Renaissance, gave him the means of producing, with his own troupe of dancers, the works he had commissioned. I agreed to accept a libretto by Albert Flament on an old subject from the *commedia dell' arte* entitled *Insalata*, a mixture of Punchinello farces and love intrigues thwarted by jealous guardians; in short, a very highly complicated imbroglio bedeviled by a series of disguises and mystifications. I took as my inspiration some ancient Italian music that Massine showed me, and used a few of the serenade themes I had brought back from Sardinia. I kept the title *Salade*, and wrote a choral ballet.

The first rehearsals were held in the lovely drawing-rooms of the Comte de Beaumont at what was formerly the eighteenth-century Spanish Embassy, and later at the Théâtre de la Cigale. A series of literary evenings, dance recitals, and musical concerts was announced to take place under the auspices of the Soirées de Paris. These included a dadaist play by Tristan Tzara called *Mouchoir de nuage* and a very abridged adaptation of *Romeo and Juliet* by Cocteau, whose startlingly original production in conjunction with the scenery by Jean Victor-Hugo, marked an important date in theatrical history. Roger Désormière, a young conductor full of talent and extremely accomplished, who directed all the musical side of the Soirées de Paris, had composed a score reminiscent of the bagpipes of the Elizabethan period. It was a very successful combination. Massine produced my ballet with décors by Braque, and Satie's *Mercure* with décors by Picasso.

In the meantime, Diaghilev's season promised to be exceptionally brilliant. The rivalry between the two troupes gave rise to quite a number of incidents and dramatic episodes, particularly as Massine had carried off with him several of the dancers of the Ballets Russes. However tempted he might have been to do so, Diaghilev could not prevent artists like Braque and Picasso from collaborating in these two ballets, but he warned Poulenc and Auric that he would ignore the success obtained at Monte Carlo by their ballets *Les Biches* and *Les Fâcheux* and would not produce them in Paris if they agreed to co-operate with the Comte de Beaumont. My two friends had to give way to his demands. To lend these young men's works more prestige and ensure their success, Diaghilev engaged André Messager to conduct them, thinking that the presence of the man who had conducted the first performance of *Pelléas* would create a favorable impression on both critics and public.

I was working on *Salade* one day when I received an unexpected visit from Diaghilev. He had come to ask me whether I would write a ballet for his next season. While holding out the lure of the immense advantages that would accrue for me from such a collaboration, he advised me to break off my relations with the Comte de Beaumont on the grounds that, in his opinion, there was no future in the Soirées de Paris. I pointed out that I was under contract, and intended to honor my commitments, but that, in the absence of any clause forbidding me to undertake any other work, I was at his disposal. Diaghilev had no real choice in the matter; he needed a new work in a hurry for the debut of the young English dancer Anton Dolin, and he knew that I worked quickly. Before finally agreeing, I consulted the Comte de Beaumont, who was most understanding. So I wrote *Salade* between February 5 and 20, and *Le Train bleu* between February 15 and March 5. I call these works my twins.

Le Train bleu was an operetta without words. By asking me to treat this subject of Cocteau's, gay, frivolous, and frothy in the manner of Offenbach, Diaghilev was perfectly aware that I would not be able to produce my usual kind of music, which he did not like. The action takes place in a fashionable resort where the elegant train known as *Le Train bleu* daily discharges new crowds of visitors who wander about the stage indulging in their favorite sports—tennis, golf, and so on. Dolin had every opportunity to perform his acrobatic feats and show his choreographic skill. Throughout the rehearsals, Messager was fatherly, charming, and solicitous. The décors were by Laurens, and the costumes by Chanel. There were no incidents during rehearsals.

On the other hand, the performance of *Mercure* at the Soirées de Paris was disturbed by a band of surrealists who organized a demonstration for motives that escaped us. They kept shouting: "Up Picasso! . . . Down with Satie!" This left Satie quite unmoved; indifferent to what these incidents might lead to, he left the box where we were all together, in order to catch the last train for Arcueil. "On my way out," he wrote next day, "I passed through a group of pseudo-dadaists, but they never said a word to me." With the exception of a strike by the musicians ten minutes before the curtain was due to go up, the performances of *Salade* went off normally. On the night of the strike, I had to play my own score at the piano, by candlelight. My singers, the faithful Bathori among them, stood around me. Massine's choreography was very vivid, bringing out some of the dramatic aspects of the subject, whereas Lifar's production at the

Opéra ten years later (with highly Mediterranean décors by Derain) was designed more exclusively to express the lighthearted, frolicsome side of Italian comedy.

Only a few days separated the production of my two ballets. Later on, I had the opportunity of conducting *Le Train bleu* at Monte Carlo and London. A year or two later both works were given on the same program in the Berlin Opera, and *Salade*, which was produced at the Budapest Opera in 1938, was put on again immediately after the liberation.

21

CROSSCURRENTS, FROM "LE ROI DAVID"

TO THE SCHOOL OF ARCUEIL

IN THE history of music, distinct and opposite tendencies have often confronted one another, and frequently have led to open strife, either in the sphere of teaching methods (for example, the Conservatoire and the Schola Cantorum), or between composers like Debussy and d'Indy, or Roussel and Florent Schmitt, who were poles apart, or again between musical societies such as the Nationale and the S.M.I., or the Sérénade and the Triton, whose programs were utterly different. I myself came up against this state of affairs when musical writers, the critics, and a number of fanatical friends systematically opposed and compared Honegger's music and mine. Our friendship and mutual admiration were strong enough to take the strain of these violent attacks.

Honegger's career is a fine example of success rapidly reached in all fields. Whereas at every one of my new works the critics bared their teeth, they accepted his at first hearing; they treated me as a legpuller and joker incapable of serious thought, but they regarded Arthur as both serious and profound. In addition, his pleasant manner and jovial character won him friends without difficulty, whereas I was sometimes violent, outspoken, and at the same time both curt and bashful.

Nearly all Honegger's compositions won him immense success. When he was asked to write a work devoid of technical difficulties, to be sung by mountaineers at the theater of Mézières, in Switzerland, he composed *Le Roi David*, and its success was so great that it was not confined to Switzerland. Performances rapidly followed in Paris, in the course of which several sections of *Le Roi David* were regularly encored. The Parisian public, which hitherto had persisted in its inability to understand modern music, now felt that it had grasped the secret. In his symphonic writings Arthur hit the bull's-eye with the same uneering aim: he sang the praises of an American locomotive in a symphonic poem, and his *Pacific 231* soon went round the world. He only had to touch the operetta, seemingly so remote from the profound thinker idolized by so many writers on music, for it to be an immediate and overwhelming success; as witness *Le Roi Pausole*, with its run of a thousand performances. When he turned to the cinema, as soon as the film-producers had agreed to collaborate with a so-called "symphonic" composer, Arthur was the only man capable of writing the scores for long films on great subjects. He has such a sure sense of atmosphere, and is so skillful in putting himself at the level of the public by the extreme simplicity of his means, that soon he was unable to cope with the innumerable demands made upon him by the film industry. After *Le Roi David* it was *Judith*, also for Mézières, but a more personal and consequently less direct work than the previous one. *Pacific 231* was followed by *Rugby*, in which he celebrated sport and agility and freedom of movement. To me his masterpieces are *Horace victorieux*, somber and difficult, and not sufficiently direct in its appeal to be played very often, and the opera

Antigone, a magnificent flowering of his personality, first produced in Essen, then at Brussels before the war, and in Paris during the occupation. Finally, *Jeanne au bûcher*, a huge fresco in which the devices used for cinema sound-tracks seem to have been called into service for the orchestral accompaniment and the choirs, which illustrate in masterly fashion Claudel's admirable version of this drama of French purity and fire.

Despite the fact that Arthur's works were admired by musicians and critics who attacked mine, while my music was appreciated by a group of young musicians who were profoundly unjust in their attitude toward his, our affection remained unchanged. We were above these petty disturbances, and were fond of giving concerts together. *Le Roi David* and *Les Choëphores* often figured on the same program, each of us reaching his own public; the rival clans looked askance at one another, with unconcealed animosity, both during and after the concert. Trends opposed to Honegger had definitely set in with the works of Auric and Poulenc, but these only served to demonstrate the independence of Les Six and the fact that they had no style in common. These trends became more marked in the work of younger musicians, especially those forming the school of Arcueil, who used them by way of æsthetic shock-tactics in a kind of election campaign.

In homage to Erik Satie, a number of young men had grouped themselves together to found *"L'École d'Arcueil."* The oldest of them was my old classmate at the Conservatoire, Henri Cliquet. (He had taken his mother's name to add to his own, and now called himself Cliquet-Pleyel.) Few of his works were ever performed, though he wrote a great deal. Roger Désormière, on the other hand, was not a prolific composer; he had not the time, devoting himself mostly to his conducting. As their emeritus leader, he became the promoter and defender of his comrades' music. Baron Jacques Benoist-Méchin was a strange fellow. Very much influenced by my music, he had undeniable lyrical gifts. Perhaps from megalomania, he chose to collaborate with only the very greatest—Shakespeare or Michelangelo. He was generous by nature, and loved to act as a Mæcenas. He bought manuscripts, and had an extensive collection of first editions of Claudel, a real "Claudelium." For a period of several months he acted as buyer for a wealthy American press magnate, sending him antiques, ancient churches, cloisters, and even a Flemish carillon that played *Tosca* and could be operated by the collector from his bathroom—at least that is what Benoist-Méchin told us, though he was a great storyteller! He published an essay on *Music in the Work of Proust*. He spoke fluent English and German; he translated many works, and himself wrote one very remarkable one on the German army. He was to become one of the ministers at Vichy during the occupation. His record as a collaborator made me feel no regret at having, for personal reasons, broken off my friendly relations with him in 1930. The artistic contribution that Maxime Jacob brought to the group was compact of aerial grace and freshness of vision. He would come and see me on his way home from the lycée, carrying his big dictionaries under his arm. He would bring me some simple, sentimental, rather overfacile piece of music written in a style not far removed from that of operetta. He was a Jew from Bayonne, and sometimes remembering his origins, he put to music fragments of the Psalms. A few years later this fashionable young man who seemed to be wedded to worldly success and easy living made the most edifying of conversions: he entered a Benedictine monastery. He did not give up music, however, but became the organist of his

164

monastery. I met him again in Paris during his father's illness, and again at L'Enclos during the war, when he came to spend his leave from the army with me. Whether he was wearing his monastic robes or a military uniform, I found him the same gifted, merry-hearted, lively man, but his eyes were deeper, purer, more luminous than before. He played a part in the Resistance, and I have had a letter from him here: all the members of his family were murdered in a concentration camp. He is back in the monastery now, and still composing: for Dom Clément, music is the very breath of his soul, a gift of God.

Of all the members of the School of Arcueil, the most un-questionably gifted was Henri Sauguet. At the time of our Saturday meetings Cocteau had brought us one or two pianoforte pieces and a melody, *Oceano Nox*, that Sauguet had sent him from Bordeaux. The talent revealed in them was still not very sure of itself, but had an authentic poetry of its own. I immediately began a correspondence with him, and invited him to come and stay with me for a few days. This brief visit enabled him to get to know us and to attend a few concerts. We were all captivated by Sauguet's charm of manner, his subtle, refined intelligence, his profound culture, and his love of fun. A year later he definitely settled in Paris. To earn his living, he occupied successively the posts of salesman in the big store Paris-France; secretary to Monsieur Maître, a very learned Oriental scholar who was a friend of Désormière; and finally a job with an oil company. In the meantime he continued his studies under Koechlin. Mme Bériza, who organized performances of modern operatic works, produced his *Plumet du Colonel*, an *opéra bouffe*, whose libretto he had also written himself. This was a charming work whose fundamental qualities made up for its inexperienced orchestration. A little later he had become

165

much more skillful and wrote with clarity and sensitivity the instrumental parts for his ballet *La Chatte*, which won such success when it was performed by the Ballets Russes that it had a run of more than one hundred performances. Saugeut's most important work is undoubtedly *La Chartreuse de Parme*, based on a libretto made by Lunel from Stendhal's novel. The music is marvelous, often lighthearted, tender, and broad in its treatment, but rising in the last act to genuine heights of emotion. I love it so much that when it was produced at the Opéra in Paris, I attended not only the last rehearsals, but also seven consecutive performances.

Office work became boring and lost all interest for Sauguet, and after the success of *La Chatte* he decided to give it up altogether and make a living by means of his literary gifts. He became a music critic, one whose utterances were feared. His violent articles attacking the artistic tendencies of Honegger and his followers succeeded in exasperating Arthur. On one occasion he even went to the length of hurling himself on Sauguet at the Théâtre des Champs-Élysées, snatching off his glasses—without these the poor fellow could see absolutely nothing—and threatening to knock his face in if he persisted in his attitude. Sitting beside Sauguet, I felt caught between the devil and the deep blue sea.

With the perspective of several years, I can now see that, though opposition is stimulating to a young artist and is even essential for his development, it is useless once works have won an established reputation; and it was with an equal emotion that I received Honegger's *Danse des morts* and Sauguet's *La Voyante*, the first recordings from France to reach me after the liberation.

22

THE PRINCESSE DE POLIGNAC, who was an excellent pianist and organist, had often given in her own drawing-room the first performances of works commissioned by herself: among these were Fauré's suite *Pelléas et Mélisande*, Ravel's *Pavane pour une infante défunte*, Manuel de Falla's *El Retablo de Maese Pedro*, Stravinsky's *Renard*, Satie's *Socrate*, Kurt Weill's Symphony, Poulenc's Concerto for two pianos and orchestra and Organ Concerto with strings and timpani, and *Pièces pour deux pianos* by Sauguet. In 1924 she asked me to write a work for her. I had for a long time been wanting to transpose an ancient myth to modern times. I was attracted by the legend of Orpheus, whom I imagined as a peasant of the Camargue, living on that wonderful plain where mirages hover above blue horizons. I wanted Eurydice to have nothing in common with him, to be a stranger to his country and his settled ways. I pictured her as one of the gypsies who go on pilgrimage to Les Saintes-Maries-de-la-Mer, and belong to a fiery, mysterious, passionate race.

Armand Lunel had now been a philosophy teacher in Monaco for several years, and I had kept up my correspondence with him. Gallimard had published a number of books by him which I admired enormously and in which I saw the fulfillment of the promise of his youth. It was with genuine pleasure that we met again at Aix each summer. I told him of my idea, and in the course of long conversations we worked out the details of a libretto that Lunel undertook to write for me. He fell in with my wishes admirably: *Orphée charmeur d'animaux* became *Orphée guérisseur des hommes et des bêtes.* The action is brief and dramatic. Orpheus lives in a little village of the Camargue, from which he absents himself from time to time to tend sick animals, even in their dens; his village friends, the Wheelwright, the Basket-maker, and the Blacksmith, are worried about him; Orpheus reassures them and tells them that he is going to settle down in the village for good because he is going to marry Eurydice, one of four gypsies who arrived in the village a few days before. Suddenly Eurydice comes in, tracked down by her nomadic relatives, who are revolted at the idea of her proposed marriage and are determined to win her back, dead or alive. The villagers advise the young couple to flee. Act II takes place in the mountains, where the lovers have sought refuge, but Eurydice has been smitten by a mysterious illness that Orpheus, for all his skill, is unable to relieve. She dies after recommending her husband to the old Bear, the Boar, the lame old Fox, and the Wolf "that has lost the taste for blood." The animals, singing a funeral chorus, carry away her mortal remains. Act III discloses Orpheus once more back in his home, a cross between a pharmacy and a natural-history laboratory, adorned with votive offerings and crutches and plaster casts of limbs. Everybody believes him to have got over his grief, but he sings now of a despair that nothing can alleviate. Blinded by false appearances, the three sisters of Eurydice, like the bacchantes who in the ancient myth tore Orpheus' body to pieces, now come to accuse him of their sister's death and to pierce him with a pair of shears. As the unhappy man expires, yearning with all his soul and all his being toward his beloved, they realize their mistake.

In Lunel's hands the libretto was beautifully balanced. He built it up in short scenes, with separate arias, duets, and choruses. This made my task all the easier, and I composed *Les Malheurs* straight off, working all day long and then, at the end of the afternoon, going out for a drive with Madeleine Milhaud, who was spending the summer with us at L'Enclos. There could be nothing more restful than to drive in the light of the setting sun, able, thanks to the motorcar, to explore roads that lay off the beaten track and to discover yet another unknown aspect of the wonderful scenery around Aix.

I invited Jean Victor-Hugo, who was staying at the time with his grandmother, Mme Ménard-Dorian, to meet Armand Lunel. We wanted to talk to him about our plans for *Les Malheurs d'Orphée*, and for *Esther de Carpentras*, on which we intended to start soon. Our projects seemed to interest Jean, and he immediately did one or two sketches. He had an admirable grasp of what Lunel had imagined: the Camargue villagers, the gypsy women with their striped skirts and long shawls, which made them look like "black and gold bees," the animals swathed in bandages, worn out with weariness and old age. We had to wait till some years later to see these lovely sketches translated into reality in Mme Bériza's production of our work; for when the opera was played at the Théâtre de la Monnaie in 1926, a Belgian painter was commissioned to do the scenery. The Honeggers went with us to Brussels to see the first performance. Vaurabourg, Madeleine, and I squeezed into the little Renault under a pile of blankets and luggage, while Arthur,

169

wrapped up in a great overcoat and wearing a sou'wester like those worn by fishermen on the Newfoundland banks, slept in the rumbleseat, heedless of the rain. Elsa and Paul Collaer attended all rehearsals. When she heard *Die Entführung*, which was being produced at the same time as *Les Malheurs*, Elsa, who was more used to hearing contemporary music than Mozart's, was as startled as most people are on hearing a modern work for the first time.

Les Malheurs d'Orphée was the first of a series of chamber operas that I wrote. The music is stripped to its bare essentials. Apart from Orpheus and Eurydice, the characters are grouped together, and while each preserves his or her own individuality and character, more often than not they sing together, thus forming a little chorus. I scored it for only thirteen instruments. I knew that such an ensemble was as capable of filling a large hall as a drawing-room, but the director of the Orchestre de la Monnaie, Corneil de Thoran, who conducted the work, doubled the strings for fear that the solo instruments might prove inadequate. He soon realized that in doing so he was destroying the balance of my score, which was based on solo instruments only, so he suppressed the doubling.

Apart from the full-scale productions at Brussels and in Paris at the Théâtre Bériza, performances of *Les Malheurs* were given both in the concert hall and on the radio. I conducted it myself at a Pro Musica concert in New York and at a concert at the Salle Pleyel devoted to works dedicated to the Princesse de Polignac. It was conducted at Königsberg by Scherchen; several recitals were given on the French radio; and the University of Chicago included it in the same program as my ballet *The Bells*, produced in 1946.

Lunel had written a comedy, *Esther de Carpentras*, inspired by old family stories and an eighteenth-century play in

Jewish dialect of the county of Avignon; and Gallimard had just published it. I found it the ideal subject for a comic opera. The scene is laid in Carpentras before the Revolution. In the first act three Jews come to the Cardinal Bishop to ask permission to present the traditional play of Esther on the town square for the Feast of Purim. The young Bishop, newly arrived from Rome, allows himself to be influenced by his valet, Vaucluse: he grants their request, but plans to interrupt their performance in order to urge all Jews to renounce their faith. Act II takes place in front of the synagogue, where all the houses are bedecked with banners. Two plots are interwoven. In accordance with tradition, the actors are recruited from among the spectators. The play is given on a little wooden stage, and all the roles except that of Esther are taken by amateurs. At first everything goes off as usual. Then, just when the famous scene of Esther is about to begin, the Bishop and Vaucluse turn up and read an edict threatening the Jews with death or exile if they refuse to be converted. Esther, unaware of the Bishop's presence, makes her entry and then plays her scene with him as if she thought he was the actor supposed to play the part of Ahasuerus. Touched by her beauty and her religious faith, the Bishop gives the Jews the right to stay in Carpentras and preserve their own religion. The choir and chapter come looking for their Bishop, disapproving of a mass conversion that would deprive them of real material advantages, and they express astonishment at finding their Cardinal Bishop in such an incongruous setting. They move away singing an anthem while the Jews intone a hymn of gratitude. "The masquerade ends in a sermon," says the producer, and the curtain falls.

Lunel treats this subject very freely, constantly mingling the Old Testament with the New. Dramatic scenes are immediately followed by scenes of comedy, and this made me hesitate a long time before deciding how to treat them. I wrote *Esther de Carpentras* in 1925 at Paris, Aix, and Malines. It was first produced on the radio in 1937 under the direction of Manuel Rosenthal; then in 1938 it was put on at the Opéra-Comique to accompany a revival of *Le Pauvre Matelot*, produced by Cocteau with décors by Monnin, and a ballet based on the *Suite provençale* (décors by André Marchand). Roger Désormière conducted the performance. I had hoped that Jean Hugo would do the décors for *Esther*, for he appeared to be interested a few years previously and had even done some sketches at the time of our conversation at Aix, but now he had lost these, and by the time the opera was produced he preferred to devote himself to painting rather than to the theater. His place was taken by Nora Auric.

23

THE DEATH OF ERIK SATIE

THROUGHOUT HIS life Satie, courageously overcoming the miseries of man's lot and drawing his strength from his own inward resources, never knew the meaning of compromise. He was very forthright in character, and as he detested certain critics, he could not bear the idea that his friends should associate with them. When therefore he found out at Monte Carlo that Poulenc and Auric had made friends with Louis Laloy, whom he regarded as his oldest enemy, he behaved as if it were a personal affront. No doubt this slight misunderstanding would have blown over if Auric had not published an unfortunate article entitled "Adieu, Satie," criticizing the music of *Relâche* (a ballet presented by the Ballets Suédois) and explaining his reasons for breaking with its composer. He seemed to have forgotten the preface to *Parade*, in which he had written: "Some well-informed critics, enamored of audacities now grown familiar and of the fantasies that made us smile yesterday, pointed to the inexperience of musicians whose lack of charm and of originality they felt obliged to denounce. Meanwhile, Art pursues its path, from which no man can make it turn aside." Satie was especially fond of Auric, and was much hurt by his attitude. The breach between them widened.

After the first night of *Relâche*, Satie fell seriously ill; cirrhosis of the liver was diagnosed. He got into the habit of coming to Paris every day after this, lunching with Derain, with Braque, or with me. He ate only very light meals, sitting right up against the fireplace with his umbrella and overcoat, and with his hat pulled down over his eyes. In this posture he would remain silent and unstirring until the time came to catch his train for Arcueil. We did not think it right that he should travel every day like this, and we were so insistent that he finally decided to settle in Paris. He tried to get into the Hôtel Istria in Montparnasse, but they could only promise him a room at a later date. Meanwhile he found a room at the Grand Hôtel, thanks to the intervention of Jean Wiéner, whose father had once been its manager. Still wearing his hat and coat and clutching his umbrella, he would spend his days sitting in a large armchair, gazing at himself in a mirror and operating the bolt on his door by a complicated arrangement of strings that he himself had contrived. He was so irritated by the telephone that we avoided calling him up, but often went to see him. His room was quiet and comfortable but Satie refused to stay there, and in spite of the noisy company of painters and students he installed himself in the Hôtel Istria as soon as he could get a room there. His state had worsened to such an extent that the doctor ordered him to bed. Poor Satie! He had never been ill before, and everything gave rise to scenes, from taking medicine to having his temperature read. Several times we asked him whether he had any relatives whom he wished to see or to have informed of his illness, but his deliberately evasive answers precluded further discussion of the matter. Yet it was becoming necessary to make some serious decisions. When the doctor insisted that he be taken to the hospital, the Comte de Beaumont, who had endowed a ward at the Hôpital Saint-Joseph, used his influence to get a private room for him. Satie asked Madeleine to pack his suitcase. As she knew he was likely to fly into inexplicable rages if things were not placed exactly the way he wanted them, she asked Braque to stand between them so that Satie might not be able to watch how she packed his case. We accompanied our friend in the ambulance as far as the little room from which he was never to emerge alive. The nun who put away his personal possessions soon realized that she had no ordinary patient to deal with: Satie's only toilet accessories were a scrubbing-brush and a piece of pumice stone, with which no doubt he used to rub his skin.

Despite his intolerable sufferings, he still retained his own characteristic brand of wit. Maritain brought a priest to see him. Satie described the priest to us next day as "looking like a Modigliani, black on a blue background." When Monsieur Lerolle came to see him about publishing *Relâche*, he insisted on being paid at once. "You never need money so much as when you're in a hospital," he remarked slyly. Hardly had Lerolle paid over the money when he hid the banknotes between the sheets of old newspapers piled up on his suitcase together with all sorts of papers and bits of string. Satie refused to allow anything to be thrown away; he loved to accumulate all kinds of odds and ends. At the beginning of his illness we had brought him several dozen handkerchiefs. Yet when Valentine Hugo asked him what he would like, he said: "I've seen some very fine handkerchiefs at the haberdasher's downstairs in the Hôtel Istria; I should like some of them"; and when, at his request, Madeleine went to get a bundle of laundry from his concierge at Arcueil, she was dumbfounded to discover that it contained eighty-nine handkerchiefs.

As soon as Poulenc heard of his illness, he asked me to beg

175

Satie to see him. Satie was touched by this, but refused, saying: "No, no, I would rather not see him; they said good-by to me, and now that I am ill, I prefer to take them at their word. One must stick to one's guns to the last." Several of his friends were at his side until his death, among them Brancusi, Wiéner, Désormière, and Caby, a young composer who had introduced himself to Satie after the performance of *Relâche*. He cared for him with intense devotion, patiently putting up with the sick man's often unjustified rages. For six months Madeleine and I went to see him every day. When we left him at the end of April to go to Aix, where we were to be married, we feared we should never see him alive again. After a visit to the Middle East, from which I returned in very poor health, Madeleine was so alarmed by Satie's condition that she insisted on my going to see him next day in spite of my own weakness. Alas, we found only an empty bed.

Our poor friend's death created a series of administrative problems, some of which seemed insoluble. To avoid a pauper's grave for him, the law required that a member of his family should be present before the funeral took place; so his brother had to be found at once, at all costs. Satie's death was announced by the Agence Havas in all the provincial and foreign newspapers. That is how his brother Conrad and his nephews came to hear about it. They went to the hospital, where they were given my address. They then came to ask me for details of their relative's illness and death. Conrad Satie showed himself at once to be a charming man: he was sincerely grieved at not having been able to look after his brother, whom he loved dearly and with whom he had quarreled for family reasons that were really unimportant. At the funeral, we were astonished to see an aged composer, Alexandre Georges, of whom Satie had never

176

spoken; yet they must have been great friends in former days for the old man to have gone to the trouble of coming as far as Arcueil for the funeral. Satie had been so much one of us that we tended to forget that he had taken part in the activities of several generations, including those of the Rosicrucians, Sâr Péladan, Debussy, and Ravel.

Conrad Satie did not know the address of his married sister in Buenos Aires. In such a case the law requires that seals be affixed to the deceased's property and a public sale held. Before this took place, Conrad obtained permission to take away all his brother's personal papers and correspondence (he had kept all his letters, as well as the rough drafts of his replies, even the most insignificant). Conrad was an exceptionally disinterested and tactful man, and his first thought was to make his brother's work as widely known as possible. He packed into the suitcase, bearing the initials E.S., which Satie had bought for his trip to Monte Carlo all the little manuscript albums and separate sheets of music that he could find. He brought them to me, for me to sort out and publish what was worthy of being saved. This was a labor of love for me. I entrusted to Rouart-Lerolle the publication of *Ogives*, *Les Préludes*, and *La Messe des pauvres*. Universal Edition accepted *Jack-in-the-Box* and *Geneviève de Brabant*, and bought the copyright of the ballet *Mercure* from the Comte de Beaumont, who owned the manuscript.

Conrad asked Désormière, Wiéner, Caby, and ourselves to help him go through his brother's effects before the public sale. A narrow corridor, with a washbasin in it, led to the bedroom into which Satie had never allowed anyone, not even his concierge, to penetrate. The idea of entering it upset us. What a shock we had on opening the door! It seemed impossible that Satie had lived in such poverty. This man, whose faultlessly clean and correct dress made him look rather like a model official, owned almost literally *nothing:* a wretched bed, a table covered with the most incongruous objects, one chair, and a half-empty wardrobe in which there were a dozen old-fashioned corduroy suits, brand-new and absolutely identical. In each corner of the room were piles of old newspapers, old hats, and walking-sticks. On the ancient, broken-down piano, with its pedals tied up with string, there was a parcel whose postmark proved that it had been delivered several years before; Satie had merely torn a corner of the paper to see what it contained—a little picture, some New Year's present, no doubt. On the piano we found gifts bearing witness to a precious friendship, the *édition de luxe* of Debussy's *Poèmes de Baudelaire,* and *Estampes* and *Images,* with such affectionate dedications as "To Erik Satie, the gentle medieval musician" and "To the famous contrapuntist Erik Satie." Behind the piano we found an exercise book containing *Jack-in-the-Box* and *Geneviève de Brabant,* which Satie thought he had lost in a bus. With his characteristic meticulous care he had arranged in an old cigar-box more than four thousand little pieces of paper on which he had made curious drawings and written extravagant inscriptions. They spoke of enchanted shores, pools, and marshes in the time of Charlemagne. There were frequent allusions to the devil or to a magician who inhabited a "cast-iron castle in the Gothic style." He had also very carefully traced tiny plans of an imaginary Arcueil, in which the rue du Diable stood near the Place Notre-Dame. Had we not also seen chalked up on the gate of the house opposite (by whom?): "This house is haunted by the devil?"

On the day of the sale, Satie's friends decided to buy in everything personal that had belonged to him. Déso stood beside the auctioneer and while forcing up the bidding, also kept an eye open for anything likely to be of interest to us. Thus the Comte de Beaumont acquired the big portrait of Satie playing the organ—a painting in the style of a stained-glass window—by Antoine de la Rochefoucauld; Braque bought the portrait by Desboutins and the old piano; I went home with all sorts of souvenirs: walking-sticks; drawings in red ink, no doubt representing the characters in the ballet *Uspud;* scrawls of what looked like plainchant, illuminated and framed; and a large painting that when cleaned turned out to be our friend's portrait by Zuloaga.

In homage to Satie, Diaghilev organized a performance of *Parade, Mercure* (by permission of the Comte de Beaumont), and *Jack-in-the-Box* orchestrated by me and with décors by Derain. The Comte de Beaumont got Déso to conduct a concert of works by Satie, at which the first performance of *Geneviève de Brabant,* orchestrated by Déso himself, was given. Ortiz designed puppets for this show. Conrad Satie conceived the delicate attention of offering Déso and me legal documents ceding all rights in these two works to us.

A year after Satie's death a memorial tablet was placed on the wretched building he had inhabited at Arcueil; speeches were made by the Mayor, a Communist Deputy, and Robert Caby, while I spoke in the name of French musicians. Afterward a concert was given in the Mairie. The program bore a reproduction of a drawing by Caby of Satie on his deathbed. Viñes played, and I accompanied Marya Freund in *Socrate.* The last words in that work assumed for me their real meaning on that day as never before: "Such, Echecrates, was the manner of our friend's parting, the wisest and most just of all men." Just Satie certainly had been, but chiefly toward himself, which is rare.

Conrad presented me with all his brother's manuscripts. When the international situation deteriorated beyond remedy in 1939, I deposited them in the Bibliothèque Nationale, with the request that M. Julien Cain, the curator, should exhibit them at the Conservatoire the following winter. This prospect would have tickled Satie, who had always been scorned and ignored by that official institution. The war prevented this project from being carried out, however. I was able, though, to exhibit at Mills College, the Boston Symphony, and the Chicago Arts Club the two or three manuscripts that I had bought from him in his lifetime and still had in my possession: exercises in counterpoint and fugue, with corrections by his teachers at the Schola—Roussel, d'Indy, and Séryex—as well as some music-hall songs that I had also kept, composed when Satie used to play the piano at the Chat-Noir. I was glad to have this opportunity of paying homage, even so far afield as America, to the memory of my old friend and master, whose fierce independence and proud hatred of compromise I so often recall. Thanks to Mrs. Robert Woods Bliss, these manuscripts are now at Dumbarton Oaks.

24

FRANCIS POULENC came to our wedding, for which Paul Claudel and my brother-in-law Étienne Milhaud acted as witnesses. The very simple ceremony took place quietly in the synagogue of Aix-en-Provence. Madeleine and I had long since planned our honeymoon; we intended to spend a few weeks in Palestine. We sailed in a ship that was due to call at many ports; the first was Naples. We went to Pompeii along a dusty road full of potholes, with trucks, farm-carts, donkey-carts, and flocks of sheep and goats milling in all directions. I still wonder how we got back alive. At Malta an elevator conveyed us up to the town, carved out of solid rock. The women wear huge double hoods, spread out like wings, to protect themselves from the sea breezes. The solidly built church of the Knights of Malta and the Governor's rococo palace form a lively contrast to the narrow streets lined with English shops and tearooms in which it was delightful, after the rather rough crossing, to sit down to cups of hot tea with toast. We stopped two days at Piræus. A motley crowd jostled around the harbor, in which the fishing-boats were anchored so thickly that they formed a forest of masts. A kind of electric railway took us to Athens. I loved the tiny chapels, lit by innumerable tapers, constantly renewed by the piety of the worshippers. Through the half-open doors I caught a glimpse of the icons glittering with gold. The perfume of incense hung over the whole town, mingling with the smell of olive oil, which is characteristic of Mediterranean towns. The very few sculptures in the Museum are all choice specimens. And at last, the Acropolis! How small and familiar it seemed to me! Viewed from a distance, the buildings seemed to stand like everyday objects on a tray, and this accentuated their character of intimacy. They seemed so much smaller than the mental image I had formed of them from reproductions, as if they had been built on an ordinary scale, accessible to the human heart, in spite of their absolute perfection.

We were looking forward to our arrival in Constantinople, but just at the entry to the Dardanelles the weather turned bad, and the celebrated Golden Horn looked as somber as a Norwegian fiord through the fog and the rain. We stayed a week in Constantinople. The political reformation had just begun in Turkey, and we saw the first signs of the emancipation of women; the abolition of the veil had been enthusiastically welcomed, especially by the older women. Naturally, we visited the Mosque of Sancta Sophia and the Cemetery of Eyoub, where the graves are a disorderly huddle of vertical stones among the tapering trunks of the cypresses. We drove along the banks of the Bosporus as far as the beginning of the Black Sea, whose name seems justified by the dark hue of its waters. The Asiatic shore of the Bosporus is bordered with luxurious villas, the summer residences of the wealthy and of the diplomatic corps, whereas the European side is more popular in character. Some cousins of my mother, the Guido Friedmans, lived in Constantinople, and offered to take us round in order to avoid the monotony of the usual sightseeing tours. In their company we visited little native restaurants, with dishes familiar to me from childhood, but I was fascinated by the desserts: rose-petal jam, loukoums, pistachio nuts covered with sugar, honey-cakes made of puff-pastry. We heard some Turkish music; the instruments played in unison, *almost*. By listening attentively, I could always detect, in one or other of them, a slight variant, so slight as to be barely perceptible. We often strolled in the Bazaar of Constantinople, and were even nearly the victims of an amusing hoax. I wanted to give Madeleine an amber necklace, and though these were rather scarce, a merchant promised to get me one. He knew where there was a superb necklace; all that was needed was to persuade the owner to part with it. A day or two later he arranged a meeting with her; she was an old woman, apparently quite poor. A long conversation in Turkish ensued. She promised to bring the jewelry to the shop next day. It looked good to us, but we had too much experience of haggling not to be mistrustful of this little comedy. We asked the advice of a friend of our cousins, an expert in antiques, who declared the necklace to be modern and of no great worth. This brought an end to the comedy, which is apparently traditionally played for the benefit of foreigners, and which had lasted several days.

At Beirut we hired a little Ford. The brakes were held together by strings, and the motor leaked. Our driver only spoke Syrian, but he brought along a friend to act as interpreter. They were lively young sparks, and treated their car with affectionate roughness. Lebanon, with its soft, clear horizons, would be rather reminiscent of the American deserts were it not for the occasional tuft of palms or a glimpse of Bedouin nomads, with their haughty, inscrutable faces, crossing the distances on their camels. After Lebanon, and Baalbek with its imposing ruins, Damascus nestling amid its greenery was a refreshing sight. The bazaar is a real roofed-in town, so huge that you go round it on donkey-back. We bought candied apricots and all kinds of attractive trash, and even, though it was June, camel's-hair cloaks like those worn by the shepherds, so Biblical in their silhouettes. When we left Damascus, our drivers seemed merrier than usual. Yet they had been playing cards all night and had lost all their money. In the middle of the mountains they stopped the car and showed us an acquisition of which they were very proud: a revolver loaded with two cartridges. Then they asked us to get out of the car with them while they tried out their weapon. Without enthusiasm we complied. Our driver stood in front of a telegraph pole, fired off his gun at it at point-blank range, and then, laughing uproariously, got back into the car with his friend. The rest of the journey was uneventful.

On arriving at Beirut, I felt so ill that I went to bed. Mme Sarrail [1] very kindly sent a military doctor immediately; he said I had amœbic dysentery. He gave me a series of injections of emetine to arrest the malady, prescribed bed for several days, and forbade any further travel. To our great regret, we therefore had to abandon the principal goal of our journey, Palestine. Madeleine then began her practice as a nurse, which has been too often hers, and which she bore with unwearying devotion and exceptional good humor. We tried to go back to France direct, but all berths had long since been reserved by government officials going home on leave. Thanks to the influence of General Sarrail, we managed to get a cabin on a crowded boat bound for Egypt, where we hoped to catch an Italian vessel, the *Esperia*, a few days later.

When we got to Alexandria, my health had improved

---

[1] General Sarrail was High Commissioner for Syria and Lebanon at the time.

somewhat, and we were able to make a few excursions. In the train to Cairo we were gripped by the spell of this magical country as we watched the villages of beaten earth flashing by. There was always the same archaic system of irrigation, worked by patiently turning horses or oxen. For a long time we ran along the banks of the Nile, a marvelous river on which craft with black or salmon-colored sails moved to and fro. We visited the museum and the Citadel, as well as the Pyramids, whose amazing dimensions took my breath away. The Sphinx seemed so tame and so familiar that one expected it almost to eat out of one's hand. On the road to Sakkara, among thickets of palms, monuments of antiquity merged with the natural surroundings.

The *Esperia* took us to Naples, where we found my friend Yvonne and her husband, Illan de Casafuerte, waiting to take us home with them. They owned a tremendous feudal castle in the Abruzzi, looking down on the ruined village of Balsorano, destroyed by an earthquake. The castle was typical of the historical buildings one visits but no one ever inhabits, with its battlements, its fifty rooms, its enormous corridors, and walls twenty feet thick. Yet the Casafuertes had contrived to create a warm and intimate atmosphere; their children and dogs, and the constant visits paid by peasants bringing produce from their farms, made this imposing mansion a comfortable and animated dwelling. Besides, there was Balsorano's permanent guest, Monsieur Larrapidie. This was an original character, an aged violinist, deeply versed in the lore of the violin and the art of making stringed instruments. Claudel had made his acquaintance in Boston, while serving as French vice-consul there. At that time, Larrapidie used to take him out into the woods of Massachusetts and try, like some modern Orpheus, to charm the birds with his violin. When Claudel was appointed to China, Larrapidie went with him. He stayed in that country for a long time, and even brought back an almost Oriental obsequiousness of manner, which never left him thereafter. He met Casafuerte at the home of his niece Madame Lara during the First World War. Larrapidie was very unhappy because he had no apartment and was incapable of solving the problems of everyday living. He used to complain bitterly. Casafeurte, who was always impulsively generous, proposed that he should go to Balsorano to live. The next day Larrapidie called him up: "Where is this castle you were telling me about yesterday? I'm leaving for it tonight!" He stayed there for twenty years, and finally died there.

I fell ill again during my stay in Balsorano. The peasant woman who brought me my meals carried up on her head all the furniture we required for our installation. She would come near my bed every day with a murmur of: "*Speriamo, speriamo!*" It was then that I began to write my Seventh Quartet. For us it will always be bound up with our memories of that journey. As soon as I felt a little better, my friends drove us to Rome, where we were to take the train for Paris. When we stopped at a little village to fill up with gasoline, we saw a lot of ancient bottles in the window of a café. Our collector's fever made us buy the lot: Garibaldis, Queens of Italy, Angels, Glocks, and Acrobats. When we got to the Hotel Flora, we had them all taken up to our room, to the great dismay of the porter. He was somewhat mollified when we offered him the contents of the bottles. He soon returned with a large empty vase, into which he poured all the contents of the bottles, regardless of the type of liqueur they contained. "This will be a treat for the kids," he said with a smile.

In 1926, cultural relations with Russia had been resumed. Monteux had had a great success there. Szigeti had been there twice and had come back full of enthusiasm. His wife asked me if I would be interested in going. I gladly accepted. Reports on the U.S.S.R. were so contradictory that I was delighted to have the opportunity of judging for myself, as well as of being the first French composer to resume musical contact with the country. Wanda Szigeti immediately got into touch with the brother of the diplomat Krassin, who was to act as impressario for my tour. He arranged for me to conduct three concerts in Moscow and three in Leningrad. Jean Wiéner was to come with me as soloist.

We set out with Madeleine in March 1926. All went well as far as Berlin, but from then on it was impossible to make oneself understood. English couldn't help us, nor the two or three words of German that Jean jabbered. This was all the more embarrassing because we were passing through many different countries and had to be continually changing money: from Estonian marks to lits, and from lits to lats, and so on. One day when we were vainly endeavoring to make ourselves understood, we heard someone talking French. Jean rushed out into the corridor and, to our great surprise, threw himself into the arms of a strange passenger. He had found an old wartime friend, who was now French Minister in Tallin. As the train was stopping there for several hours, he invited us to lunch and showed us the town and the Parliament, a very bold modern building erected on the foundations of a former prison in which Estonian patriots had been locked up before the country won its independence. He also took us out into the surrounding countryside to admire a famous view, but the car got stuck in the snow, and we had to run to catch the train.

Crossing the Soviet frontier in the middle of the night was quite impressive. A wooden arch covered with foliage bore a banner with the inscription in several languages: "Workers

187

of the world, welcome." Soldiers in long greatcoats supervised the customs formalities. Newspapers and books were examined one by one as a precaution against any attempt at capitalist infiltration.

Leningrad seemed asleep on the banks of the Neva. Since the government departments had abandoned them, the red and green palaces appeared to have remained uninhabited. The sky was blue, the sun warm, and the thaw had set in. It was a curious sensation not to be able to read the name of a street or boulevard, but the government made up for this inconvenience by supplying a young musician to act as interpreter and go with us wherever we went, to help us in all our difficulties. Every day the Commissar of Fine Arts responsible for cultural relations rang up to know what we should like to see at the theater, and reserved seats for us. All productions were most elaborate and enthrallingly interesting. We had gone to the Opera the very day we arrived in Leningrad. *Boris Godunov* was being given. The brilliantly decorated hall was crowded with men and women wearing overalls and dark clothes. Later on we saw Prokofiev's *The Love for Three Oranges* and *Russlan and Ludmilla*, a prodigious work by the great precursor Glinka, which is unfortunately never given outside of Russia. The actors, as state employees, rehearsed for as long as the director wished. Meyerhold invited us to a rehearsal of Gogol's *Revizor* (*The Inspector General*). It was the hundredth rehearsal, and yet how many times he made them repeat the same gesture! In *Howl of China*, a political play, an important part was taken by the supers. They represented Chinese coolies in a port. They had studied their parts so long that every move and gesture had its own significance, thus approximating the art of choreography.

We were keenly interested by the Persimfans Orchestra.

It played without a conductor. The musicians assembled in groups and were free to express opinions and criticisms during rehearsals. For the actual performance, attacks and entries were discreetly indicated by the leader. The experiment had been fully successful, but it had been a politically inspired effort, and a conductor would have obtained the same results, no doubt a little faster. At all events, this demonstration of collective discipline was confined to the Persimfans.

Our concert was a great success; the players were docile and very understanding, and what an extraordinary audience! What love of music! There were in Leningrad a number of musicians who had grouped themselves around the musical critic Glebov. They were all eager to know the new French works, and we met on a number of occasions. Popov, Kamiensky, and Dechevov played their own compositions and those of their comrades. When Wiéner played them some syncopated music, they were amazed. Kamiensky, the "giant with a heart of gold," who was an excellent pianist, tried vainly to imitate these new, unfamiliar rhythms. We enjoyed the company of such unconventional and undeniably gifted young men. In Moscow, academic influences were much more in evidence; the youthful musicians were more argumentative and inclined to hairsplitting. They were full of curiosity and asked questions about all sorts of things: about Monsieur Poulenc's ideology, the origin of the "Groupe de Six," and the percentage of sons of workers included in it. (Our reply: "They are all sons of bourgeois," must have been a great disappointment to them.) Generally speaking, the atmosphere seemed to us to be more formal and intellectual than in Leningrad. Nevertheless, a young man with dreamy eyes hidden behind enormous spectacles came to show me a symphony which, in spite of its rather conventional form and construction, showed genuine gifts,

189

and even a certain greatness, if it is remembered that its composer, Shostakovich, was only eighteen at the time and still a pupil at the Conservatoire.

The Conservatoire was directed by Glazunov. I called on him, but he was cut off from the world by a veil of vodka fumes and was absolutely indifferent to human affairs. The tradition established by Anton Rubinstein was still flourishing, and there was a marvelous school of piano-playing. We heard several amazing sixteen-year-old virtuosos. I remember Kagan (what became of him?). Vladimir Horowitz, who arrived in Paris a few weeks later, is a brilliant example of the Russian musical education at that time. We also watched pupils practicing, and saw very careful performances, including one of *The Fair of Sorotchinsk*, acted and produced entirely by students. These performances, instinct with the purity and fire of youth, were most pleasing.

Of course, we visited all the museums. At Tsarskoye-Selo a former servant of the Tsar showed us the mansion. He was living in an essentially bourgeois atmosphere reminiscent of the 1880's, surrounded by innumerable photographs and memories of his masters. Jean Wiéner was pulled up short at the sight of the Tsarevich's toys; he would have liked to take them home to his own little boy. He missed his wife and family very much and seized the slightest opportunity of talking longingly about them. In Moscow we stood in line with peasants who had come from the most distant parts to see Lenin's tomb. Corridors draped in red led to the little room in which he lay in a glass coffin, exposed to the view of visitors. A former counselor to the Soviet Embassy in Paris, escorted by an officer, managed to gain admission to the Kremlin for us. This was temporarily prohibited because of official meetings then going on. In this way we saw, among other things, the little chapel, which is a real jewel.

Apart from ikons (of which we saw some superb examples in the Icon Museum), there was never any real Russian school of painting, but in the museums there are magnificent collections (forty Rembrandts at the Hermitage, and many pictures by the Impressionists and from Picasso's "blue" period in the Chukin and Morosov collections). The education of the people was organized on a remarkable scale; everywhere one saw groups escorted by specialist guides who were giving talks on the exhibits.

The Russians led an arid and difficult existence. They were overcrowded, often several to a room; their clothes and furs were worn out; the food was poor; but the will to reconstruct their devastated country was manifest in all their actions. They lived austerely, rarely going out, and never visiting dance halls or cabarets. The intellectuals met in their clubs to talk and smoke. One evening, however, we were invited by Krassin to a so-called clandestine night club, or rather one winked at by the authorities. Our host turned up at about two in the morning, when we were preparing to leave. He persuaded us to stay, and we had a party at which our healths were drunk, and Jean's. Jean was persuaded to have a drink. It was all very innocent and delightful. But the telephone kept ringing, and this did not fail to set us thinking.

One morning the official from the Ministry of Fine Arts, who asked me each day what I would like to do, proposed that I should choose between a visit to a factory, a hospital, and a school. No doubt he was disappointed to hear that I was no more interested in visiting a factory or a hospital in the U.S.S.R. than I should have been in my own country, but I said I should be glad to see a school.

The children greeted us by singing the *Marseillaise* and the *Internationale*, and, to our great astonishment, we found every classroom adorned with banners bearing such inscriptions as

191

"Long live the Commune!" and a huge portrait of Louise Michel. It was customary to surround the pupils with objects illustrating the period of history they were studying, and for the Russian children Louise Michel was a legendary figure. In the school entrance there was a wall newspaper, edited and illustrated by the pupils, commenting on school affairs and the main political events.

Our parting from our young friends in Leningrad was a melancholy occasion. Sadly we wondered whether we should ever see one another again. For a journey to Soviet Russia was as rare an event as a visit to western Europe for a Russian. Back in Paris, we were assailed by questions and the eternal: "But of course they didn't really show you anything?" Good heavens, what did they show one in Belgium, England, or Switzerland that was so special?

No sooner had I got back to Paris than I found myself obliged to compose a new work for a tour in the United States. This had been organized by Robert Schmitz under the auspices of Pro Musica, of which he was president, and whose aim was to spread the knowledge of contemporary music. There were branches of Pro Musica throughout the country, so that our trip promised to be an interesting one. I beguiled the time by stringing together twelve extracts from *Salade*, images of characters from the *commedia dell' arte* which seemed all ready to take part in a carnival, so I grouped them together and called them *Carnaval d'Aix*.

Once again I disappointed the American reporters by telling them I was no longer interested in jazz. It had now become official and had won universal recognition. The Winn School of Popular Music had even published three methods: *How to Play Jazz and the Blues*, in which syncopation was analyzed—I might even say dissected. The various ways of assimilating jazz were taught, as well as writing jazz style for the piano, and improvisation; its freedom within a rigid rhythmic framework, all the breaks and passing discords, the broken harmonies, arpeggios, trills, and ornaments, the variations and cadences that can return ad lib in a sort of highly fantastic counterpoint. You could also find instructions on playing the trombone, including the principal types of glissando and the way to make the sound quiver by a rapid little to-and-fro movement of the slide; and there were clarinet manuals exploiting all the new technical possibilities opened up by jazz. Even in Harlem the charm had been broken for me. White men, snobs in search of exotic color, and sightseers curious to hear Negro music had penetrated to even the most secluded corners. That is why I gave up going.

I played my *Ballade* with Walter Damrosch at one of the series of concerts of modern music promoted by him under the title: "Pleasant and Unpleasant Music." Before each piece, the old maestro addressed the members of the audience and asked them to classify the music as pleasant or unpleasant. I regarded this procedure as definitely "unpleasant," whatever the verdict of the audience might prove to be.

Before I started to play *Carnaval d'Aix* with the New York Philharmonic Orchestra under Mengelberg, I suffered a slight contretemps, for a piece of chewing-gum had got stuck to the sole of my shoe just as I came on the stage. I played the *Carnaval* again at Boston with Koussevitzky, who engaged me to play it again under his direction in Paris, where he was in the habit of conducting a few concerts every spring and presented new works. It was in this way that I came to hear Aaron Copland's *Music for the Theater*, which first roused my admiration for its composer.

This was a period of prosperity in the United States.

193

Welte-Mignon, a pianola firm, gave me a profitable contract, as did Baldwin, whose pianos I had always used. Sales of mechanical pianos had been considerably boosted during recent years, for they enabled all the details of an orchestral score, which it was impossible to render on an ordinary piano, to be given. The Pleyela company had obtained exclusive rights from Stravinsky to publish all his works in pianola rolls. He had been given a studio for this purpose in the Pleyel building, and throughout one winter he himself played "pleyelized" versions of his works so as to ensure the correct reading, and supervised the perforation of the rolls, which was all done by hand, as well as all the musical details to be added to this preliminary version. Jean Wiéner and I recorded a piano duet of my *Bœuf sur le toit*. Welte-Mignon was less bold than Pleyela. They asked me to play a few *Saudades* and some of Mendelssohn's *Songs without Words*. As I was no virtuoso, I considered it absurd to play works other than my own, but I was told that was just what the public would like to hear: Mendelssohn interpreted by a contemporary composer. Personally, I think it was merely a way of getting me to play one less of the *Saudades*! In any case, it did not matter, for the firm went bankrupt before the recording was published. The development of the radio and the phonograph rapidly cut across that of mechanical music, and all these experiments came to nothing.

Gieseking and Casella were staying at the same hotel as we were, and we often saw one another. Casella several times invited us to his room to hear his latest compositions, never failing to say: "I think it is my best work." We had lunch with Charles Ives, a pioneer of American music. He received few visitors, and worked unremittingly. Schmitz, who had taken me to see him, knew his compositions well; they were

194

hard to play (and almost unreadable in manuscript), but bore the imprint of an extremely original personality.

We spent my holidays in Birmingham, Alabama, with Jeanne Herscher, who was teaching in the conservatory there. She was interested in the local folklore, and a Negro pastor assisted her in her research. In her company, we attended a religious service in a little Negro church all hung with white draperies and carefully decorated for the Christmas celebrations. The church was packed. We were the only white folk, and occupied places reserved for us by the pastor. The sermon began in an extraordinary way, reminiscent of those recordings of Negro sermons like: "The black train of Death is coming, you must have your ticket in your hand!" The preacher's voice rose to a sort of melopœic chant, now wheedling and now violent, but always awe-inspiring. The congregation responded by cries of "Lord!" or "Amen!" which rang out all over the church. There was a sort of undertone of excitement; when it reached its paroxysm, the preacher suddenly lowered his voice, and gradually the fervor subsided. Then the sermon continued and the preacher spoke of the relations between white folk and colored folk: "Why are we so badly treated? And yet the white people entrust us with their dearest possession, their children!" The tide of his eloquence began to swell once more. His lyrical outbursts had an astonishing effect, the cries of the congregation following the inflections of his voice as a shadow follows the body that casts it. Those who fell into trances were immediately looked after by persons specially designated for the purpose. When the pastor judged that he had had a sufficient effect on his hearers, he brought his sermon to an end in a quieter and calmer voice. He asked his aged mother, a former slave, to stand, and then he introduced us to

195

the congregation as French people who were friends of the Negro. Next day we were to have witnessed a baptism of two thousand Negroes in the waters of the Mississippi, but the ceremony was unfortunately postponed owing to rain.

In New Orleans the gulf between whites and blacks was even deeper, and their ways of life lay quite apart: the colored folk had to use special staircases and designated seats in the buses and trains. We were told that any white doctor who treated a Negro was irrevocably compromised in the sight of his clients. We were refused admission to a little Negro theater where an operetta was being given. They apologized for not being able to let us in, but the laws were rigid. As we insisted, however, they got the manager, to whom we explained that we were French musicians, whereupon he invited us to watch the show from his office, in which there was a little window overlooking the stage.

We stopped for one day at the Grand Canyon, which impressed us enormously. From the plateau itself, we looked down on a huge abyss whose rocky walls were colored as vividly as any picture postcard. We visited Portland, Denver, Chicago, St. Paul, Minneapolis, and Montreal. Wherever we went, we met admirers and supporters of Robert Schmitz. On our return to the United States thirteen years later, we found that most of the branches of Pro Musica no longer existed, which is a great pity, for Robert Schmitz had been a real pioneer of contemporary music. In addition to my visit, he organized similar tours by Roussel, Ravel, Honegger, and Tansman.

Although it was tiring, the journey was tremendously interesting. Very often we reached a town just in time for the concert, and left immediately afterward. Several consecutive nights were spent in the train. So it was a joy to be able to stay for a few days in Los Angeles. The lady president of

Pro Musica was waiting for us at the hotel and immediately asked us what our plans were. These were quite simple: we wanted to walk as far as the Pacific, upon which we had never set eyes before. She offered to take us there in a car, and when we declined she became so insistent that we finally gave way. It was a good thing that we did, for we certainly covered more than twenty-five miles before she pointed to a grayish expanse of water and said: "There it is." It was nightfall aready. We did not even have the courage to get out of the car. When she brought us back to our hotel, she invited us to a Hollywood *première*. The prospect was tempting, but as it was due to take place an hour's drive away from Los Angeles, we declined.

A day or two later we visited De Mille's film studio, where he was producing *King of Kings*, based on the life of Christ. He appeared before us in the midst of his apostles in a black-and-white landscape mounted on movable platforms. Mary Pickford and Douglas Fairbanks, then at the height of their fame, asked us to tea. They were delightfully informal. With all the exuberance of a child, he told us about the tennis match he had just been umpiring. She asked Madeleine, with the utmost naturalness, to take off her shoes so that they could compare heights.

Next, we spent a few days at Santa Barbara, at the home of Henry Eichheim, a most pleasing composer who had lived for long periods in the Far East and had brought back many lovely old instruments. He lived with his mother, who was ninety-six years old (the same age my grandmother Précile would have been had she lived). She was lively and full of animation. She thoughtfully placed a footstool under Madeleine's feet, much to Madeleine's confusion. She was afraid of dying, and had had a bed set up in the garden for fear of the slight earthquakes so common in that region.

No concert had been arranged for San Francisco, but we wanted to go there. We arrived at night by ferry, and the spectacle was absolutely fairylike. As we drank in the city's unusual atmosphere, I little dreamed that for several years we should live so near it.

WHILE JEAN COCTEAU was spending a holiday at Le Piquey, he was greatly struck by a news item he read in the local paper: the son of some poor Romanian peasants had been entrusted at an early age to relatives who were setting out to seek their fortune in America, and had had no further communication with his parents. He became a brilliant student, and set out for Romania to see his father and mother again. When he got to his native village, he had the idea of staying the night in his parents' house without letting them know who he was. They thought he was a wealthy foreigner, and murdered him. Cocteau took this story as the basis of a libretto for an opera. His poetic version, written rapidly without any erasures, appealed to me. Cocteau had meant it for Auric, but as the latter was very busy, he agreed to let me have it.

The plot of *Le Pauvre Matelot* is simple. A sailor's wife has been without news of her husband for several years. In spite of her father-in-law's insistence, she refuses to remarry. The husband returns unexpectedly, and goes first to a neighbor, who tells him of his wife's virtuous behavior and of her poverty. The husband wants to "see his happiness from the outside." He passes himself off to his wife as a friend of her husband, tells her the poor fellow is still a prisoner, suffering from disease and the lack of money, and confides in her that he himself has been more fortunate, that he is rich. He asks to spend the night at her house. She agrees, and kills him "in order to rescue her husband." The curtain falls before she has had time to realize her mistake and the crime she has committed.

Le Pauvre Matelot was composed at L'Enclos in 1926 and scored for a normal orchestra. It was produced in the following year at La Monnaie and the Opéra-Comique, but in very different ways. As it lasted only forty minutes, the Opéra-Comique put it on in conjunction with *Werther* or *Tosca*, which pleased neither the usual audience, bored by modern music and forced to put up with it in this way, nor the amateurs of contemporary music, who had to sit through an opera by Puccini or Massenet. What was more, there was a strange union rule, still observed in the opera houses at that time, to the effect that any musician, even if he had previously taken part in rehearsals, could get another to take his place at the performance. The substitute would often be reading the score at sight even on the first night. This custom, which might possibly be tolerable in a piece from the repertory, was sheer madness in the case of new work. Thus for the first performance of *Le Pauvre Matelot* I was favored with seventeen completely new players. Naturally the result was catastrophic. Understandably enough, the public and my friends to whom the work was unknown held me responsible for the cacophony, whose origin they were not in a position to suspect. As, on the other hand, the Brussels production of *Le Pauvre Matelot* was faultless, one of my composer friends who had attended the first-night performance in Paris, asked me in all innocence whether I had not reorchestrated my score for the Théâtre de la Monnaie. All misunderstandings were obviated in Brussels by including *Le Pauvre Matelot* on the same program as Honegger's *Antigone*, and the fact that both librettos had been written by Cocteau conferred a very special unity on the whole entertainment.

Further performances were given at the Opéra-Comique, but the difficulty persisted. One evening when I was up "in the gods," the man next to me said with a heavy suburban accent: "There's a pillar in my way; do you mind if I move up closer to you?" All through the performance of *Le Pauvre Matelot* he was pressed tightly against my side, following very closely, frowning and breathing heavily. When the curtain fell, he leaped to his feet, muttering: "Nasty piece of work!" and disappeared.

La Pauvre Matelot was my most widely performed opera. Written for four singers, with no change of scenery and with plain modern costumes, it is easy to produce. It ran for three consecutive years at the Opera on the Republikplatz, Berlin, and was revived in Berlin immediately after the war. It was also shown in more than twenty German cities, as well as Vienna, Salzburg, and Prague.

I conducted it myself in Barcelona, with Jane Bathori and singers I had brought from Paris. Although it was snowing, which was an exceptional event in Barcelona, Bathori was tireless in going from shops to exhibitions and from museums to churches. The theater was icy cold, we all wore several sweaters, and my singers were even able to keep them on on stage, fortunately! The performance was given in a concert hall. The walls were adorned with modern-style muses whose florid vulgarity was one of the secrets of the beginning of the century. The rudimentary scenery was barely lit, and the props were nonexistent. A makeshift curtain had been rigged up for the occasion, and as it was to be operated by one solitary stagehand perched in the flies who could not be informed in any other way, Madeleine, who was prompting the singers, had to pull a cord attached to his foot, whereupon the curtain would hurtle down—I can still hear the frightful din it made—and send clouds of dust through the hall. As there was no pit for the orchestra, the musicians sat in the stalls, and I conducted from the midst of the audience.

I was asked by Scherchen to score *Le Pauvre Matelot* for fifteen instruments. He wanted to put it on at the same time as *L'Histoire du soldat*. The first performance was given in Geneva. Ramuz produced *L'Histoire du soldat*, and Cocteau took the part of the Narrator with his clear voice, so luminous and distinct. He was also responsible for the mise-en-scène of *Le Pauvre Matelot*. (It was used again for the revival in Paris in 1937.) It was a highly simplified kind of improvisation, owing something to the slow-motion technique of the cinema: two benches, a few screens, actors in jerseys, with their faces daubed with violent colors as in the Chinese theater, to catch the light. Scherchen produced these two works in Turin and Florence. The "Vienna Studio" troupe, including Herta Glaz, also produced *Le Pauvre Matelot* in Vienna and Salzburg. Fritz Reiner conducted it in Philadelphia and New York. It was played in Paris and Rome after the liberation, and recently in England, in Chester and London and over the radio.

During our travels in the United States in 1927, when we had been running through a collection of old French-Canadian songs, we had noticed *Le Funeste Retour*, which described how a cabin-boy went to spend his shore leave with his mother, who had not seen him for a long time and who murdered him. It is curious how this theme is constantly recurring in literature and folklore. Albert Camus took a similar situation as a basis for his *Le Malentendu*, and in *L'Étranger* (*The Stranger*) he relates an analogous adventure:

> One day, when inspecting my straw mattress, I found a bit of newspaper stuck to its underside. The paper was yellow with age, almost transparent, but I could still make out the letter print. It was the story of a crime. The first part was missing, but I gathered that its scene was some village in Czechoslovakia. One of the villagers had left his home to try his luck abroad. After twenty-five years, having made a fortune, he returned to his country with his wife and child. Meanwhile his mother and sister had been running a small hotel in the village where he was born. He decided to give them a surprise and, leaving his wife and child in another inn, he went to stay at his mother's place, booking a room under an assumed name. His mother and sister completely failed to recognize him. At dinner that evening he showed them a large sum of money he had on him, and in the course of the night they slaughtered him with a hammer. After taking the money they flung the body into the river. Next morning his wife came and, without thinking, betrayed the guest's identity. His mother hanged herself. His sister threw herself into a well. I must have read that story thousands of times. In one way it sounded most unlikely; in another, it was plausible enough. Anyhow, to my mind, the man was asking for trouble; one shouldn't play fool tricks of that sort.

After reading this passage I wondered whether the theme of *Le Funeste Retour* was not destined to live on like those of Greek tragedy.

26

MINIATURE OPERA AND GRAND OPERA

BETWEEN 1922 and 1932 Paul Hindemith was organizing concerts of contemporary music, first at Donaueschingen under the patronage of the Prince of Fürstenberg, then in Baden-Baden under the auspices of the municipal authorities, and finally, in 1930, in Berlin. Hindemith was absolutely his own master, and tried out all kinds of musical experiments. In 1927 he asked me to compose an opera, as short as possible. Henri Hoppenot wrote a libretto for me, *L'Enlèvement d'Europe*, offhanded, poetic, and slightly ironic in its treatment, and containing all the essential elements on a miniature scale. It was produced in conjunction with *Die Prinzessin auf der Erbst* by Toch, lasting one hour; Kurt Weill's *Mahagonny*, lasting thirty minutes; and Hindemith's *Hin und Zurück*, lasting fourteen minutes. Emil Hertzka, the managing director of Universal Edition, did not consider the publication of my work to be a commercial proposition: "What an idea, an opera that lasts only nine minutes! Now," said he, "if you would only write me a trilogy—" The idea appealed to me. Once more I had recourse to Henri Hoppenot, who in spite of his official duties (at that time he occupied a post in Berlin) dashed off two more librettos of the same kind as the previous one: *L'Abandon d'Ariane* and

La Délivrance de Thésée. The three operas together lasted twenty-seven minutes. The trilogy was immediately produced at the Operas of Wiesbaden and Budapest, and I made a recording for Columbia. I have never been able to understand why the firm did not make more publicity of the fact that each opera occupied only one record.

In the following year various cantatas and works I had written for the radio were produced at Baden-Baden. Scherchen conducted my *Cantate de l'Enfant-Prodigue.* Hindemith took an active interest in the development of contemporary music for amateurs and wrote works specially for them. In the course of a concert given in the forest, both ancient music and his cantata *Frau Musica* were sung by peasants.

Another year they put on music specially written for the cinema, and on this occasion I wrote a score to accompany a film of Cavalcanti's called *La P'tite Lilie.* I recorded it in Berlin a few weeks before the festival. Hindemith's concerts and classes took up so much of his time (he was composition teacher in the Berlin Hochschule) that he was caught unprepared and right up to the last moment was feverishly composing his pieces for the festival. I shall always see him scribbling furiously and passing each page as he finished it to two of his students, who immediately transcribed it to a pianola roll. It was a score for an imaginative film by Richter called *Vormittagspuck.* For an animated cartoon, *Felix the Cat,* he used a synchronizing apparatus invented by a German engineer, Robert Blum. By means of this it was possible to run off the film at the same time as a reel of similar size bearing two staves on which the music was written, so that the music could follow the slightest movement of the picture. During the performance the musical score was thrown on the conductor's desk at the same time as the images were projected on the screen. In this way the conductor was enabled to synchronize his playing exactly with the film. Hindemith proposed that I experiment with this apparatus and, having nothing better to do, I accepted: I got hold of the newsreel of the week and, using the Blum machine, I wrote a suite of short pieces for a small orchestra. Among the French visitors to the festival that year were André Gide, Marc Allégret, Marie-Laure and Charles de Noailles, and Annie and Jean Dalsace.

Diaghilev came to Baden-Baden for a few days to try to persuade Hindemith to write a ballet for him. He was accompanied by an eighteen-year-old composer, Igor Markevich, whose work already bore the stamp of originality and maturity and evident signs of mastery. It was painful to see how ill Diaghilev looked, and we were scarcely surprised to hear the news of his death a few weeks later. This fulfilled the prediction by a gypsy that he would die on the water. In fact, his friends accompanied his corpse to the cemetery in Venice in gondolas.

The festivals in Baden-Baden were more to my liking than those given by the International Society for Contemporary Music. The latter performed great services, but as it was more catholic in its tastes, it had to open its doors too wide. There were I.S.C.M. committees in every country; works were submitted to these, and a choice was made; then the final program for the festival was fixed by an international jury. Each year it took place in a different city (Salzburg, Zurich, Siena, Barcelona, Frankfurt, Liége, Paris, Warsaw, London). A large number of musicians, chiefly from central Europe, attended these festivals, as well as those of Baden-Baden, but in the latter case the atmosphere was more intimate, and the programs, thanks to Hindemith's exacting standards and judicious choice, were of unquestionable æsthetic value. During the war the American section of the

I.S.C.M. organized an international festival to be held at the University of California at Berkeley, only a short distance from the college where I was teaching. I was a member of the jury.

There was a very active section at Basel, which had often commissioned works, including Bartók's Sonata for two pianos and percussion, and Roussel's *Sérénade*. In 1946 I was asked to compose a work for them, and wrote a group of six *a cappella* settings of some lovely poems by Jean Cassou: *Six Sonnets écrits au secret*.

We went to stay for a few weeks in 1927 with Emil Hertzka, whom we held in great affection. He had a house in the suburbs of Vienna, at Grinzing, a charming place famous for its little inns buried deep in flowers, where, as in the days of Beethoven and Schubert, whose mighty ghosts seem never very far away, you sit and drink new wine to the strains of Viennese waltzes. Audrey Parr, whose husband was now secretary to the British Legation in Budapest, invited us there for a week at Easter. How delightful it was to explore the city and the countryside, dazzling with flowers, in Audrey's ancient Rolls-Royce! We all went to call on Bartók, with whom I had some slight acquaintance and who had recently been rather ill. I was an admirer of his music, and knew that he had made long stays in remote districts of Transylvania and the Carpathians, where by dint of patience and unremitting effort he had succeeded in getting the peasants and mountaineers to sing him their songs, all of which he had recorded. Bartók's servant refused us admittance to his house. We explained to her at great length who we were, but the door remained bolted. We were so insistent that we finally attracted Bartók's attention, and he allowed us to come in. I asked him to play us some of his recordings. He put on one or two waxed rolls on a phonograph that emitted nasal sounds through a copper horn. There was an extraordinary lilt to these dance tunes and songs sung to the accompaniment of a cimbalom and a violin.

On our return to Grinzing, I composed *L'Enlèvement d'Europe* and the polka for *L'Eventail de Jeanne*. The latter was intended for Jeanne Dubost, a charming friend of ours, for performance in her drawing-room, where musicians, artists, and left-wing politicians regularly forgathered. She used to organize musical evenings in honor of foreign artists and occasionally offered her friends some curiosity or other. One summer's evening the Russian Obukov sang, or rather wailed, one of his mystical cantatas, greatly to the alarm of the passers-by who had gathered in front of the open ground-floor windows. Another time, it was a red Indian chief who uttered his war-cries as he strode up and down her exquisite drawing-room. Her husband did not take any great interest in these artistic functions. He had little or no sympathy for her "mountebank friends." Most of them did not even know him, so that they were amazed to see this unknown gentleman always arriving very late and the butler hastening to serve him. On the day when the redskin was there, M. Dubost came in just as the former was planting an enormous feather in Mme Dubost's hair. After a moment he made her a discreet sign that she should take it out, but she exclaimed: "But it's wonderful, darling, it's just as if he had given me the Legion of Honor!"

As a token of our thanks for all she had done for us, Auric, Delannoy, Ferroud, Ibert, Roland-Manuel, Poulenc, Ravel, Roussel, Florent Schmitt, and I decided to give her a surprise. We each wrote a little dance, and had them all performed in her drawing-room by pupils from the Opéra. My Polka was danced by little Tamara Toumanova, who was then eight. Marie Laurencin, who was one of Jeanne's personal friends, did the décor as well as the organdie costumes and plumed headdresses. It was such an enchanting show that M. Rouché decided to put it on at the Opéra. I was afraid that our works, written for a drawing-room, would be lost in a theater, and besides, I had composed so many works that had never been performed at the Opéra that it hurt my pride to make my bow there with a little polka, dashed off one morning in May in Vienna. So I remained on my high horse, and refused to attend either the rehearsals or the performance.

It was also during my stay in Vienna that I first made a start on *Maximilien*. A series of extraordinary coincidences had induced me to choose this subject. On the boat coming back from the United States in 1927, I borrowed from the ship's library a book that was an account of the Mexican expedition by a Belgian officer who had taken part in it. I was greatly interested to read his descriptions of the forests and mountains and of the works of art that remain to bear witness to the marvelous Aztec civilization; but what interested me more than anything else were the details of the expedition, for I had never studied the history of that period. My notions of the Mexican expedition were confined to Manet's paintings of *The Execution of Maximilian* or some relic piously preserved by friends in honor of an ancestor who, like the Douanier Rousseau, had fought beside the Belgians and Austrians who had vainly striven to shore up the already crumbling empire of Maximilian. I was immediately struck by the human, timorous character of this Habsburg, thrown into a tragic adventure by the boundless ambition of his wife, Charlotte, and the political scheming of Napoleon III, combining to force upon him an improvised throne in a country so utterly unknown to him that he had no inkling of the extent of the revolutionary movement that was to raise part of the country up in arms against him. I told Madeleine how interesting it would be to write a historical opera based on the character of Maximilian. Hardly had I got back to Paris when I saw the new *Maximilian and Charlotte* of Count Corti in the window of the bookshop opposite my house. I hastened to buy the book, which was full of details concerning their tragic lives. A few days later I was conducting a concert in Brussels when the papers announced the death of the aunt of the King of the Belgians, the former Empress Charlotte, who had been living in retirement in a château in Belgium ever since her reason had given way during her voyage to Europe at the time of the dramatic events preceding the tragedy of Querétaro. The weekly papers were full of photographs and illustrations; my material was collecting itself without any help.

More and more I thought about the subject; so when Emil Hertzka found me deep in one of the volumes of Count Corti's biography and asked me what I was reading, I told him I feared he would find out only too soon, for it was very possible that an opera would come of it. Far from discouraging me, Hertzka told me to read Werfel's play, *Juárez and Maximilian*, which was then having enormous success in Germany and central Europe. I knew Werfel slightly, having met him in the company of Alma Mahler, whom he later married. I got in touch with him immediately. As he spoke only German and I was unable to do so, our interview was very brief, but my luck still held good: the very next day he sent me a French translation of his play which he had just received. I read this and decided that with a few alterations it could be used as a basis for a libretto. We worked in collaboration. Dr. Hoffman, a specialist in translations for musical purposes, wrote a libretto under his direction, and

Lunel agreed to make a free adaptation of the German text. He preserved the order of the scenes and the broad dramatic outline, but pruned the text and enlivened the dialogue by interpolating arias and duets on traditional operatic lines.

I wrote at once to Mexico to the writer Alfonso Reyes, whom I had met in Paris as Mexican Minister, to ask him to send me some folk tunes and soldiers' songs dating from the time of Maximilian. The Mexican Minister of Education sent me a political song, a popular refrain *Mama Carlotta*, and a collection of songs. There was one beauty, which I used as a song for soldiers mounting guard at night.

I was just going to make a start on *Maximilien* when I received a letter from Claudel asking me to come and see him at once. I knew he wanted to show me the first part of *Christophe Colomb*, which had long been on the stocks. Sert had been the first to ask Claudel to write him a brief scenario for a choreographic divertissement on music by Manuel de Falla, to be given at the court of Alfonso XIII, King of Spain, but Claudel had refused to treat such an enormous subject in a few lines. Some years later Sert suggested this subject to Reinhardt for a show or a film to be made in Hollywood, with music by Richard Strauss. The idea appealed to Claudel, who suggested me as composer, on the strength of our having worked together so often. We motored out to the Château de Brangues in the Isère, where Claudel was spending his vacation with his family. While croquet was being played on the lawn, picnics were being planned, and the merry cries of children resounded on all sides, Claudel worked in his big library, far from all this activity. It was to that room he took me to read me his new play. I immediately realized the possibilities it opened up for me, with its myriad intermingling strands of lyrical and epic inspiration. A week or two later Claudel left for Washington. He had several interviews with Reinhardt, and the telegrams I received led me to suppose that the project would be carried out. I therefore set to work and had finished the first part of *Christophe Colomb* when Claudel and Reinhardt fell out as a result of differences of opinion on artistic matters. I finished the composition of my opera the following summer and showed it to the director of the Berlin Staatsoper during my brief stay in that city for the recording of *La P'tite Lilie*. He decided to produce it the following year and to start rehearsals at once.

When Madeleine had recovered from the long illness that succeeded the birth of Daniel, we set out for Berlin to attend the last rehearsals for *Christophe Colomb*. Altogether there were one hundred rehearsals for the choral parts and twenty-five for the orchestra. I couldn't dream of a more perfect production. Our stay in Berlin was pleasant. Many French people were there at the time, and we used to run into one another at the Embassy or at M. de Margerie's home, where we met M. and Mme André Maurois, the Jean Paulhans, and Henry Bernstein. André Gide was staying at the hotel where we were stopping. He used to love to go to the zoo, especially in this early spring season, which disturbed the animals in the same way as human beings. Much to Madeleine's joy, he took us there, and together we visited a crocodile farm where twelve hundred of these creatures, of all sizes, seemed to have adopted an immovable position regardless of the awakening of nature.

After a concert I conducted for the Berlin radio, we had dinner with Hindemith's brother-in-law, Hans Flesch, who confided in us his anxiety concerning the political situation and his fears for the future. Unfortunately, he was right, for he was one of the first victims of the Nazis. We saw the Hindemiths often, for Paul was in Berlin at the time. We

Milhaud and Fernand Léger, 1938

Watercolor by Raoul Dufy presented to Milhaud
after première of Maximilien, Paris, 1932

Milhaud rehearsing the Fantaisie pastorale *with the Boston Symphony Orchestra and Stell Anderson, December 1940*

Milhaud conducting the CBS Orchestra, New York, August 4, 1940

decided to attend the first night of my opera together, and I asked for a little box on the side in order not to be seen. The management ignored my request, and put us right in the center of the theater, in the box formerly reserved for the Kaiser. It was a remarkable performance, and Kleiber's conducting was superb. The *mise en scène* was particularly clever: the curtain had been suppressed and the stage prolonged on either side of the orchestral pit throughout the whole length of the theater, so that the chorus could sing without impeding the action on the stage. At the back of the stage was a movie screen; the idea of the introduction of the film was to intensify the scenic effects. When Christopher Columbus is reading Marco Polo's travels, blurred images of tropical landscapes flit across the screen as in a dream; in the scene when Columbus takes leave of his family, the same actors enact the episode in a different setting, thus duplicating and hence reinforcing the effect; when Columbus questions a sailor concerning a piece of wreckage found near the Azores, the same scene, immensely magnified, is thrown on the screen in a way that seems to prolong its mystery into an inner universe opening out from our own. The technical resources of the Staatsoper were able to cope with rapid shifts of scene, which was invaluable as there were twenty-seven tableaux.

Christophe Colomb was an enormous success and ran for two seasons. Thereafter it was given in the form of an oratorio, which can be done quite easily, each scene being linked to the next by the Narrator. I owe the first French production of my work to Pierre Monteux, who put it on in Nantes with the excellent town chorus under its leader, Mme Le Meignan. Conducting a chorus calls for great tenacity of purpose, and Mme Le Meignan had plenty of that. When the city council refused to let her go on rehearsing in one of the rooms of the former castle of the dukes of Brittany, as her funds did not permit of hiring premises, she threatened to hold her rehearsals on the public highway. They knew her, and realized that this was no idle threat. It was deemed wiser to restore the use of the château.

A few months later *Christophe Colomb* was conducted by Manuel Rosenthal on the French radio, with the Raugel Choral Society. I myself conducted it in London, where it was sung in English. It was given in Czech in Prague, and in Flemish and French on the Belgian radio.

Certain prominent personages expressed astonishment that my work should have been given its first performances in Germany. I have always submitted my works to the Opéra, in spite of the hardly encouraging reception they have been given. Was I not told concerning the *Euménides*: "What an idea to choose such a subject!" I thought that Æschylus had proved its worth. Be that as it may, the fact that *Christophe Colomb* had been produced first in Germany excited a good deal of comment, and was even mentioned in the Chamber of Deputies. As a result of this incident, the Opéra was determined to produce one of my works, no matter which. I had just completed *Maximilien*, and this was accepted.

For a state-owned theater, the subject of *Maximilien* was rather a delicate one. While rehearsals were going on, therefore, the Ministry of Fine Arts judged it wise to submit the libretto to the Belgian Embassy (because of the Empress Charlotte), the Austrian Legation (because Maximilian had been a Habsburg), and finally the Mexican Legation. Fortified with the approval of the representatives of the three countries in question, I imagined that I should now be left in peace, when suddenly I received a letter from the grandson of Marshal Bazaine requesting an interview with me. He was a very tall man, extremely solemn, and his anxiety was

214

touching. He was afraid that the presence of Bazaine on the
stage of the Opéra might provoke a demonstration. I tried
to persuade him that no one could possibly have any such
idea, his grandfather having been utterly above suspicion
during the Mexican expedition. To reassure him, I showed
him the libretto, and he asked for a slight alteration in it. He
was afraid of the disagreeable juxtaposition on the stage of
Bazaine and López, the officer who was ultimately to betray
Maximilian. I was able to set his mind at rest by substituting
another officer for López in this short scene.

In treating a fairly recent historical subject, I ran the risk
of encountering people who had actually known the originals
of my drama. After the first performance I received a call
from Colonel Hans, who had remained at the Emperor's side
at Querétaro up to the time of his execution. In spite of his
great age, he had an astonishing memory, and his recollec-
tions were circumstantial. He criticized the color and shape
of the beard worn by the actor playing the part of General
Mejía, on the ground that they did not conform to the original.
We saw a lot of him, and it was fascinating to hear him
relate so many intimate details concerning the characters I
had tried to re-create. Then General Malleterre's daughter,
who had been named Charlotte in memory of the Empress,
asked me for seats in order to relive the moments of her
childhood, when she had so often heard her father tell the
tangled story of all these events. I also learned that the
widow of the Republican General Porfirio Díaz, Juárez's
right-hand man and successor, had attended one of the performances, at which she had no doubt seen her husband as he
might have been at the time of their betrothal. The performances of *Maximilien* were excellent, and Pedro Pruna's
décors and costumes brought out the character of the work
in the most tasteful fashion. Although the press seemed to

have grasped the meaning of the work, it really let itself go this time. I was abused, torn to tatters, and dragged in the dust.

Les Choëphores was produced on the stage in Belgium. Claudel, who was French Ambassador there at the time, was invited to supervise the production. For the costumes and décors, he called on his faithful collaborator Audrey Parr, who, as for *L'Homme et son désir*, did her best to translate in her sketches the exact ideas he endeavored to express to her in words. The part of Clytemnestra was taken by Mme Ida Rubinstein, and that of Orestes by Jean Marchat. The roles of Electra and Orestes were both spoken and sung, the singers and actors alternating with one another. The spoken choruses were delivered by "Les Renaudins" under Madeleine Renaud-Thévenet, whose interpretation followed Claudel's own idea of what he had been trying to convey so closely that this was the start of a fruitful collaboration between them.

Apart from *Les Euménides*, which in any case involved one serious difficulty in the way of execution, all my works for the theater have been produced. The Finale of *Les Euménides* was given by Louis de Vocht and the admirable Cœcilia Chorus at a concert in Antwerp in 1928. The audience was gripped by the triple chorus of the voices of Athena, the Eumenides, and the people of Athens, and made no attempt to conceal the depth of emotion it roused: carried away with enthusiasm, a dense crowd besieged the car of M. Fester, president of the choral society, in which I was seated, and ran after us for a long way. I was deeply moved. Some of my Parisian friends who had attended the concert decided to form a guarantee fund to ensure a repetition of it in Paris with the same performers. The program had also included *Les Choëphores* with Claire Croiza magnificently playing the speaking role. The same success was repeated in Paris. Like the Belgian audience, the Parisians appeared chiefly impressed by the exaltation and power of the voices under the electrifying direction of de Vocht, whose fervor and enthusiasm had a superhuman effect.

It was after this performance that Columbia made recordings of extracts from *Les Choëphores* and of the Processional that concludes the Finale of *Les Euménides*. These records did a great deal to make my music more widely known. The work was never performed in the United States, and yet I found that, thanks to the record-collections in the various universities and colleges, it was well known to most music-lovers.

27

VISIT TO MANUEL DE FALLA

WE HAD become great friends with Jeanne Fernandez, whose combination of charm, high spirits, kindness, and courage we found particularly attractive; she had got into the habit of visiting Aix regularly and had bought a little house there called Le Couffin. She spent her vacations there and was often joined by her son Ramon. As he had given a series of lectures in Madrid that had been extremely favorably received, he asked me whether I should like to go there. It was an opportunity to take Madeleine to a country I loved and to renew contacts with Spanish musicians. Ramon put me in touch with the University of Madrid. This was in 1929, under the regime of Primo de Rivera. The aristocracy of Madrid took an interest in the intellectual functions held at the University City, which was to become the last bastion of freedom during the fighting around Madrid.

At Madrid, I came into contact once more with Ernesto Halffter and Adolfo Salazar, who included among his gifts as a composer and writer on music a talent for the role of cicerone. With unaffected simplicity and lighthearted solicitude, he shepherded us everywhere, from the cafés in the Puerta del Sol, where we sat dipping doughnuts dripping with oil in cups of thick chocolate flavored with cinnamon, to the *terrasses* of the cafés on the main streets, where at cocktail time we regaled ourselves with *percebes* that looked like the feet of some kind of marine elephant. He took me to see Gustavo Pittaluga, son of the famous surgeon, who was a very sick man at the time, and whom we were to meet again in Paris a few years later on the first stage of his exile, which finally took him to the United States.

In addition to the lectures I gave in Madrid, I conducted some of my works, and played *Le Carnaval d'Aix* under the direction of Fernández Arbós. Together with Artur Rubinstein, this eminent musician was one of the most entertaining characters I have ever met. Chance brought them together on one occasion in Paris, when each sought to outdo the other in wit and petulance. It was a duel of anecdotes. During the same stay in Madrid, I was asked to repeat my lecture in Bilbao a week or two later. This gave us time for a trip to Granada and Seville.

It was a cold and rain-drenched day for our arrival in Granada. Muffled in a long overcoat, with a thick scarf over his face, Manuel de Falla was waiting for us at the station. This was a most touching attention, especially as I knew his own health to be delicate. He took us to our hotel. From the balcony of our bedroom we could look out over the forests that cover the hill of the Alhambra. When the rain stopped, an intoxicating scent of jasmin invaded the room, and a hundred thousand nightingales burst into frantic song across that sea of fragrant green leaf. The silhouette of Charles V's unfinished palace stood out against this background of interwoven flower-scent and bird-song. Next morning Falla called for us to show us the Alhambra and the Generalife.

These gems of architecture are located in such a marvelous landscape that we were torn between our admiration for the arabesques that adorn the walls, and enthusiasm for the astonishing loveliness of which we caught glimpses through every casement. Falla took us to his home at Antequeruela Alta for lunch, looking over a hillside inhabited by gypsies who dwelt in caves carved from the living rock. As we passed by, children and old men came running with outstretched hands. On all sides typical gypsy women appeared, wearing voluminous skirts and long shawls, with a carnation stuck in their hair above huge combs. Guitars were playing, and their chords merged with the words sung by exquisite husky voices practicing the *cante jondo*, and a delicious odor of saffron, tomato, and garlic hung over the scene. All three of us went on foot, under a sun as fierce as molten lead. The only living thing we met was a cart or two raising clouds of dust that compelled Falla to cover his mouth with a large handkerchief and hide in the bushes until the air had cleared again. Falla lived with his sister in a charming white house. They gave us a delicious meal of different kinds of pancakes, made with cheese, with fish, and with jam. We lingered long over our meal, chatting rather drowsily because of the heat from the brazier that warmed our feet in spite of the precocious spring weather. Then Falla showed us the room where he worked, and where he had been composing the *Atlantide*. When I was starting on *Christophe Colomb*, he had written to tell me that Columbus was to be one of the secondary characters in his own next work. He had warned me in case I should be annoyed that we were both introducing the same character in our works. I answered that it was not of the slightest importance, as Columbus was the central figure in my opera. These circumstances and my admiration for Falla induced me to dedicate *Christophe Colomb* to him. After lunch we went for a long ride in a carriage and then took our leave. I was keenly sorry not to be able to return Falla's delightful hospitality when some years later he and his sister came to Aix unexpectedly, the day before we left for Portugal.

Our favorite way of passing time in Seville was to stroll along the little streets too narrow for vehicles to pass through. There are picturesque shops and clubs for men. Behind a huge bay window on the ground floor you can see them drinking and playing cards as if they were sitting in a shop-window. We visited the Cathedral, where Columbus's logbook is preserved. Looking down from the top of La Giralda between the spires, you can see the whole city and the Guadalquivir outspread at your feet.

In Bilbao I gave my lecture to a very likable group of young artists. The charming Basque city was split into two opposing camps: those who liked chocolate with cinnamon, and those who liked chocolate without cinnamon. Happy days, when the only subject of discord was the taste for one particular spice!

VISIT TO FRANCIS JAMMES

I HAD not seen Jammes for a very long time, and I wanted him to meet Madeleine. In 1928 we decided to return to Paris via the Basque country. The Jammeses had left Orthez, where they had lived for so many years, as a result of an extraordinary chain of circumstances: poetry did not provide them with enough to live on, for they had a lot of children; Ginette Jammes was ill and had been ordered to a spa; and they had been given notice by the owner to quit the house they lived in. So they were passing through a particularly difficult time, when Jammes made a novena, and his prayers were granted. On the very ninth day the postman brought him a letter from a lawyer informing him that he was the heir of an aged, recently deceased spinster who wished to leave her property to a good Catholic with a numerous family, thus disinheriting the rightful heir, an unmarried nephew or cousin, who was a free-thinker. In this way the poet came into possession of a beautiful house and several farms in the heart of the Basque country.

It was there, at Hasparren, that I went to see them, and found them as friendly and affectionate as ever. There were now seven children around their grandmother, Jammes's mother, who also lived with them. Bernadette, the eldest, acted as her father's secretary. They gave us a lovely room adorned with old engravings, most prominent of all being a little frame containing the medal awarded to Ginette's father during the Mexican expedition. Jammes was in good health, working hard and taking an interest in all the affairs of the village. He loved to go for walks through the countryside with its blue horizons, but he was a little homesick for his native Béarn.

We used to get up late, to the sound of all the familiar noises that mingled with the hum of conversation, little disputes about a mislaid newspaper, comments on the mail from Paris, and the indignation of the servant, who could not get used to hearing sermons in the Basque language at the local church. It was all such a hubbub that Jammes would have to leave his study, where he had been trying to concentrate, and shout in stentorian tones: "Be quiet! You'll wake the Milhauds!"

After dining with the Abbé Dibildos, director of the Stanislas School, Madeleine and I did our best to play my score of *Christophe Colomb*. It was after hearing this that Jammes wrote a little account of it that was published in three numbers of *Le Divan*. One Sunday, we squeezed all the Jammes family into our little car to go and see *"les trognons"* (apple cores or cabbage stumps)—Jammes's nickname for his two youngest girls, who were boarders at a convent in Fuenterrabia. We stopped for lunch at Hendaye, where Jammes ordered an impressive quantity of oysters and wood-pigeons, those delicious birds the hunting of which he describes in one of his books. As we left the dining-room of the hotel, an old gentleman with an owl-like profile bowed to him. It was Miguel de Unamuno, who softened the bitterness of exile by living just across the frontier, and from the balcony of his bedroom could gaze at his native land.

Hardly had we crossed the frontier when Jammes waxed lyrical. Trees, houses, old women playing cards in front of their hovels, all seemed to him as marvelous as if he had landed in a distant island, for the whole of our friend's universe was circumscribed within a very small space, no more than a few hours' traveling time between one part of it and another. Homeland: the Béarn; land of exile: the Basque country; the borderland of romance: the Spanish frontier—a universe filled with wonder for the purest of poets.

VISIT TO FRANCIS PLANTÉ

ON LEAVING Hasparren, we stopped at Mont-de-Marsan because I wanted to pay homage to the oldest living French pianist. It was thrilling to meet one of the greatest virtuosos of the nineteenth century, a living witness to a period of music so remote from our own. Planté lived on a magnificent estate. In spite of his great age, he was still very active and year after year indulged in his favorite sport of hunting. Every morning in bed he had the latest works of contemporary pianoforte music brought to him, and amused himself by annotating and fingering them. He gave me the pleasant surprise of hearing him play one of my works, using his own fingering. He was the very incarnation of a pianist, and especially marvelous interpreting his beloved romantics, for playing which special qualities of precision, elegance, and subtlety in the use of the pedals are required. Here his technical mastery was particularly superb. He would comment on them as he played: "Pretty modulation . . . lovely passage. . . . Bravo! Bravo! Bravo! Chopin!" He talked of Liszt and "young Wagner," whom he had known. Planté did not play at concerts any more, except for local charities. When he had completed his program, he still kept on playing, murmuring: "Bravo! Bravo! What do you think of this tune? Adorable!"

Our parting from him was rather melancholy. With a plaid shawl round his shoulders, he came as far as the car with us. The sunlight was gilding the trees, whose yellowing leaves already spoke of autumn.

28

UNDER THE SHADOW OF ILLNESS

FOR THE past few years my health had been getting steadily worse; recurring attacks of rheumatism confined me to bed for weeks at a time and racked me with atrocious pain. During these periods of illness my darling Madeleine was also a prisoner, nursing my sickness and giving me moral strength through her unconquerable optimism, unalterable good humor, patience, and infinite devotion. How often she spent the night in an armchair, seeking in every way possible to bring me relief. During the lengthy convalescence that succeeds each of my attacks, the use of my legs only gradually returns. Soon I could go about only in a car, for even a few moments' walking sufficed to bring on a relapse or even a violent attack. How often I had to cancel a tour or a concert! Like Offenbach, whose life I had just been reading, I depended on chance for the outcome of all my plans, and like him, too, I often attended rehearsals leaning on two sticks and wrapped in a shawl.

During the night of February 8, 1930, I dragged myself to the living-room on my crutches while Madeleine was in labor in the bedroom; our son, Daniel, was born next day. He spent his first night beside my couch in the living-room. Every now and then he would utter a little cry as shrill as a cricket's chirp. The first gift that greeted his arrival was a rattle that Sauguet brought, and then a marvelous flowering almond that Picasso sent to Madeleine, which we had transplanted in the courtyard. Was this a gift from the fairy that presides over the art of painting to mark the destiny of Daniel?

When we came back from Berlin, we sent Daniel off to Aix with his nurse, Marinette, a charming girl from Béarn, while I went to Vittel, to take the waters. What a dismal time that was! Twenty-one consecutive days of rain spent under the galleries, waiting for the hour when I should swallow a glass of water. How slowly the days dragged by! Fortunately, we met Ambroise Vollard and Marie Dormoy, and soon her gaiety and Vollard's highly original personality lightened our horizon. There was an "Ubu" side to his character which captivated us. He had known so many painters that he never ran out of anecdotes or personal memories. He took us for rides in his car, and we attended together a show in the Théâtre du Peuple at Bussang, where a very interesting experiment in decentralization was being carried out, with performances organized by the workers. We kept in touch with Vollard in Paris. It was quite impressive to have lunch opposite a gentleman sitting beneath a portrait of himself in the costume of a toreador, painted by Cézanne.

For a number of years, I had been having homeopathic treatment, for this was the only thing that seemed to do me any good. The waters of Vittel had aggravated my condition, so we decided to go to Lausanne to consult Dr. Nebel, one of the most famous homeopaths in Europe. He was an amazing character, who examined his patients by means of a pendulum, and was able to base his diagnosis on a photograph. But though this wonderful doctor detected the cause of illnesses by such mysterious means, the astonishing cures he effected were owing to his medical science. Dr. Nebel did not conceal from me the gravity of my condition, but the treatment he prescribed soon began to do me good. For several years running, he sent me to Ragatz, and then to Cauterets for homeopathic treatment: to the amazement of the other patients, I only swallowed a few mouthfuls of water, and took baths lasting two minutes. Sometimes, it became necessary to have recourse to more mysterious aids to rid myself completely of my painful attacks. In 1934 I was bedridden, with pains in the feet, the knees, and the right arm. The months were slipping by, and nothing was doing me any good. I was trying all kinds of treatment without success. I was slightly feverish and incapable of working or reading. Only the visits of a few faithful friends brought me a little distraction. Then I started to throw shadows on the wall by my bed, using the light from my bedside lamp. Patiently, for hours, I tried to make profiles and portraits, and by dint of practice I managed to move my fingers independently of one another to an unusual extent. By slight alterations in the position of the various joints, I achieved some likenesses that were well-nigh perfect. This was a wonderful source of distraction for me; my collection included Sauguet, Poulenc, Satie, Hindemith, Prokofiev, Cocteau, Marguerite Long, the Princesse de Polignac, and the Comte de Beaumont. I regret not having had photographs taken of these silhouettes, for I never managed to do them again once I was cured. I was out of practice, my fingers were as rusty as those of a pianist who had not been working hard enough.

This distraction, however, was doing nothing to cure my illness, which still went on. At my cousins', the Allatinis', I had met a Dr. Feral. He had done my mother a lot of good, releasing her from a most rigorous diet she had been following for years. Dr. Feral had studied in Vienna and also with witch doctors in Abyssinia. He could not practice in Paris, for he was a foreigner. He had set up a beauty parlor on the left bank and earned a living in this way. He would give medical attention only to one or two friends, and came to see me. My feet looked to him as if they were dead. He gave me some magnetic treatment through the blankets themselves. His fingers exuded a gentle warmth that tired me tremendously. He did not lose heart, though my feet were still terribly swollen. He told me of a treatment he would like me to follow, but could not himself prescribe because he was not recognized as a doctor in France. He brought a dark, silent, bearded physician to see me. They had a mysterious colloquy, as a result of which they decided that this treatment would be premature, and the laying on of hands was resumed at more frequent intervals. A few weeks later another consultation took place, as serious as if it had been a question of amputating my legs, and the doctors decided to apply cotton wool and court plaster to my feet in alternate layers.

After swaddling my feet in huge woolen socks, they recommended me to keep on all this paraphernalia for two days. Next day, when Madeleine came in after stepping out for a moment, she was astonished to see me standing up, leaning on my crutches; two days later I left for Brussels to see the performances of *L'Annonce faite á Marie*, for which I had written the incidental music.

Dr. Soulié of Moran practiced acupuncture, a Far Eastern medical method of the greatest antiquity. It consisted of superficial applications to the skin, without ever drawing blood, of needles of gold, silver, or other metals, at points corresponding by reflex action to some tonic effect. The treatment was not at all painful. I tried it; it was successful every other time. It should not be inferred that I am always

ready to submit to any outlandish treatment. I have always
been afraid of healers whose gifts were not supported by
medical knowledge, and who might therefore be extremely
dangerous. Nevertheless, my last adventure deserves to be
related. At the beginning of the war, I was rather ill, and had
had several relapses. *Medée* was being produced at the Opéra
in May, but as I could not even slide from my bed to an armchair, I had, reluctantly, to abandon the idea of being present.
A day or two before the first performance Daniel came into
our room very early in the morning, followed by an air-raid
warden who wanted to give us a summons for a chink of light
showing from a second-floor window. Yet all the windows
had been painted with blue paint. What we had not bar-
gained for was that Daniel would scrawl all over them with
his finger: "Down with Hitler!" and "Long live France!" I
tried to excuse myself, but the warden would not listen; he
asked me why I was in bed. I explained to him in a few words
that I was ill, and that this was preventing me from going to
Paris to see my opera. "Say no more," said he. "Don't worry,
you shall go to Paris!" And without another word he threw
his helmet into a corner and started to lay on hands. He was
no liar: two days later I was able to set out.

Here in California, during the longest attack I ever had to
endure, when I started to write down these memoirs, how
often have I regretted that some Chinese magician did not
come and offer me relief. . . .

29

CONGRESSES, FESTIVALS, THE SÉRÉNADE

AND THE TRITON

Aʟᴛʜᴏᴜɢʜ I take comparatively little interest in the sort of speeches made at musical congresses, I like to attend these functions because they provide an opportunity for seeing other countries. In September 1931 the Portuguese government organized a Critic's Congress, to which I was invited, as was Bernard Shaw, who refused, and Pirandello, who accepted. I was not required to take part in the discussions or in the work of the congress. I was merely asked to conduct one of my own works at a concert to be given in Lisbon. I have rarely had any contact with critics, and this was an opportunity for me to meet some of the men who had been dragging my name in the mud for years. I was amused by the prospect, for I never take notice of criticism. I was delighted to find that my old enemy Robert Kemp was a charming man—provided you kept him off the subject of music—and that he had a very extensive literary culture, as well as a fund of high spirits that helped to make the journey agreeable. The congress was admirably organized by Antonio Ferro, the director of Portugal's propaganda services.

The whole country seemed to be out to greet us. One

evening we were offered a celebration by the inhabitants of one of the ancient popular quarters of Lisbon, Alfama, which looks down over the river. The narrow streets were hung with flags and with banners bearing the inscription: "Long live Criticism!" (critics have never been feted like this before or since) stretched from one upper floor to another in this working-class district. Through the half-open doors of ancient palaces that had now fallen on evil days could be seen tables groaning with all kinds of dainties. They were like fairy-tale palaces temporarily abandoned by their inhabitants to make way for the members of the congress. Fireworks exploded in all directions to express the charmingly childlike joy of the populace. I heard songs and refrains that I was to hear again a few days later in the excellent Portuguese film *Maria del Mar*, about life in a fishing village.

We stayed at Estoril, in the suburbs of Lisbon. We all went off in a boat to see a bull-fight, like those of the Camargue, to which we had been invited. The traditional picnic was a riotous affair. Lunch was served on the banks of the Tagus (near where we sat whole sheep and oxen were being roasted), and we were waited on by young peasant girls in gaily colored costumes while guitarists accompanied the melancholy refrains of the *fados*. To finish off the proceedings, we saw a bull-fight in the courtyard of the farm. Riding an immensely valuable thoroughbred, the *torero* tries to remove the cockades and rings attached between the animal's horns. His movements have to be executed with speed and precision if his horse is not to be wounded. In the north of the country, we were also received with banqueting and festivities. Pirandello took part in all these entertainments like the rest of us. He was reserved, silent, and retiring, leaving everything to his secretary, Saul Colin, whose activity as a publicity agent left him little respite. He was particularly appreciative of a visit to the university city of Coimbra, where young students in their traditional black gowns grouped themselves around him in respect and veneration. I was greatly impressed by the harbor of Oporto, where trucks and animals milled around in all directions. High above it stand the enormous iron bridges built by Eiffel connecting the two upper parts of the town. The Critics' Congress concluded with an enormous reception. Our hostesses, most of them members of the nobility, had put on in our honor the superb traditional costumes handed down in their families for generations. The popular dances were more lighthearted than in the south, and the *viras* livelier than the *fados*. Later I wrote a suite for the piano called *Automne* based on my memories of this lovely journey: *Septembre*, *Alfama*, and *Adieu*. There is one melody in *Adieu* consisting of a *vira* in slow time, whose feelings sum up for me the whole of the little suite.

I have several times been invited to attend the musical festival held at Florence in May each year. It was pleasant to meet old friends and foreign composers, and our visits were usually very gay affairs. We would all lunch in a band in one of the little *trattorie*—Berg, Křenek, the Malipieros, Casella and his wife—and then go off on some excursion together. The formal inauguration of the congress was held in the great hall of the Palazzo Vecchio, and presided over by one of the princes of the blood. The speakers each used his native language, their reports being immediately repeated in Italian by a genuine virtuoso of the art of translation, Mme Preobrazhenska. The concerts organized by Labroca and conducted by Vittorio Gui were highly polished performances. But what an audience! They were still hissing Debussy's *Nocturnes*. I saw some very remarkable theatrical performances. I also heard *Simone Boccanegra* for the first time. The festival of Il Maggio Fiorentino also engaged foreign producers. Copeau gave some Shakespeare in the Boboli Gardens, and a play about Savonarola on the Piazza del Palazzo Vecchio, on the very spot where its protagonist had been burned.

The 1937 festival was particularly interesting because it also included the celebrations in Cremona of the bicentenary of Stradivarius. For this occasion instruments had been brought from all the corners of the world, and the whole represented an exhibition of a unique character. Unfortunately the concert for strings was rather disappointing, either because the players were not accustomed to handling such sublime instruments or because they were quite simply not sufficiently skilled. With the Collaers I went as far as Mantua, where we visited the Gonzaga Palace. The portraits of the illustrious Gonzaga family form a collection of human faces mostly of uncommon ugliness. From the balcony of the room where Monteverdi's *Orfeo* was first given in 1607, we gazed for a long time out over the huge plains flooded from the marshes bordering the Po.

The last festival of Florence that I attended happened to coincide with the visit of the Führer. There was still complete freedom of musical expression in Italy, and the absurd story of degenerate art had not yet been adopted. The festival therefore went off as usual, though everyone was a little nervous. Mussolini had given orders for the whole town to be cleaned; every roof had been painted, as had the Ponte Vecchio. Fountains and lions of papier-mâché were arrayed outside the station to impress Hitler on his arrival. German policemen were checking the identity of passers-by and searching all hotels. But a considerable section of Florentine society left the city on the day he arrived, an overt demonstration of hostility. The Rietis took us in their car to Ravenna.

The Festivals of Venice were held biennially, and represented yet another wonderful opportunity to see my musician friends. The highly varied programs included well-known works such as Verdi's Requiem given on the Piazza San Marco, as well as contemporary works conducted by their composers. In the little conductor's dressing-room at the San Carlo it was not unusual to see Stravinsky's mackintosh and Constant Lambert's tweed overcoat hanging near my two walking-sticks modestly tucked away in a corner, while Pizzetti would be putting up a mirror, opening a silver toilet-case, and arranging flowers, his wife's photograph, and a sheaf of telegrams. Rieti's delightful little chamber opera *Teresa nel Bosco* was given. The last time I visited Venice, Stravinsky conducted his *Capriccio* with his son as pianist, a happy collaboration; Markevich presented his *Icare*; and I gave the first performance of *La Suite Provençale*. Unfortunately, owing either to the damp or to the tiredness induced by the lack of cars, so that I was obliged to go everywhere on foot, not only to rehearsals but also to the Café Florian to savour their delicious *gelati*, my legs began to give me trouble, and I was afraid I was going to be bedridden again. As soon as I had finished conducting my piece, therefore, Madeleine whisked me off to the hotel and started to pack our bags. After a few hours in the train I felt considerably better.

There were in Paris two active chamber-music societies, the Sérénade and the Triton. The latter had been founded by P.-O. Ferroud, who was killed in a motor-car accident in Hungary. It had a very large selection committee, including foreign composers resident in France such as Honegger,

Mihalovici, Harsányi, as well as many French composers. The programs were highly eclectic, and many new works were performed. Madeleine gave Hindemith's *Hin und Zurück* in her own translation. The orchestra, conducted by Munch, occupied a small corner of the platform. The tremendous efforts made by Hindemith to sponsor works designed for amateurs had inspired me to write my *Cantate pour louer le Seigneur*, written for chorus, solo voices, and orchestra, and easy to perform. The work was presented by the Abbé Caillet in the cloisters of the Cathedral of Saint-Sauveur at Aix-en-Provence. Durand started to publish under my direction a series called "Music for the Family and for Schools." Armand Lunel wrote the words for *Un Petit Peu de musique* and *Un Petit Peu d'exercice*, and René Chalupt provided me with a little play with twelve songs entitled *A propos de bottes*. These were all children's pieces. For several years I had been following with interest the extraordinary results being obtained by Mlle Pelliot by means of the Gédalge method, in which she had sole rights and of which she was the principal exponent. When Hindemith's *Wir bauen eine Stadt* and my *Un Petit Peu de musique* were given at the Triton, I asked her to provide the children's choruses, and I was amazed to see the speed with which these children, aged from eight to ten, drawn from elementary schools in the Bastille quarter, learned to sing and mime our playlets. The violins and cellos in the orchestra were selected from the pupils of private schools. In my score, as in Hindemith's, the music did not go beyond the first position.

The selection committee of La Sérénade, presided over by Yvonne de Casafuerte, was less catholic in its tastes than that of the Triton, and based on more clearly defined æsthetic standards. Its members were Auric, Poulenc, Markevich, Nabokov, Rieti, Sauguet, and myself. Thanks to the generosity of the Vicomtesse de Noailles, we were able to present Kurt Weill's *Mahagonny* and *Der Jasager*, for which the soloist Lotte Lenja and the conductor Maurice Abravanel came from Germany, as well as a group of children, for *Der Jasager* was written specially for schools. I was lecturing in Holland at the time the concert was given, and in the train that was bringing us back to Paris, I told Madeleine that we should no doubt find that the city had been taken by storm. Little did I know then how true this was, for the delirious enthusiasm aroused by these two works lasted for several days. The Montparnasse set used the concert as a pretext for political diatribes; it saw in it an expression of the moral bankruptcy and pessimism of our times. Smart society was as carried away as if it had been the first performance of a Bach *Passion*, in mentioning which I am merely repeating what was said to me by one of my friends, a lady somewhat infected by the captivating snobbishness that enabled the Sérénade to keep going. We also presented festivals of the works of Stravinsky, the first performance in France of the *Dumbarton Oaks Concerto*, Henri Sauguet's *La Voyante*, and Francis Poulenc's *Bal Masqué*. The children's choir of the Armenian church, directed by Baron de Van, sang plain chant as it was sung in the year 1000, accompanied by cymbals and castanets, amazing music whose tempos were extremely rapid. On one occasion, the Sérénade gave a concert at the Church of the Trinité, consisting of Satie's *Messe des pauvres*, Sauguet's exquisite *Messe pastorale*, and works by Olivier Messiaen, the composer whose works enjoyed an enormous vogue after the liberation.

Among the first performances that I gave at the Sérénade, I should like to mention *La Mort du tyran*, based on a text to which my attention had been drawn by Daniel Halévy. It was a passage by Lampridius, translated by Diderot in his *Disserta-*

236

tion sur la Poésie rythmique and quoted as an example of rhythmic movement raised to the point of transport. In it the author depicted the outcry and imprecations of the Roman populace on the death of the Emperor Commodus, and their hopeful cheers for his successor, Pertinax. I wrote this work in 1932 for voices, percussion, and a few instruments capable of making themselves heard through the greatest possible tumult of sound: the piccolo, the clarinet, the tuba. When the dancer Alanova asked me for a work for chorus and percussion, I offered her *La Mort du tyran*. She gave a choreographic interpretation of it at the Sérénade, under the direction of Désormière, together with the Gouverné chorus, who were responsible for both the spoken parts and the singing. The orchestra was a small one, and the six percussion-players each performed on several instruments. On this occasion the dancing was only a pretext for the music. *La Mort du tyran* is essentially a work for the concert hall. It was given in Brussels with a chorus and the Renaudins. It was ideal to be able to entrust one of one's works to this group, so highly trained in the expression of the most violent dramatic feelings and using the most powerful elocution. Claudel was delighted with their work, and it was in co-operation with them that he arranged the spoken choruses that provide the off-stage noises in *L'Otage*, a kind of genuine verbal orchestration in which sentences uttered in high tones or in low stand out against a background of hammer-like repetitions of onomatopœias and disjointed phrases. A recording of this was made, and used for the performances at the Comédie-Française.

The Sérénade had a little sister society in Rome called the Concerti di Primavera, organized by Rieti and a few other Italian musicians under the patronage of the Contessa Pecci Blunt. I was engaged by them on two occasions. In 1934 their

program included the Viola Concerto dedicated to Hindemith, and given its first performance by him at Amsterdam
under the direction of Monteux, and repeated in Rome. *Un
Petit Peu de musique*, excellently translated by Rieti, was sung
by children wearing the Balillas uniform. Hindemith and his
wife stayed with the Labrocas, and often came to see us at
Rieti's home. Hindemith would sit down at the piano and, as
he had a phenomenal memory, would play whole operas by
heart. One evening he was joined by Mimi Pecci, and they
sang together at the top of their voices choruses, duets, and
arias from one of Verdi's operas. The noise was deafening
and the effect extremely comical, but as it was Good Friday,
our neighbors were shocked and banged on the wall to make
us be quiet. Fortunately, they never knew that one of us was
the niece of Pope Leo XIII.

Our stay in Rome coincided with the canonization of Don
Bosco. We wanted very much to be present at the ceremony,
but were unable to reserve any seats. Mme Charles Roux
was good enough to offer us two in a little gallery. We arrived at St. Peter's at six in the morning, to find that eight
hundred persons armed with invitations of the same kind as
ours had already tried to get into the little gallery, which held
only eighty. We did not abandon all hope, but sought out a
suitable place of vantage where I could lean against a balustrade. The multitude presented an unforgettable spectacle:
sisters of charity, priests, peasants, and women with their
heads covered with black veils that were indistinguishable
from their black clothing, were squeezed into every corner of
the church, mercilessly jostling one another with their elbows. A Red Cross tent had been erected at the entrance to
the basilica. Once you had got inside the building, there was
no way out. The congregation, having left home at dawn,
relieved themselves with no heed for their neighbors, while

others tranquilly ate the food they had been wise enough to bring with them. The arrival of the Pope's curule chair and the fan-bearers caused tremendous excitement. The papal benediction, vibrant with spiritual power, produced a surprising reaction. Instead of bowing their heads or prostrating themselves with religious awe, the crowd suddenly broke out into applause and cries of "*Viva il Pappa!*" Losing the most elementary self-control, a nun climbed up on the platform against which I was leaning in order to get a better view, and practically climbed on my shoulders to reach a balustrade. Others were clinging to statues or perched on the holy-water fonts. At first I was taken aback by these demonstrations, but little by little I was touched by their spontaneous, child-like familiarity, as of children greeting their father.

I returned once more to Rome for the Concerti di Primavera, and Yvonne Astruc played the *Concertino de Printemps* that I had composed for her in 1934. Jacques Ibert had just been appointed director at the Villa Medici. Ably supported by his wife, Rosette, he upheld the prestige of French art, a task that grew more and more difficult with each year that passed, in a most efficient and meritorious manner. Thereafter I never went back to Italy because of the racial legislation, and soon my music was banned in that country.

CHAPTER

30

MUSIC FOR THE THEATER AND

THE CINEMA

For a long time the so-called symphonic composers were ostracized in film circles, and as a class rather looked down upon by film-producers in search of composers capable of writing music that would be both popular in appeal and a commercial proposition. Gradually the serious musicians managed to win their way into the studios by putting on false noses—that is, by disguising their music in a style calculated to earn the approval of film-producers and directors. Once it had been proved that fine scores like Auric's music for *A nous la liberté* or Honegger's for *Les Misérables* could win popular success, these musicians' reputations were established and their services were much sought after. The first round had been won. Soon Roland-Manuel, Ibert, and Delannoy were writing music for the screen. While their scores contained all the simple elements needed to attract the general public, they remained personal works, stamped with their author's personality from the very first bars. French musicians are accustomed to orchestrate their own scores, a fact that helps to preserve the personal aspect of their works, contrary to what usually happens in Hollywood, where there are professional

240

orchestrators who churn out on a commercial scale musical pathos *à la* Wagner or Tchaikovsky.

Of all the "symphonic" musicians I was no doubt the one who roused most mistrust, so the number of film scores I have written remains strictly limited. My first film was *Madame Bovary*, a film by Robert Aron, who, in spite of the intellectual qualities and undoubted culture of the director Gallimard and the producer Jean Renoir, was unable to spare me a rather inquisitorial visit from these gentlemen to hear what sort of music I was writing for their film. I believe that in spite of the scant courtesy with which they heard it out in silence, they must have felt reassured, for I never heard any more from them. My music was composed during a long illness, and I was still very unwell on the day for the recording. I had myself taken to the studio and remained in the sound cabin all day long, on the assumption that my presence would be of more use to the sound engineers than to Désormière, who had had a great deal of experience of the film industry.

It rarely happens that a score written for the cinema is also suitable for concert performance, for it is usually too fragmentary and too descriptive, solely adapted to the requirements of the screen (for purposes of illustration, scenes of *bals-musette*, village bands, fairground scenes, and so on). Nevertheless I managed to extract from the music for this film a piano suite suitable for amateurs: *L'Album de Madame Bovary*.

Désormière, Honegger, and I collaborated in *Cavalcade d'amour*, which deals with the same subject at three different periods (Middle Ages, 1830, and 1930). I chose the first. Later on I used this music in a suite for wind quintet: *La Cheminée du Roi René*. Sometimes, but very seldom, a film out of the ordinary run gives a composer the opportunity to make fewer concessions and ignore the commercial angle. This was the case for Cocteau and Auric's *Sang d'un poète* (*Blood of a Poet*), which was commissioned by Charles de Noailles. Some documentaries may also give an opportunity for more original scores: one or two of those written by Delannoy and Taille-ferre were given concert performances. The only chance I ever had to do the like was for Malraux's *Espoir*. The film depicts a poignant episode from the war in Spain, and music was not required until shortly before the end of the film when the peasants are carrying home the bodies of the Republican air-men who had bombed the bridge of Teruel and crashed in the mountains. This very moving funeral procession lasted eleven minutes, and it was for it that I wrote my *Cortège funèbre*, the first performance of which I gave on the C.B.S. radio network in New York in July 1940 in memory of those killed during the war.

Music for the theater involves highly complex problems that may be dealt with in widely differing, often contradic-tory ways. When the producer plans the production of a new play, he attends to the function to be played by the music with the same minute care that he devotes to the lighting, and he often asks the composer to make alterations in the course of the actual rehearsals, so that the musician must be highly adaptable. But when the incidental music has been written with no view to immediate performance, as I had done for *Les Choéphores*, *Agamemnon*, or *Protée*, it is quite another problem. Now it is the producer who must endeavor to con-form wholly with the work previously completed by the authors.

Claudel has always imagined the role to be played by music in his various plays. It is an exciting experience to fol-low his lyrical outbursts as he tries to express the ideas he wants to convey. In the published version of *L'Annonce faite à Marie*, very precise indications are given as to the musical accompaniment. Claudel never ceases to ponder over his plays. This is why there are several different versions of the same work. *Protée* was published in 1913, in two acts. Claudel added a third during a voyage to Japan. *La Jeune Fille Violaine* was rewritten and became *L'Annonce faite à Marie*. The fourth act was shortened and simplified not long before war broke out in 1939. At the first performances of *L'Annonce* a score composed by the Abbé Brun was played, but when a few years later a lavish production of the play was planned for the Théâtre Pigalle, Claudel asked me to produce a more elaborate score. He came to L'Enclos to see me and work out the general plan in my company. He wanted the music not only to intervene when the text called for it (fanfare and liturgical choruses) but also to provide a kind of enhancement of the sound of the poetry, sometimes by means of the repetition of fragmentary phrases or by offering a pretext for a song, or a sung commentary on the action, or for bird song and a long melody celebrating noontide and the sweetness of summer. All this had to accompany the action of the play without in any way holding it up: the speech was to have a sort of musical shadow accompanying its every movement. The idea was fascinating, but Claudel was carried away by the interior flood of lyricism which sweeps him along like a veritable force of nature, and did not stop there. From Washington he sent me a lyrical commentary on every sentence in his opening scene —tremendously interesting, but likely to make it last three times as long. I was therefore obliged to stick to the plans we had worked out in Aix. I scored my music for the instruments most suitable for the microphone (organ, piano, flute, clarinet, two saxophones, two Ondes Martenot, and percussion) and for vocal quartet. Theoretically, the music was to be recorded for going on tour, but the theater management changed hands and the project was abandoned. *L'Annonce*

243

was produced at the Palais des Beaux-Arts in Brussels. The singers and orchestra were beautifully handled, but the actors were only amateurs. It was most interesting to see the scenes in which the effect of duplication was employed, the music and the singing proceeding independently of the action on the stage. It was a case of reinforcing the dramatic effect rather like the visual experiment that had been tried out in *Christophe Colomb* when a scene similar to the one depicted by the singers was thrown on the screen. A series of performances of *L'Annonce faite à Marie* was given at the Théâtre du Parc. When Jouvet toured South America in 1942 he wrote to me to send him the score, but as my copy of it had stayed behind in France, I decided to write some new incidental music. I kept strictly to the stage directions in the printed text, and composed a very different score, less lyrical and having a quality of austerity that linked the play even more closely to medieval music. As soon as my work was completed, I sent it off to Jouvet, but I had not foreseen that in wartime an envelope containing music and Latin words might arouse the censor's suspicions. It was held up long enough to guard against any dangerous eventuality and reached Jouvet too late. He had been compelled in the meantime to ask an Italian refugee composer, Massarani, for his collaboration. I turned the new music for *L'Annonce* into nine Organ Preludes and five *Prières* for voices and organ based on Latin texts.

In 1933 André de Richaud asked me to collaborate with him on *Le Château des papes*, a new play for Dullin to open the season with. I did not know Richaud, but I had admired his play *Village*, the sheer movement of which was positively amazing. I had seen all of Dullin's productions, and his use of music had always been interesting and original. He exercised great care and discernment in his choice of musicians: Maxime Jacob for *Voulez-vous jouer avec moi* by Achard, and Auric

Milhaud, Carlos Chávez, Madeleine Milhaud, and Otilia Chávez,
Mexico City, June 30, 1946

Milhaud and Madeleine Milhaud, Mills College, 1950

*Milhaud
and his son Daniel,
New York, 1946*

Arthur Honegger and Milhaud, Paris, 1952

for *The Birds*, *Volpone*, and *The Silent Woman*; for *Antigone* Honegger had written an enchanting musical motif for oboe and harp; and Sauguet had composed music for Roger Ferdinand's *Irma*, Delannoy for Aristophanes' *Peace*, and Ibert for *The Pleasure of Honesty*. It is not always easy to evoke and describe a character in a phrase lasting only a few seconds. In *Le Château des papes* there were in addition choruses that had to sing between scenes and in isolated sentences. Dullin and Richaud had taken up their quarters in the Château de Lourmarin. The former came as far as Aix to give me his instructions. He had locked up Richaud in the château, to make sure that he would work on the play instead of setting out in search of the liquid moonlight he writes about so much in his books. There was nothing hidebound about Dullin, no ready-made formulas, and though it was more expensive, he always preferred to use "living" music rather than recordings. I scored my music for two pianos, one trumpet, and a Martenot. I believe it was the first occasion on which this valuable instrument was tried out in the theater, with its almost unlimited range from high to low, its tremendous power and soft tones just within the limit of the audible. An arrangement of loudspeakers in the body of the theater and in the roof enabled the sound to be projected from several different points at once. My vocal quartets were sung by groups of actor singers, among whom was that charming Mme Limosin who a few months later perished in dramatic circumstances at sea with all her family. What a thrilling experience rehearsals at L'Atelier were! Disregarding what he has prepared in advance, Dullin works with the living model, constantly altering and revising, rarely satisfied. For days he goes over the same passage. Changeable because ever aspiring to perfection, he makes the musician's work hard. "Don't you think it's too long?" "Yes, perhaps you're right," you reply, and the scene is cut. Then the next day he will say: "Don't you think it's a little weak to support the opening theme?" You alter it, or speed it up, and as likely as not come back to what was suggested in the first place. This is excellent training for those who collaborate with him. Dullin is in agony, overcome with despair, passing without transition from tears to laughter: some trifling incident such as a clumsy move by one of the actors is enough to make him forget his worries and soon recover his spirits and optimism. In the *Château des papes* one scene describing the Black Death gave us enormous trouble. We worked on it all night, but next day Dullin had a sudden inspiration that made him alter everything—*and he was right.* All this preparatory work revived Madeleine's love of the stage. She had abandoned her dramatic studies in deference to her father's wishes, but now, by arrangement with Dullin, she attended his classes and those given by Mme Dullin and Arnaud. We did not like to be parted for long, however, and she decided to go on the stage only after the financial reverses that left her mother without resources.

For Dullin I composed music for *Le Faiseur* and *Plutus,* very cleverly adapted by Simone Jolivet, and for *Julius Cæsar,* in which the importance of the crowd scenes and of the battle sequence raised difficult problems. We thought of mingling recorded sounds with those made by the actors themselves, and of then superimposing my score (for seven instruments) upon them. The mechanical aspect of these experiments seemed to us to be incompatible with a living performance, and the idea was abandoned. In fact, a roll on the drum *sounds* more real in the theater than a recording of actual sounds. It was as a sequel to these performances of *Julius Cæsar* that I was asked by the Old Vic to write a score for Michel de Saint-Denis's production of *Macbeth.* There too preference was expressed for living music, but I was limited to five instruments. A young conductor deeply versed in the requirements of theatrical music showed remarkable adaptability, especially in the scene with the three witches, in which the music and the words must be absolutely synchronized.

For the translation of *Romeo and Juliet* by Jouve and Pitoëff, I wrote a suite for oboe, clarinet, and bassoon based on themes from Corrette, a *petit-maître* of the eighteenth century, very freely handled as regards both harmony and melodic line. This *Suite d'après Corrette* was published and recorded. It was very pleasant to work with Pitoëff. With the manuscript open before us, we would pick out the passages in which music was required and work out the timing together. Then I composed my music, which corresponded exactly to the spoken text. In addition to *Romeo and Juliet*, I wrote for him music to René Lenormand's *La Folle du ciel*, using harp, Ondes Martenot, and voice (my songs were sung with great charm and feeling by Ludmilla Pitoëff); *Amal* by Tagore and Gide; *La Première Famille* by Supervielle; and Anouilh's *Voyageur sans bagages*. From the last-named I extracted a Suite for piano, violin, and clarinet. The smallest orchestra I ever used was undoubtedly for *Le Bal des voleurs* by Anouilh: it consisted of one single player, a clarinettist, who mingled with the actors on the stage—sometimes, it is true, he played the saxophone.

I have only on one occasion worked for Jouvet, at the Comédie-Française in *Tricolore* by Lestringuez, and once too for Copeau, in André Obey's *Le Trompeur de Séville*. Unlike Pitoëff and Dullin, these two producers used to have the music recorded. Whereas the fact that the players only had to be paid once made it possible to have a bigger orchestra and thus obtain a greater variety of timbres, in my opinion there is no real substitute for *living* music. For the fanfares in *Le Trompeur de Séville* I used one or two eighteenth-century themes that recurred later in the score from which I drew my *Suite provençale*. During the performances of Henriette Pascar's production of *Golden Boy* I had a little adventure. The plot is a simple one: a young violinist decides to abandon his career for that of a prize-fighter. At the end of Act I he plays the violin for the last time (I had written a little melody that had been recorded); then he sadly lays the instrument back in its case in front of his sorrowing parents. At the dress rehearsal, the sound of the violin was only heard a moment after the violin had been put back in its case. The stage manager offered his apologies, and next day the music was on time, but unfortunately he lost his head and put on a piano record by mistake. The effect was startling!

Henriette Pascar had been responsible for some delightful plays for children, on subjects adapted by Charles Vildrac. I composed the music for *Le Médecin Volant*, and later based the first and third pieces of *Scaramouche* on it. I also introduced in the middle of this suite the theme of the brief overture I wrote for Supervielle's *Bolivar* at the Comédie-Française. Although I had written a full score for this work, I did not use any part of it in the opera I was to compose later. I did, however, take from it the *Trois Chansons de Négresse*.

In 1936 the Popular Front government decided to celebrate its accession to power by a gala theatrical performance that would also be a patriotic and political pageant. They chose Romain Rolland's *Quatorze Juillet*, and commissioned music from Charles Koechlin, Albert Roussel, Honegger, Ibert, Auric, Daniel Lazarus, and myself. My piece was intended to accompany the funeral procession for the burial of Necker. My orchestra consisted solely of woodwinds and brass, and was conducted by Désormière. I was unable to attend the performance owing to illness, but I was able to judge the popular enthusiasm aroused by the show when it was broadcast on July 14. Later on I rescored this piece and called it *Introduction et Marche funèbre*. A few months later another collective gala was given under government auspices, on the central theme of Liberty. Numerous musicians and writers collaborated. The idea was a noble and moving one, but it was translated into reality in a lame and heterogeneous fashion, with no unity of effect. With the exception of one or two scenes, it was a failure, and terribly "hammy."

Nearly every year I went to Orange for the Fêtes. Whether it was a solemn and majestic opera by Gluck, or the sun-drenched music for *L'Arlésienne*, or Paul Mounet bawling out poetry, for me the effect was always unique of its kind. The theater's acoustic qualities never failed to astonish me: a sigh or the most lightly breathed syllable could be clearly heard by eighteen thousand spectators. The orchestra was crystal clear in texture, with each instrument's line standing out, unblurred and stripped of extraneous sound. The city presented an amusing spectacle, hotels and boarding-houses being taken by assault, and streets and cafés filled to overflowing. In the evening, a huge crowd streamed out silently, almost majestically, toward the theater. There was a quite extraordinary atmosphere of quiet beauty and popular rejoicing. I had the great good fortune to be able to take part in it through my music for Valmy-Baisse's *Bertran de Born*, which included a ballet and songs, *Moyen Age fleuri*, for which I used eighteenth-century Provençal themes. The *Chansons de Troubadour* were later taken from this work, other fragments of which were included in the finale of the *Suite provençale*. I thought the rehearsals in the Theater of Orange even more beautiful than the actual performances because of the sunlight and the golden glow of the stone. The stage was conventionally floodlit and stood out sharply against the nocturnal vault of the heavens, in which on these moonlight nights there glittered millions of stars. Some fragments of the *Suite provençale* were included in *La Coupe enchantée*, produced at the Orange Theater by Pierre Bertin the following year.

Among other of my works based on music for the theater I should mention *Fragments dramatiques*, derived from the incidental music for Jean Mistler's *Le Conquérant*, produced at the Odéon.

During this period when my efforts were divided among so many fragmentary works, I wrote two important works of a religious character. It is curious how often a chance encounter or an unexpected detail may lead to the creation of a considerable work. In 1936, at one of Mme Long's receptions, we met Mme Ida Rubinstein and talked to her about the Ohel players from Palestine, who differed from all the other Jewish theatrical companies, usually strongly under Russian influences, and were playing at the Théâtre de l'Ambigu at that time. The primitive, rustic style of production, its savagery almost, and the authentic flavor of the acting, so delighted us that we had gone several times. Mme Ida Rubinstein asked to be allowed to accompany us. At the end of the evening she asked me if I should be interested in writing for her a work based on a Biblical theme. I suggested a collaboration with Claudel, and she enthusiastically agreed. I had worked with her before; since *Le Martyre de Saint-Sébastien* she had appeared in one show after another (*Amphion* and *Sémiramis* by Valéry and Honegger, *Perséphone* by Gide and Stravinsky, and ballets by Auric, Sauguet, and Ibert). In 1938 she had commissioned me to orchestrate some waltzes by Schubert and Liszt for a ballet called *La Bien-Aimée*, with décors by Benois. Although the subject was a simple one, it involved some ticklish problems in the situation arising when a young pianist throws a spell on those around him through his playing. What I had to do was try to exceed the virtuosity of Schubert's waltzes, those adorable short pieces, only a few bars long, already difficult enough in Liszt's *Soirées de Vienne*. I was only able to do this by means of the Pleyela. This was for me an amusing experiment from every point of view, for the mechanical rigidity of the Pleyela compelled the conductor to follow it as if it had been the most implacable soloist imaginable.

I stopped at Brangues to see Claudel, who at first refused point-blank to agree to a Biblical subject. What? Which one? No! He would not do it. Next morning at breakfast Henri Claudel told me that his father had asked not to be disturbed, as he was working. About eleven o'clock he came in with the completed scenario of *La Sagesse*, based on the parable of the Wedding Feast. A month or two later, Mme Ida Rubinstein asked me to approach Claudel for a scenario on *Jeanne d'Arc* for Honegger. I caught him on his way through Paris to Brussels. "What!" said he, "another Joan of Arc? No, I won't do it." The rhythm of the train must have touched off his imagination, for on his arrival in Brussels, his plan for *Jeanne au bûcher* was already drawn up, and Mme Rubinstein received the precious manuscript a few days later.

La Sagesse and *Jeanne au bûcher* were to have been produced together at the Opéra, but the project was postponed several times. Honegger's oratorio was given in Basel, and later in Orléans for the Feast of Joan of Arc, an official occasion graced by the presence of representatives of the government, the church, and the army.

La Sagesse slumbered in Mme Rubinstein's archives until 1946, when, within a few months of one another, Rosenthal and Collaer presented it on the French and Belgian radio respectively. The recordings of these two broadcasts were sent to me in California to bear witness to the excellence of the performances.

My second Biblical work was *Le Cycle de la Création* by Don Luigi Sturzo, the Italian priest who had been the leader of the Christian Democrat Party and who had left the country for his own safety after the murder of Matteoti. Several years before, he had asked me, through Emil Hertzka, whether I would be willing to set his text to music. He came to me from London, where he had taken refuge, accompanied by a group of producers who were interested in his work. He handed me the manuscript, on which he had noted the prosody of the Italian, to facilitate my work and avoid unnecesary errors. In spite of the incredible number of projects accepted for stage and screen, *Le Cycle de la Création* has never been performed.

I have always regretted that before the Second World War there was never any serious move toward decentralization in France, especially in view of the success obtained by some provincial companies. In Marseille there was a band of very talented young men, inspired by Louis Ducreux, who were introducing the local audiences to ancient and modern plays previously unknown to them. Henri Fluchère, who was an *agrégé* in English and was teaching in the lycée of Marseille, translated and adapted for them Elizabethan plays as well as T. S. Eliot's *Murder in the Cathedral*. These enthusiastic young actors cheerfully faced all difficulties and turned them to their own advantage. I saw a performance of *The Beggar's Opera* in the Salle Pins at Marseille which enchanted me. There was no real stage, merely a kind of platform at either end of the hall, like those provided for the orchestra in a ballroom. Their dimensions were so small that the scene-shifting took an unconscionable time, almost too long to be practicable. Louis Ducreux produced his play by using the two platforms alternately, requesting the audience to turn their chairs round in order to see the scenes to be performed at the other end of the hall. I harmonized and orchestrated the melodies of *The Beggar's Opera* for him, and later published a selection from them under the title *Carnaval de Londres*.

Another effort toward decentralization was that of the Compagnie des Quinze. Michel de Saint-Denis hoped to be able to enlarge its activities and produce plays in old marketplaces, châteaux, or the arenas suitable for play-acting such as abound in Provence. A house in the neighborhood of Aix-en-Provence was turned into a scenery workshop and school of acting. Saint-Denis also hoped to interest Provençal artists in the enterprise. He asked Jean Giono for an adaptation of the *Odyssey*, and wanted me to do the music for it. I had met Giono several times at Manosque. He had read me the manuscript of *Le Serpent d'étoiles*, which I had thought an admirable subject for a cantata. He had also told me how he came to write this book, which further added to my enthusiasm for it. While out walking he had chanced to come across a hilltop from which he had seen numerous flocks of sheep converging on one particular point. This had surprised him, for it was not the season of the transhumance, and he had learned that the shepherds were going off to their annual gathering, at which there would be an impromptu performance of a play. Giono had been fascinated and, borrowing an exercise book and pen and ink from a little village girl, had had himself taken by cart to as near the rendezvous of the shepherds as it was possible to go. There were thirty thousand sheep surrounding a narrow space marked out by lanterns like will-o'-the-wisps. Speaking their patois, in which all the dialects of the Mediterranean were mingled as in a melting-pot of poetry,

253

the shepherds enacted a pastoral drama on a cosmic theme. Giono had noted it down and translated it into French. He offered to take me to the Feast of the Shepherds the following year, so that I might steep myself in its atmosphere before composing my music. He promised to inform me of the date by telegram. I waited in vain for some sign from him, and after I wrote several times, a telegram arrived to tell me that the feast had taken place without his being informed. When I met Giono again, I had the impression that he had been romancing, and he readily confessed that the cosmic drama had never existed outside his own imagination—and was none the worse for that!

All this artistic activity in Aix and its surroundings made me long even more to see the city become an important art center for musical and theatrical festivals. A university city where studious youth can labor and meditate amid its eighteenth-century buildings steeped in tradition, and the amazing beauty of the surrounding countryside, made familiar through the landscapes painted by Cézanne, my native Aix seemed peculiarly fitted to become the center for a Mediterranean festival.

IN SPITE of the difficult period that followed the adoption of the Popular Front government's social reforms (forty-hour week, vacations with pay, organized leisure) and the disturbances, lockouts, and sit-down strikes, preparations for the International Exposition of 1937 went ahead and were eventually crowned with amazing success. Yet the mutter of sinister threats and portents was already to be heard. There was to be an Austrian pavilion, but the evil forces of the *Anschluss* were never very far away. Picasso's *Guernica* adorned the walls of the Spanish pavilion, but the Republic had been murdered. Placed face to face, the German and Soviet pavilions seemed to challenge each other to mortal combat. One evening as we watched the sun set behind the immense mass of flags of all the nations that fluttered above the Pont d'Iéna, Madeleine clutched my arm in anguish and whispered: "This is the end of Europe!"

The arts were well represented. Great painters, both French and foreign, had produced panels and frescoes; sculptors had been given an opportunity of showing off their prowess, and architects of demonstrating their new ideas The national broadcasting system had a studio with walls of glass so that the public could see all that was going on. The broadcasts were relayed over the whole exposition by means of a system of loudspeakers, and music seemed to have found its natural home in space. One autumn evening I listened to the pure crystalline notes of one of Mozart's concertos dropping at our feet like leaves from the trees. Another time it was Debussy's *Nocturnes* that merged with the lights that twinkled in the peacefully moving waters of the Seine. But the government did more than this to familiarize the public with music. It ordered some twenty-odd scores for the Festivals of Water and Light. The architects Beaudoin and Lodz invented a special device that made it possible to synchronize, to within one second of one another, the playing of fountains and firework displays. I was asked to write music for the "Festival of Light." My score ended with a poem by Claudel specially written for the occasion. The rehearsals had a charm all of their own; the music merged with the passing scene, and was not even noticed by the onlookers. But after dark, people watched and listened in perfect silence; skyrockets and showers of colored lights, tinted smoke-clouds and multicolored balloons mingled with the voice of Elena Fels, to which three singers responded: "O blessed light!" and with the changing play of fountains and lights.

The Musée de l'Homme had mustered all the most modern techniques for the presentation of the ethnographical collections previously displayed dismally in the antiquated Palais du Trocadéro. The Vicomte de Noailles and Henri Monnet asked me to write a cantata for the inauguration of the museum. Robert Desnos, who was as capable of writing genuine poetry as occasional verse, wrote the words for *La Cantate pour l'Inauguration du Musée de l'Homme*, which was performed before a tightly packed crowd in the lecture-room of the museum.

Official ceremonies followed one another thick and fast, as

if to add to the brilliance of that brilliant season. The government decided to celebrate the seventy-fifth anniversary of Aristide Briand's birth by a ceremony at the Sorbonne, in which speakers from all countries would be invited to take part. Anxiously I asked Marguerite Long, who had been deputed to commission a work from me, what singers and players would be available. "The band of the Garde Républicaine or the Manécanterie des Petits Chanteurs á la Croix de Bois," she replied. As Claudel had for so long worked under Briand and admired his policy, I got him to collaborate with me in a choral work. He selected a number of verses from the Bible, and together we wrote *La Cantate de la Paix*.

The Abbé Maillet, founder of the Manécanterie, had his quarters in the heart of Belleville [1] and welcomed there any child who wished to sing. Although the musical gifts of the children might be small, they were given special attention in an attempt to develop whatever potentialities they might have. Even when the result was nil, at least the children had the benefit of healthy surroundings and benevolent care. Rehearsals were quite devoid of severity or constraint. The children did what they liked, sitting on the ground or standing in a corner, with fingers in their noses, with their feet on their neighbors' chairs, but always attentive to the words of the Abbé, whom they adored. Their voices were supported by a group of grown-ups for the bass and tenor parts, but what carried me away was the absolute purity of the soloists' unbroken voices. I was amazed by the speed with which they learned my music. The Manécanterie included the *Cantate* in its repertoire, and the Petits Chanteurs á la Croix de Bois often sang it on tour as well as in Paris. The Abbé told me it was not unusual, when they were traveling, for one child to sing a bar or two from the *Cantate* and the others to join in

[1] One of the poorest quarters of Paris. (Translator's note.)

the chorus and sing it right through to the end. Filled with enthusiasm for our young interpreters, Claudel and I wrote for them *Les Deux Cités*, the first performance of which was given by them at the Sérénade; a few days later they sang it again at the Church of Saint-Etienne-du-Mont during Holy Week. Later still I wrote the music for a documentary film on the Manécanterie.

I have always had a great liking for the cantata form. Through Francis Poulenc, I was asked by the Chanteurs de Lyon to compose one for them. I immediately made a start on the *Cantique du Rhône*. In 1937 I used fragments from the Song of Songs for a cantata to celebrate my parents' golden wedding. After a number of family parties and a tea for some of our friends and the women from my father's factory, some of whom had been with him for fifty years, I conducted a concert on the Marseille radio, in which my parents had the pleasant surprise of hearing *La Cantate Nuptiale*.

Marguerite Long was accustomed to make her pupils learn contemporary music. (Had Madeleine not played a Debussy *Arabesque* in the presence of the composer in 1911?) She asked a group of musicians to compose some pianoforte pieces on the theme of the exposition, and had them played by her pupils, among whom was the granddaughter of the President of the Republic. My modest contribution was played by an eight-year-old boy, Jean-Michel Damase, later to be a Prix de Rome.

Also at this period I composed a piano work that gave me more than usual trouble. It was a suite for two pianos, to be played by Ida Jankelevitch and Marcelle Meyer. I took some passages from two sets of incidental music for the stage, and called the mixture *Scaramouche*. At once Deiss offered to publish it. I advised him against it, saying that no one would play it. But he was an original character who published only works that he liked. He happened to like *Scaramouche* and insisted on having his way. In the event he was right, for while sales of printed music were everywhere encountering difficulties, several printings were made, and Deiss took delight in informing me: "The Americans are asking for five hundred copies, and one thousand are being asked for elsewhere."

When I left for the United States in 1940, Deiss's friendship for me was such that he let me know through my mother that he authorized me to have reprints made of any of my works published by him, so that his American agent was able to keep up sales. It was a real grief to me to learn of the death of my excellent friend. He was actively engaged in the Resistance, and on being captured during the occupation, he was beheaded with the ax.

During the exposition various foreign companies succeeded one another at the Théâtre des Champs-Élysées. I saw a memorable performance of *The Doll's House* given by the Oslo Theater company. Why is Ibsen always played so slowly, as if to drive every syllable home? These Norwegian players were swift in speech and movement; Nora had all the careless freedom of a bird. At the Théâtre d'Essai, companies of young actors were given a chance to win their spurs. I wrote the incidental music for Webster's *Duchess of Malfi* in Ducreux's production, and for the *Hecuba* of Euripides, adapted by André de Richaud and produced by Marchat and Herrand. Richaud had traveled widely in Greece, and hoped to transport the whole production to the Theater of Epidaurus. They sounded me on the subject, as well as Derain, who had already designed some lovely costumes and prepared plans for making use of the actual landscape in the décor by hanging drapes from giant cactus plants.

In 1940 I visited the New York World's Fair, but I did not

find the atmosphere that had so entranced me at the Paris Exposition. I was particularly disappointed by the lighting displays, a pale imitation of our own. There was no contemporary music: the spectators were drenched in a flood of canned music. The day I went, there was nothing but Wagner!

32

THE PREWAR YEARS

T HE IDEA of war was increasingly becoming an obsession: for years it had never been completely absent from our thoughts. I remember the anguish we felt when, on leaving the Chinese Theater in New York in 1926 in the company of Copeau and Bourdet, we saw the headlines announcing the Italo-Albanian Treaty and the mobilization of our fleet. Next day it was forgotten: we could see the events in their proper proportion. How many fire-eating speeches had not been made by Mussolini during the previous twenty years or so? From 1933 on, the obsession grew. I was present at a debate in the Chamber of Deputies after the remilitarization of the Rhine. Protests were made against the violation of the treaty and the threats that had been uttered, but no action was taken. One evening when we arrived in Paris from Aix, our rest was disturbed by the news-vendors shouting the news of the murder of Dollfuss. Then came the Abyssinian crisis, the slaughter of Abyssinia before the very eyes of the impotent League of Nations, whose sanctions were incapable of preventing the crimes of the monster in the Palazzo Venezia. The *Anschluss* and the murder of Austria, with no one saying a word! The sinister sequence of events in the Sudetenland; the dismemberment of Czechoslovakia after Munich, and

261

the war in Spain, a dress rehearsal for the Axis troops! The murder of Republican Spain. And yet life went on as before; it was still peacetime, was it not? There was one's work to be done, one shut oneself up in it; what else was there to do in a world gone mad and caught in an iron grip that grew tighter day by day? One more turn of the screw, each day one turn more.

In 1938 it was decided to celebrate together the twentieth birthday of the Pro Arte concerts in Brussels and the concerts run by Mrs. Elizabeth Sprague Coolidge. They had both done yeoman service for music, and had grounds for feeling pride in their achievement. In homage to them, I composed a cantata in which I hoped to group together all our friends in a kind of Franco-Belgian family party. I chose some poems by a young Belgian poet, Maurice Carême, taken from his delightful volume entitled *Mère*. I called my work *La Cantate de l'Enfant et de la Mère*. In order that all our little band of friends might take part in this work, I wrote it for rhythmic recitation (so that Madeleine could join in too), piano (for Collaer), and quartet (for the faithful Pro Arte). I conducted the performance in the enormous concert hall of the Palais des Beaux-Arts in Brussels on May 18, 1938. It must have looked like a flea-circus, for our soft music and tender, intimate poetry recital came after some bravura pieces executed by the military band of the Guides, in full-dress uniform and energetically conducted by Arthur Prévost. The air still rang with the sublime din of wind and brass, through which the lightning of the cymbals seemed to flash above the thunder of the drums.

The state bought paintings and works of sculpture for its museums. It commissioned architects to erect official buildings. But it did nothing to help musicians. The director of the Beaux-Arts, Georges Huysmans, ever a friend to artists, thought that it would be a good thing to encourage musicians by official patronage, for in difficult times like ours it no longer paid to write operas; taking a long time to write, and longer still to orchestrate, even if it were ever played, of which the composer could never be sure, one of them could be performed only six times in a season because of the subscribers, who would not want to see the same work more than once. In 1938, therefore, commissions were given for a three-act opera by Marcel Delannoy, a one-act opera by Henry Barraud, an operetta by Georges Auric, a symphony by Elsa Barraine, and a cantata by Germaine Tailleferre. I was asked to do a ballet or an opera in one act. I chose the opera. For a long time I had been wanting to depict the character of a jealous woman whose passion would drive her to crime as the inevitable conclusion of her exacting, boundless love. Medea seemed to me the ideal subject for such a theme. The previous summer Madeleine had, for her own amusement, selected scenes from Euripides and Seneca. Thanks to her sense of the theater and her knowledge of my predilections, she was able to write a libretto, reviving the character of Creusa, who occurs in Corneille's *Médée*, to serve by her innocence and sweetness as a foil to the violence of Medea herself. I composed my *Médée* during the summer of 1938.

A concert-manager in the United States, Albert Morini, had often commissioned works from me for artists of his bureau (a series of duets with orchestral accompaniment; *La Fantaisie pastorale* for piano and orchestra; a dance, *L'Oiseau*, for orchestra), and now he came to me in Paris to persuade me to conduct some of my works in America. I liked the idea, but it could not be carried out, owing to the political situation. In view of my ill health, I did not want to go without Madeleine, nor did I wish to leave Daniel behind or let him interrupt his studies, so I put off my acceptance of Morini's proposal. In 1939 Hitler occupied Prague, and Czechoslovakia vanished into the silence of the European chancelleries. This could not happen again, however, because France and England had given their guarantees to Poland, Greece, and Romania. Not only was war constantly in our thoughts, but it was in our imaginations too, for we could see two thousand bombers bombing Paris without any declaration of war. Madeleine said to me: "You ought to send your manuscripts to Kurt Weill in America." I only wish I had done so! Instead I sent them to my brother-in-law, who was a justice of the peace in a little Normandy town called Domfront, which you would think to be the safest place in France. We also thought it would be wise to buy a little house on the outskirts of Paris in case of emergencies, but we set about it too late, for so many Parisians had the same idea that they invaded the agencies, buying up everything, whatever the price. All the agent could offer us was a little café in the heart of the country. It was a well-built little house, and it was fun arranging it to suit us. There was a big bedroom on the first floor, with one window looking out over the vast plain and the other on to the forest of Molière, where you can still occasionally meet deer. Although there was no practical means of transport available to get to Le Petit Séran, we finally bought it. Up to the time of writing, we have never had a chance to live in it.

A new star was rising in the theatrical firmament: Jean-Louis Barrault. The stage setting for *Autour d'une mère*, based on a story by Faulkner, was startling, though it owed something to the rather dated æsthetic ideas of the Jooss Ballet. I could find nothing wrong with Cervantes's *Numancia*, with décors by André Masson. The play contained allusions that seemed made to fit the Spanish war. In April 1939 Barrault asked me for some music for an adaptation of Laforgue's version of *Hamlet*. I scored it for five instruments. Barrault made an unforgettable Hamlet, who had been imagined by Laforgue as a representative of absolute decadence.

The Opéra-Comique put on a most painstaking production of three of my works on one program: *Esther de Carpentras*, with décors by Nora Auric; *Le Pauvre Matelot*, with a setting by Cocteau; and *La Suite provençale*, as a ballet with a décor by André Marchand.

Two new phonograph companies branched out magnificently in quite opposite directions. L'Oiseau-Lyre issued recordings of Couperin, Rameau, and medieval music, with a few contemporary works such as Sauguet's *La Voyante* and my *Suite d'après Corrette*. Le Chant du Monde, on the other hand, published a vast collection of folk music. This involves a twofold problem: either it should be left intact, classified in the archives of a musical library, or it should be freely handled by a musician and incorporated in his own musical personality. Le Chant du Monde asked Koechlin, Auric, Jaubert, Delannoy, Honegger, Désormière, Hoérée, Loucheur, Sauveplane, and me to harmonize French songs (I dealt with four from Provence). The same firm also published an admirable series of songs of the Spanish Republican armies, with a most attractive harmonization and orchestration by Gustavo Pittaluga and Rodolfo Halffter, both refugees in Paris at the time.

For two years we had been going to Mayens de Sion for a month before going to Aix. This enchanting part of Switzerland, in the canton of Valais, dominates the valley and twisting course of the Rhône. The hotel-keeper was pastry-cook, baker, grocer, and café-keeper all rolled into one. The inhabitants of the chalets and the peasants all came to him to purchase their provisions and drink Fendant wine or eat *la raclette*. We loved this spot, perhaps out of fellow-feeling for dwellers in the Rhône valley, and Madeleine had told the hotel-proprietor: "We shall come back every summer, unless something dreadful occurs." On the other bank of the river, the Hindemiths had been living in a little village between Sierre and Crans: they had finally decided to leave Germany, as Paul's music had now been banned and he himself was prohibited from teaching. Next door to them lived Blanche Honegger, who one afternoon played us the Concerto for violin and flute that I had composed for her and her father-in-law, Marcel Moyse. On our way back to Mayens, we made a little detour to visit the village on the hillside where Rilke lies buried. That summer I composed the *Quatrains Valaisans* for *a cappella* chorus, based on poems written in French by Rilke.

It was during this stay in Switzerland that Daniel's taste for painting first manifested itself. On our way to Mayens de Sion by car, we had stopped in Geneva to visit the exhibition of paintings from the Prado which was provisionally housed there. It was a very hot day, and a dense crowd prevented us from seeing the pictures properly. We were in a hurry to reach Mayens before nightfall, so we were dragging Daniel along behind us as we hurried through. A few days later he expressed the desire to go back. We thought this a childish caprice, and refused to go down to the plain again. He insisted, however, so one rainy day we took him back to the exhibition, and much to our surprise we found that he had remembered all the pictures he had seen during his previous visit. He asked us to buy a great many reproductions, which he himself selected with unfaltering sureness of what he wanted.

The day before we left for Aix, I had a telephone call from Paris from Mr. Henry Voegeli, manager of the Chicago Symphony Orchestra, asking me on behalf of Frederick Stock to compose a work for the fiftieth anniversary of the orchestra. When we arrived in Aix, Vladimir Golschmann came to see me to ask for a *Fanfare* for the sixtieth anniversary of the St. Louis Symphony. Morini's letters proposing a tour in the United States were growing more and more pressing. But the international situation was growing too dark for me to take such a decision. I fell ill in the bargain, and it was from my sickbed that I heard on the wireless the news of the invasion of Poland, which led to the declaration of war by England and France.

33

THE WAR

WE DECIDED to stay on at L'Enclos. Bedridden and incapable of working, I listened to the radio night and
day. When I think back to that time now, it seems like some
interminable period of waiting, in which the predominant
feeling was one of impotence and frightful anguish, of daily
anxiety for all our friends who had been mobilized. The
official communiqués posted up in chalk on a blackboard outside the Sous-Préfecture during the 1914 war, had been replaced by announcements read on the radio, to which we
never wearied of listening wherever we might happen to be.
The accounts of the Polish campaign were terrifying. In even
the remotest places you felt the shadow of an impending
doom. Illusory hopes and radio bulletins and still more waiting: that was the "phony war," when everyone said: "The
Germans would never do that to us!" or put their faith in the
Maginot Line. The only enemy seemed to be the boredom
that reigned in the front line. We were asked to supply packs
of cards, checkerboards, and radios for the troops. Why did
they not rather give them arms? One captain wrote from the
Maginot Line to the wife of a retired general whom he had
asked for some games: "It's your lotto sets that are winning
the war." At that very moment Poland was perishing beneath

the onslaught of the motorized divisions and the dive-bombers.

My parents went back to town at the end of the summer, but we stayed on at L'Enclos with my mother-in-law. In November I was able to crawl out of bed and go down to the little dining-room, the only room with any heat in it. I had had the piano brought in there from the drawing-room. I had no heart for work, and yet I had to deliver a work for the anniversary of the Chicago orchestra. The idea that it would be the only French work on the program helped me to shake off my torpor, and I made a start on my First Symphony.

That winter we were never alone. Many friends came to spend a few days with us: Hélène Hoppenot, Francis Poulenc, Rieti and his wife; still others dropped in on their way back from Paris. Madeleine had the idea of organizing a little theatrical company to give performances in hospitals and barracks, and this was easily done by roping in two of the young Paliards, Jane Bathori, Andrée Tainsy, and Jacques Denoel, one of her pupils, aged seventeen, who had come from Lorient at the age of fourteen to attend her classes at the Schola Cantorum and was now spending the winter at Aix in order to go on with his studies with her. Thus the house was transformed into a place for rehearsals. A deputation of nursing orderlies from the hospital at the École Normale, and one of their number who was also a Dominican, came and asked Madeleine to produce a play they had written about their hospital. In it they made amusing references to their inaction and poked gentle fun at some of their comrades. The principal authors, an active member of the Marseille streetcar workers' union and a cinema operator from Joinville, supervised the rehearsals, after which one of the orderlies who had been a steward with the Messageries Maritimes ceremoniously served coffee. It was a great satisfaction for us to be in daily contact with so many good souls. Friends who had been mobilized had noticed, like ourselves, that the excessive bustle of the life we had been living in Paris had made us forget the gaiety and generosity of workers and peasants.

Once my symphony was finished, the ice had been broken, and I went on composing. Since the foundation of the synagogue in Aix-en-Provence in 1840, when a speech of which I still possessed a copy had been given by my great-grandfather, first my grandfather and then my father had acted as bursar for it, and I wished to compose a cantata to celebrate its centenary. As Aix was the last refuge of the Comtadin sect, I set to music three of the prayers in their liturgy, selected and translated by Armand Lunel: the prayer for the souls of the victims of persecution, one for the day of reclusion, and one for the pope (as temporal lord). In each I incorporated a fragment from the great mystical poem by Gabirol, translated by Mardochée Venture, who had published, at the end of the eighteenth century, prayer-books for the use of French Jews. I also composed a suite called *Le Voyage d'été*, melodies on poems by Camille Paliard in praise of vacations in prewar days.

The Paliards, friends of my mother, often came to see us at L'Enclos. Jacques Paliard was a professor of philosophy in the University of Aix. Camille wrote poetry, and poetry was for her a natural and habitual form of expression. Sometimes we would visit them. In their drawing-room reigned an atmosphere of enchantment, through which could be faintly heard the bells of the near-by convent and bugle-calls from the barracks. The Paliard children talked and Boudou, the dog, gamboled around us as we lingered to chat and read verse beside the stove that had gone out and on which, heaven only knows why, there always stood a flatiron.

Near Aix, in the Camp des Milles, enemy nationals were interned, and some refugees well known to be anti-Nazis were soon released. This was the case of Ernst Erich Noth, whose fine novel *Le Désert*, written directly in his adopted language, French, had just been published by the N.R.F.

In October my *Médée* was produced, together with Richard Strauss's *Daphne*, by the Flemish Opera Company of Antwerp. Was this an illusory gesture on behalf of a neutrality that did not make sense? One of the performances of *Médée* was broadcast. We huddled around the set, listening to my opera, and after each aria there was a news bulletin, preceded by the inevitable: "At the third stroke the time will be exactly . . ."

In February we received a brief visit from Dom Clément (Maxime Jacob), who was now a hospital orderly and came to spend his leave with us. He had not changed, but his eyes had a purer, happier look. I asked him what his impressions of military life were. "I feel like a civilian again," he answered, slipping his tie underneath his collar. He played me some of his music, in which religious and secular inspiration alternated, lively and touching songs of a popular character being followed by peaceful, austere religious chants. During his stay there was an admirable performance of *Christophe Colomb* in Flemish on the Brussels radio. We listened to it with him at my parents' house, Le Bras d'Or.

I had a relapse in March. I had taken to bed again, and should have seen nothing of the Provençal spring had not Madeleine brought some sprays of almond blossom into my room. This was when I received the visit from the wonderworking air-raid warden which I have described elsewhere. Two days after his treatment I was able to go off in the car with Marcelle Carmona and Madeleine. We had a serious breakdown along the way and had to continue our journey by train. Contrary to all our anticipations, I reached Paris in time for the last rehearsal. The Opéra had made a remarkable effort. The score had been minutely rehearsed by Gaubert, and Marisa Ferrer gave a wonderfully powerful and grandiose performance in the part of Medea. I had persuaded M. Rouché to let Dullin prepare the stage setting. Dullin had been keen to tackle the problems of an operatic production, but he had soon been disheartened by the insuperable difficulties he had to contend with. In particular, the chorus was a thorn in his flesh. Finally he found an admirable solution. He arranged them in rows on either side of the stage like a human wall, while dancers expressed the emotions of the characters. Masson's scenery and Dullin's absolutely unconventional production made the show a most memorable one. I have often thought of this last gift to me from the Opéra in Paris, on the eve of the great disaster. The first night was as elegant an occasion as any prewar gala performance, but the muffled sound of anti-aircraft firing could be heard. Next day we had news of the invasion of Holland. Hélène Hoppenot implored me to go back to Aix, and insisted that we should leave by car. I took a taxi to Lyon, where we picked up our little Fiat. Madeleine, Marcelle Carmona, and I gazed at the countryside, torn between sadness and wonder. Never had it seemed more beautiful or more sublime.

The days that followed passed swift and slow, and implacably the Battle of France was fought. All the roads were jammed with refugees, all of whom seemed to be wanting to get to Aix, both those from Holland and the north fleeing before the Germans, and those coming from the south and abandoning the coastal areas for fear of the Italians. The fall of Paris, the advance of the Germans, Marshal Pétain's decision to stop the fighting, came to rend our hearts as we sat in a little bistro in the Vieux-Port at Marseille. All around us people wept in despair. On our way back to Aix we met an uninterrupted line of trucks carrying away the men of the R.A.F.

I had had too many contacts with German, Austrian, Czech, and Italian refugees not to have a good idea of what an occupation would mean. I realized clearly that the capitulation would prepare the soil for fascism and its abominable train of monstrous persecutions. Madeleine proposed that we should leave the country. I was powerless, incapable of running away, or even of hiding if need be, but such a decision was a bitter pill to swallow. When one of our young friends, who was later to become a very gallant member of the Resistance, said to Madeleine, who was confiding in him how much she was worried: "All we've got to do is to drop England and sign a fifty-year pact with Germany," she realized the full horror of our situation and set to work immediately to organize our departure. Already all the consulates were besieged by a tightly packed crowd of British citizens trying by every means possible to get out of France. At Cook's, where we reserved seats on the clipper, we met the Werfels, who were in despair because they had been refused visas in view of their being Czechs. In desperation, they took a taxi for Bordeaux, where they hoped to get their papers. Sadly and with foreboding we took our leave of them. For us, however, everything went off well. I had in my possession all my correspondence with my manager and pre-war newspaper articles announcing my symphony, so that the American visa was granted immediately. As for the Portuguese visa, the official at the consulate was kind enough to give it to me without even telegraphing his government. At the last moment the driver who had undertaken to take us to the frontier refused to go. Madeleine loaded up the little Fiat, and we said good-by to our relatives. We set out in an exceptionally violent thunderstorm. We were stopped several times along the way for our papers to be examined. The road-blocks grew more and more numerous because the Minister of the Interior had just put a ban on all movements by road. We had to explain our position and show our passports and our tickets for the clipper.

Some soldiers were hard to convince—the Senegalese, for example. We drove on till late at night, and when we came to a square in Narbonne the blackout was solid—you could see exactly nothing. Madeleine asked a passer-by the way to a hotel. "You won't be able to find room anywhere, dear," said a woman's voice. "You'd better come home with me." The good woman, a market-gardener, gave us her bed, made us some coffee, and insisted on giving us breakfast before we left. We carried away with us a warm memory of her open-hearted hospitality.

At Cerbère we left the car in a garage and crossed the frontier. We were searched by young Falangists wearing scornful and triumphant expressions on their faces. We nearly missed the train because they insisted on weighing every tube in our stock of homeopathic remedies and looking up every name in the dictionary. The trains were not running regularly, and there was only a limited number of seats. We should have preferred to buy through tickets to Lisbon, but were not allowed to do so. The tickets were issued only by sections, and no one was able to give us even an approximate idea of what the total cost would be. We traveled third-class, with goodhearted peasants who marveled at Daniel, who never stopped drawing. They all insisted on sharing their food with us. We reached Madrid about midnight and suddenly, to our horror, noticed that Daniel had disappeared. Panic-stricken, Madeleine ran off to find the entrance to the station, but there were several of these. She came back to me, and I went on shouting his name at the top of my voice. This is what saved the lad. He heard me and found his way back to us. Half asleep, he had been following a lady whom he took to be his mother.

We stayed two days at a little hotel, waiting for the train to Lisbon. It was then that we learned that we should not be allowed to take any Spanish money out of the country. We therefore decided to spend all our pesetas, much to Daniel's amazement, for he had never had so many presents before in his life. We traveled in a sleeper, and what a relief it was to cross the Portuguese frontier! The officials were kindly and sympathetic. At Lisbon, we rushed to the clipper office, but our tickets were no longer valid. They had been paid for in Marseille, and the franc had lost its value. We had no means of making up the difference in price, having brought out only the sum authorized by the government—namely, twelve thousand francs for the three of us. We had not even enough money to take passage by boat. While we waited on events, we moved into a little hotel. I wrote letters to Kurt Weill, to my manager, to Mrs. Claire Reis, to Pierre Monteux, and to Mrs. Coolidge. I told them where we had got to, and these good friends set about organizing a future for me in America. Antonio Ferro, the Minister of Propaganda, let us know that the Portuguese government would be responsible for all our expenses while we stayed in Lisbon. Ernesto Halffter, Falla's favorite pupil, together with his Portuguese wife, came to see us with offers of assistance. I conducted a radio concert organized by Freitas Branco. I conducted *La Cantate de l'Enfant et de la Mère*, recited by Madeleine. I also gave a lecture on Poetry and Music at the Conservatoire. Several of our friends attended it. How apt Péguy's saying: *"Il faut qu'une sainte réussisse!"* (a holy woman is bound to succeed) seemed to me then!

The Baronne de Goldschmidt-Rothschild, who had managed to escape from France with her children in a little car into which she had packed some of the pictures from her amazing collection—works by Van Gogh, Manet, Cézanne, Cranach—was in Estoril at the time, and told me how disappointed she had been when the bank had refused to let her send some money to her gardener in Toulon. I saw in this a way of salvation for us. I got my father to send the money, and she paid me, so in that way I was able to leave.

On board the *Excambion*, I was handed a telegram from Mills College offering me a teaching post, my name having been put forward by my friends Pierre Monteux, Robert Schmitz, and the members of the Pro Arte Quartet. It was only then, after the wrench of departure, that I realized I was entering on a new phase in my existence. I should find new copies of my orchestral works in America. Deiss was the only publisher engraving my scores, and he had sent copies regularly to his agent Elkan Vogel in Philadelphia. But the agent for Universal Edition would not have many of my works in stock. I should have to start work afresh to cope with any demands that might be made by concert societies. Lying in a deck-chair beside my wife and son, I felt how privileged I was to be able to be working with them at my side, and I can never be grateful enough to Providence for not having parted me from them at this time of ordeal.

That was a gloomy crossing. There were a few Frenchmen on board: Jules Romains and his wife, Robert de Saint-Jean, Lévy-Strauss, the Duviviers, and the American writer who is such a Frenchman at heart, Julien Green. Like ourselves, all were filled with inconsolable grief. I remember

276

Jane Bathori and Milhaud, Paris, 1950

Milhaud and his son Daniel at a rehearsal of Bolivar, *Paris, 1950*

Bolivar: *the scene at* la mairie

Bolivar:
Roger Bourdin as Bolivar

now the desperate, profound sadness that fell upon us on that July 14, 1940, when we forgathered in my cabin.

When we arrived in New York next day, my faithful friends Kurt Weill and his wife were standing on the dock to greet us.

As we had only a few suitcases, the customs formalities were soon over. We had lunch with Claire Reis. This delightful friend, the founder and director of the League of Composers, was doing her best to get me lectures and concert bookings, and had gathered together in my honor all the most eminent journalists. In the afternoon, we went with the Kurt Weills about a hundred miles in a car to see Dr. Thaddeus Ames, treasurer of the League of Composers, who had written to me in Lisbon as soon as he heard I had arrived there: "As you are traveling with your child, I think you would like to have a few days with your family in the country before doing anything else!" We had eagerly and gratefully accepted his invitation. We found him, accompanied by his sons, halfway to Old Lyme, Connecticut. They took us to their lovely house, filled with antique furniture and old trinkets, where Mrs. Ames was waiting to receive us with open arms.

Summer was scorching, the countryside green, and great rivers near at hand. Our hosts were devoting their vacation to various forms of sport. Slowly we readapted ourselves to the blessings of peace. After a few days of most welcome

278

relaxation, we settled in New York in a little hotel opposite the one where Elsie Rieti was staying; Vittorio was due to arrive from France in August, and we decided to wait for his arrival before going on to California. Exile strengthened the bonds of friendship which already united us, and the comparable friendship that sprang up now between our children has never ceased to grow stronger. Although Fabio was a little older than Daniel, they got on well together, having in common a taste and talent for painting. We took nearly all our meals in the hotel, where we had a tiny kitchenette with a little refrigerator and an electric plate at the bottom of a cupboard in the entrance hall. Whenever we went out together, people would hear us talking French and would stop us to ask us questions on the events that filled them with consternation, and would immediately tell us of their sympathy for us and of the anxiety they felt.

I got in touch at once with the agents of my publishers to ask which of my works they had in stock. The result was rather discouraging. Heugel had no representative in the United States. The Associated Music Publishers, agents for Universal Edition and for Eschig, had the scores and parts of only *Les Saudades*, *Sérénade*, and *La Création du monde*. Elkan Vogel, of Philadelphia, had copies of all my works published by Deiss, who had always taken the precaution of sending them to him as soon as they came out. As Deiss had the good sense to write to my mother from the Occupied Zone to say that I had his approval in advance for any decisions I might reach with regard to my works published by him, and that I could have reprints made if I thought it necessary, I was able to have a new one of *Scaramouche* printed.

On August 4 I conducted my *Cortège funèbre*, the score of which I happened to have with me. The parts were prepared by the Columbia Broadcasting System, which always remained faithful to me, and gave me an engagement every time I passed through New York.

Ballet Theatre, which in 1939 had given performances of *La Création du monde* under the title of *Black Ritual*, with Negro dancers and choreography by Agnes de Mille, was playing in the open-air Lewisohn Stadium at the time. We went there one evening at the invitation of Alexander Smallens, who conducted the orchestra and was thinking of commissioning me to compose a ballet for them. Daniel, who was now ten, and on the threshold of a new existence, we could not leave alone in the hotel, so he accompanied us wherever we went. They were giving *Giselle*, and Daniel, who had never seen any ballets before, suddenly exclaimed: "But Mamma, I didn't know they had such fun in cemeteries!" Smallens's plans succeeded; he introduced me to the director of the company, Richard Pleasant, who asked me next day to write *The Man of Midian*, based on the life of Moses. I composed this music on arrival in California, and the ballet went into rehearsal at once. Financial complications arose, however, and the company changed hands. Under the new management the choreographic rights were kept independent of the musical side, and the ballet was never produced. Pierre Monteux gave the first concert performance under the title of *Opus Americanum No. 2*, for it was the second work I had written in the United States, the first being my Tenth Quartet, or *Birthday Quartet*, which I had completed in New York, and which had been asked for by Mrs. Coolidge, to be played on October 30, 1940 at the annual concert she gave in Washington to celebrate her birthday.

As railroad tickets to California for the three of us would have cost the same as a second-hand car, we bought a Ford, which is still with us, and traveled to Oakland by road. Our first stop was at the home of the dancer Ruth Page, to discuss a project for a ballet, which was put into effect a few years later: *The Bells*, on the poem by Edgar Allan Poe. The lovely bungalow in which Ruth used to spend the summer stands on the shore of Lake Michigan, a few miles from Chicago. We took advantage of the opportunity to see the Chicago Art Institute, which is absolutely marvelous. Our journey through the Middle West continued uneventfully, through the farming districts, with the huge farmsteads set in the midst of unending fields of corn. This way of traveling was a great novelty for us. We spent the nights in the open country or on the outskirts of cities in "motels" or "cabins," little bungalows, very comfortably furnished, consisting of one or two bedrooms, with a shower and a garage. We used to pay the proprietor on arrival so that we could set out early without having to wake him, and we endeavored to cover as much distance as possible before the sun was high.

The mountains of Wyoming were like a beneficent oasis, and the desert plateau horizons reminded us of the Lebanon, or of certain landscapes by Salvador Dali. Then we crossed the great desert, where the heat was stifling. For eighty miles we were dazzled by the glitter of the salt crystals that cover this huge area, which starts as soon as you leave the capital of the Mormons and runs parallel to Great Salt Lake, with its heavy, sluggish waters, across which the railway runs on a viaduct like a road through the midst of the waters. As we left the desert, we came again to the treeless mountains, with curiously shaped rocky pinnacles like huge pre-Columbian sculptures, of ochreous hues; and then there were another three hundred miles of near-desert country to cross. How often during this long journey I should have been filled with anxiety if it had not been for the numbers of cars we met! After passing over some wooded sierras, we had the first glimpse of the fertile Californian plains, stretching away as far as the eye could see to the dim line of yellowish hills on the horizon. Later I came to know that these hills turn green with the first autumnal rains.

Once more my destiny in the United States was bound up with that of Robert Schmitz and his wife, for they lived quite near the college, where their daughter Monica was completing her studies. They very kindly offered us their hospitality until we could find somewhere to live, which was no easy matter. First we rented the house of one of the professors who was on leave of absence at the time, and then, after his return, a cottage that we had to leave because we adopted a dog. Our third dwelling was very pleasant, but too far from the college during the summer school; so we settled for six weeks in a diminutive bungalow before moving on to the house which the college had built for us. It stands on a little height from which we can catch a far-off glimpse of San Francisco Bay, and is surrounded by all kinds of trees—mimosas, palms, camellias, magnolias, and all the varieties of plants that grow in the warm temperate zone. The animals have no fear of man, for they are protected on the campus, and whole tribes of partridges, hares, and squirrels wander across the lawn. There are innumerable birds—big robins, jays as blue as those of Europe are black, and, above all, myriads of humming-birds with vibrant wings and frantically hurried flight, the metallic red of their throats flashing in the sunlight like summer lightning. We lived in this garden of enchantment, but with our ears glued to the radio, for our hearts remained attached to our native shores, and our thoughts were ever with those who had to live in the midst of the tragedy that had engulfed our world.

Mills College is a foundation for girls, with seven or eight hundred students. It grew in numbers and in fame thanks to the outstanding personality of its great president, Dr. Aurelia

Reinhardt, whose successor, Dr. Lynn White, a distinguished medievalist, has carried on its humanistic traditions.

I knew America well, but this was my first experience as a teacher. American colleges have an atmosphere all their own. They are like little islands, set apart in time and space, where young people eager for learning may find all that they need: libraries, often crammed with priceless treasures; laboratories; an open-air Greek amphitheater; a theater; a concert hall; an exhibition gallery; studios for sculpture, ceramics, photography, weaving; an elaborate swimming pool; tennis courts; stables; an observatory.

American musical education is very different from ours. Whereas in France absolute specialization is required, and music can be studied only in the Conservatoire or other specialized schools, here music forms part of general cultural studies and is even taught to very young children. They are given classes in musical appreciation and the history of music, with phonograph illustrations: every school has a large collection of phonograph records. The children play in the band or a little orchestra, or else they sing in the school chorus. This program continues right up to college or university, at which stage the student may, if he desires, specialize in music.

At Mills College, four years are normally required to obtain the degree of Bachelor of Arts, and during this time the girls study harmony, counterpoint (up to four-part), and orchestration. They study Bach's chorales until they are able to compose varied or extended chorales. They follow lectures on the history of music (symphonic music, chamber music, etc.), including a year's course on Bach alone. They learn to read and to conduct an orchestral score. Finally, they compose and study, in absolute liberty, every possible form of musical expression. In addition, they play in the orchestra or sing in the chorus, and have to be capable of giving an instrumental recital (piano, violin, flute, etc.) or a vocal recital before their course is completed. After graduating, they may if they so desire stay on a year or two to prepare for their Master's degree, the course for which includes the study of fugue, the composition of a large-scale work, or a thesis on some musical subject. For these advanced courses, some young men are admitted to Mills College, and after the war, in accordance with the "G.I. Bill of Rights," I had a number of ex-soldiers studying with me. American women students are usually extremely gifted, but I can never get over the surprise of seeing with what ease, at the opening of the course, when asked to compose something—that is, to write a line of melody—they carry out the exercise, and after only a few lessons are writing songs, little pieces, or even a whole sonata movement. They are self-confident and free from complexes and inhibitions. They do not look upon composition as something solemn or momentous, but rather as a subject like any other, not reserved for exceptional beings, but something to be done with greater or less success, and always with ease and gusto. Each year my students take part in two public concerts. In the spring it is a ballet composed by themselves and danced and produced by dance students; later there are two concerts of works composed in class (suites for piano and other instruments, songs, chamber music, chorales, etc.).

I have had some excellent colleagues at Mills, and I get on very well with the members of my department. My "chairman," Luther Marchant, has always shown great understanding and made my tasks easier. He teaches singing and organizes the college concerts. Moreover, he is entrusted with the often delicate mission of collecting donations for the concerts, the library, or the scholarship fund. Another teacher, Marguerite Prall, has the secret of opening up before her pupils the whole vast field of musical knowledge without filling them with dismay. Before the girls come to my class, they are thoroughly grounded in their preparatory studies by young teachers who are composers. In 1940 Arthur Berger was responsible for this work, and when he left to become a music critic on the New York *Sun* and later on the *New York Herald Tribune*, Charles Jones for five years taught advanced harmony, counterpoint up to four-part, and preliminary work on Bach's chorales. His successor was Howard Brubeck, a young Californian who took his M.A. at Mills in 1941 and stayed on as my assistant. These two young composers have been invited by Monteux to conduct their works with the San Francisco Symphony Orchestra.

I teach right through the summer, so that I have little in the way of vacation. The summer school lasts six weeks, and those who attend it are teachers and students of all ages who want to cram into their course as much as possible. An excellent resident quartet gives twelve concerts of classical and modern quartets, and each year plays the whole series of Beethoven's. Quite apart from the fact that I like writing quartets, the excellence of their playing led me to compose four quartets during my first long stay in America. During the summer session, the departments of dancing, dramatic art, and music give classes similar to those given during the year, except that they take place every day and work is carried on at high pressure. The remainder of the session is devoted to Hispanic studies in the Casa Panamericana and the study of French in the Maison Française.[1] There are teachers and assistants teaching literature, grammar, style, conversation, and diction. I believe that Mills College is the

[1] The head of the Maison Française is Mlle Réau, who has worked disinterestedly since 1918 to spread the knowledge of our literature and language.

only school in the United States to engage a French writer for the summer session every year. Jules Romains and Pierre de Lanux were there before the war. In 1940, after the collapse of France, there was an alarming falling-off in the numbers of those studying our language. American students tend to be highly impulsive, and political events may lead to explosive reactions on the cultural plane. This was the period of the "good neighbor policy," when French was abandoned in favor of Spanish. It speaks volumes for the strength of character of President Reinhardt that the 1941 summer school was placed resolutely under the sign of French culture, through the engagement of Fernand Léger, André Maurois, and me. Maurois's classes were highly popular, and he spent another summer at Mills. In 1944 it was Julien Green's turn. He had just published his first book to be written in English, and it was moving to note that in it he had evoked his memories of his childhood in Paris. René Bellé, who was teaching in Los Angeles, came several years running; his naturally lovable character and his immense culture endeared him to us, and I am especially grateful to him for the interest he took in Daniel, in whom he awakened a real love for our literature.

Madeleine taught every year in the Maison Française, and also gave classes in diction and literature at the college in the winter. She produced French plays, a task that involved complicated problems, for none of her actresses had studied dramatic art and they were handicapped still more by speaking in a foreign tongue. Nevertheless, by dint of patient rehearsal and hard work, the performances were excellent. She has produced plays by Molière, Regnard, Labiche, Supervielle, Vildrac, and others, with music by Lully, or scores specially composed by Brubeck, Jones, and Livingstone Gearhart. Life was hard for Madeleine: there are no servants in the

United States except at wages higher than the salaries of university professors, allowing for the fact that they also have to be fed and housed. I admire my American colleagues who lend a hand with the housework. Madeleine has had to cope with it all unaided: cleaning, buying provisions, cooking, and washing up—and we always have a constant stream of visitors. She also acts as chauffeur for me, and has to snatch a few moments here and there for her own work and reading. You see that the title of the little piano suite I wrote for her: *La Muse ménagère*, is no fanciful allusion.

As for Daniel, he attended school here in America, but soon realized that painting was his true vocation. In the beginning he was greatly aided by the presence of Corrado Cagli, who instructed him in the rudiments of the art. Elsie and Fabio Rieti came to stay a month or two in Berkeley. From childhood on, in Italy, Paris, and New York, Fabio too had been trained by Cagli. This was one more link between the two boys, and when Corrado left for the war, Fabio as the elder was able to help Daniel a great deal. We also found some of our family in Berkeley, for our cousins Georges Valabrègue and his wife left France with their three children at the same time as ourselves, and settled in California. It was only by chance that I found how our destinies had run on parallel courses. They became for us the symbol of the family, coming to lunch on Sundays and joining us on holidays.

We loved going to San Francisco, which is only thirty-five minutes away. From the gigantic bridge connecting the city with Oakland you can see the lovely hills faintly traced against the horizon, their colors constantly varying with the changes in the transparency of the atmosphere. San Francisco is full of character. From its steep hills you can always catch a glimpse of some new corner of the bay: Chinatown, or the Italian quarter with its innumerable *pizzerie*, or even the new quarters with the white apartment houses piled up like a child's blocks, high above the Pacific, all with a personality of their own.

We were often invited to San Francisco, where we have a number of charming friends who are always ready to welcome us. How many times we have been invited to one or other of the operas or concerts during the season by Mrs. Sydney Ehrman, or Mrs. I. W. Hellman, Mrs. Marcus Koshland, Mrs. Sigmund Stern and their charming daughters! Our old friends the Monteux spend twenty weeks of the year in San Francisco, and it was a great joy to meet them again at the other side of the world. Pierre Monteux has succeeded in welding the San Francisco Symphony Orchestra into an admirable ensemble by his brilliant conducting, and I was able to judge for myself of its excellence when I conducted my First Symphony. Monteux gave several of my works, especially the Second Suite (*Protée*), which he has recorded. Many soloists, meteors flashing across our country horizon and lighting up our Western seclusion, have paused at Mills to have a meal with us: Casadesus, Francescatti, Thibaud, Rubinstein—and their fleeting visits conjured up memories of Paris and Provence.

Apart from the Symphony Orchestra, there are no local musical resources in San Francisco; visiting companies bring the New York successes of a year or two before. The Ballets Russes give performances of their latest creations and new scores, not always under the best of conditions because of the vast amount of traveling they have to do and the limited time for rehearsals; but it is alway a joy to see them and to applaud the works of Stravinsky or Copland, the scenery by Dali or Eugène Berman, whose painting every day acquires new greatness, wringing tragic expression from all the pomp of baroque and the distress of suffering humanity, in sublime amalgam of tattered clothes and crumbling palaces. For six weeks in the year the San Francisco Opera engages some of the stars from the Metropolitan in New York to sing and play their usual repertoire, to which the subscribers greedily listen two or three times a week. In this way we had the pleasure of meeting once more Lili Djanel, Martial Singher, Herta Glatz, who sang *Le Pauvre Matelot* with the Salzburg company in the United States, and, above all, dear Lily Pons, for whom I wrote *Quatre Chansons de Ronsard* with orchestral accompaniment—she has sung them often, and recorded them, with her husband, André Kostelanetz, conducting. There are several museums in San Francisco, and we are great friends of the curator of the Museum of Modern Art, Grace Morley, who not long ago was appointed to the American section of UNESCO in Paris. This gifted woman was always ready to offer one of the rooms in the museum for some function connected with French culture. Chamber-music recitals are also given there. I have always enjoyed listening to music in picture galleries. What lovely performances were given by the Budapest Quartet amid Alexander Calder's mobiles and Lurçat's tapestries!

At least once a year we visited Los Angeles. This is a city, or rather a vast expanse of country, peopled by a whole *world* of artists, writers, and musicians from every country, all living great distances apart. Some of them have been attracted rather by the climate than by the proximity of the film studios. Schönberg bought a house there, to live out his old age, surrounded by the happy din made by his two little boys, whom even the gentleness of their mother and sister has been powerless to subdue. The Stravinskys live here too. Igor is now composing the masterpieces of his maturity, and Vera tends the flowers and fruit trees, and with her peaceful smile welcomes the old friends who drop in nearly every evening to see them: Catherine d'Erlanger, the Sokolovs, Eugène Berman, the Tansmans and their two adorable little girls, refugees since 1942. We always stay with Sacha. Colette has been doing much the same as Madeleine here. When they went back to France, some months ahead of us, we missed their delightful hospitality and felt a little lost when we went to Hollywood.

The world of the cinema is a world apart, and I know very few film producers, except René Clair, whose marvelous imagination found difficulty in sprouting as luxuriantly as his friends would have liked in the Hollywood jungle. I do not think I should ever have written any film music in America had it not been for a chance conversation with Noma Rathner, a young American woman attached to the State Department during the war, who was just back from Paris, where she had been very friendly with the Désormières. She suggested me as a composer to her friend Albert Lewin, who was making a film of *Bel-Ami*. He liked the idea, as did his musical director, Rudolf Polk, who rang me up immediately. I stayed in Hollywood for five weeks, writing my score. Although in Hollywood most of the orchestrations are not done by the composers, but by musicians specially employed for the purpose, I was given the right to score my own music, conduct it, and be present at the synchronization. I have a clear memory of that film: there were no upsets or snags, everything passing off in an atmosphere of mutual confidence and friendliness. Albert Lewin is a highly cultured man and, what is even rarer in those circles, genuinely modest. In the evenings I went to see the Stravinskys or George Antheil, to recover from my exertions. Since the days of *Le Ballet mécanique* Antheil had developed enough to write huge symphonic frescoes or even cowboy songs for the films. I also sometimes went to see Erich Zeizl, an Austrian pupil of mine who had fled from his country at the time of the *Anschluss*, and I spent some delightful evenings with Toumanova, my little dancer for *L'Éventail de Jeanne*, who had since become a great star. I greatly relished these quiet moments after the arduous work of the day, and feeling so remote from the bustle of excitement that usually swirls in the wake of the kings and queens of the cinema. The first signs of financial success with them inevitably consist of a luxurious swimming pool and a picture by Renoir, without which their houses would not be complete.

The entry of the United States into the war did not have much immediate effect on the life of the college; the students waited until they had completed their studies before joining up. The war made itself felt but slowly; yet in spite of our remoteness it still kept creeping in. Is it fair to criticize a farmer of Iowa or Texas for not realizing the significance of Hitler's threat to the rest of the world? How many Frenchmen had understood the meaning of the fighting in Spain at the very frontier of their own country? The attack launched by Hirohito's aircraft precipitated events. We ought to thank him for that!

As the college had a month's vacation at Christmas, I took advantage of this to give some concerts in the East and to get in touch with my friends again. I used to stop regularly in Chicago to lecture at the Arts Club and to give some concerts. I conducted the Chicago Symphony Orchestra three times, twice in my First Symphony, which I had written for the fiftieth anniversary of the orchestra, and again for *Opus Americanum No. 2* and *La Suite Française*. I myself played my Second Piano Concerto, which I had composed at the suggestion of my manager that I should have one of my own works to play—that is, one written for a soloist who was not a real virtuoso. The parts for the old war horses I had previously used for this purpose, the *Ballade* and the *Carnaval d'Aix*, were not in America. I nearly always stayed with my friend Bobsy Goodspeed, whose house was a rendezvous for all artists and writers passing through Chicago. When I had arrived in the United States, Golschmann had asked me to orchestrate two extracts from *La Sultane* by Couperin. I conducted them with his orchestra in St. Louis and also gave a concert in Cincinnati, where I spent a week with Lucien Wulsin, the proprietor of the Baldwin piano firm, whose instruments I used in the United States. In his house there reigned a delightful, home-like atmosphere, and all his children spoke French fluently. His mother had lived in France for a long time. In 1940 I conducted in Boston the *Cortège funèbre*, the *Suite provençale*, and the *Fantaisie pastorale*, for which the soloist was Stell Andersen, the pianist for whom I had written it. In 1946 I conducted the Second Symphony, which I had composed at the request of the Koussevitzky Foundation in memory of Mme Koussevitzky. The distinguished conductor had been with the Boston Symphony Orchestra, regarded throughout the world as one of the best in the United States, for twenty-five years. Musicians such as he show extraordinary adaptability when dealing with new works, and a quite unusual spirit of understanding and co-operation. Every summer Koussevitzky devoted the whole of his time to the Berkshire Music Center, founded by himself, where he organized very large festivals and ran a school of music which is especially famous for its classes in conducting. This school always invites some foreign composer to share the teaching with Aaron Copland. Hindemith, Martinu, and Honegger have gone there and I hope to go there myself when I return from France.

Shortly after the landings in North Africa, Henri Hoppenot, who represented the Algiers Committee in Washington, was placed in charge of the operations for the liberation of the

Antilles. He went there on a warship, was acclaimed by the Gaullist population, and received the capitulation of Admiral Robert. In local folklore, the name of Hoppenot is now honored like that of an angel of deliverance. The Governor sent me some musical material that he thought might interest me and some popular melodies that I used in *La Libération des Antilles*. I could not resist using the popular songs, which included words like: "Mawning, Massa Minister Hoppenot." I used the same material in *Le Bal martiniquais* for two pianos, which I later arranged for orchestra. While Henri Hoppenot was engaged in these operations, his wife, Hélène, had come to spend a few weeks at our house, and I met Henri again in 1944 when I went to Washington to conduct a concert there. Another great joy was to meet Saint-John Perse again. Since the armistice he had been engaged in a modest post in the Library of Congress, occasionally publishing, from the height of his lofty exile, a few noble poems.

I went to stay in New York with Marion and Pierre Claudel and was touched by the affectionate greeting they gave me. In their apartment all was orderly and peaceful, and they had four lovely little girls. I wrote some piano pieces for the two elder girls, Violaine and Dominique, and made them promise to play them to me when I came again, but I did not get back to New York until 1946, for I fell seriously ill on my return to Mills.

A few weeks later I heard the news of my mother's death. I had always been haunted by the idea that I should not be at my parents' side when they died, but I had never imagined that six thousand miles and insuperable obstacles would lie between us. When my father had died in 1942 at the age of eighty-nine, the thought that my mother was all alone in her ordeal had been unbearable to me, but I had consoled myself by remembering that she had tended my father's illness with loving devotion and that right up to the end his faithful doctor, Dr. Charpin, and two devoted servants, Emmanuel and Suzanne Lhinarès, had been with him. It was also a consolation to know that he had been able to stay at home, whereas so many Frenchmen had been torn from their families. Up to the invasion of the Unoccupied Zone, my mother had written regularly. Thereafter she had to endure the presence in her house of seventy Germans, and nightly visits from the Gestapo. In 1943, when it became necessary for Jews to hide, she took refuge with her nurse in Dr. Roman's clinic, opposite the Bras d'Or. It was there that she passed away, without pain, but completely alone. In spite of the occupation she had gone on writing to me and many of her letters, forwarded by friends in Lausanne, Buenos Aires, and Tangier, reached me during the war; others were held up by innumerable censors and I received them only long afterward. This was a real miracle, as if my mother had been still alive.

The day after her death there was a real house-to-house search in Aix, and once again the Lhinarès proved their devoted friendship. For several weeks they sheltered my mother-in-law at the risk of their own lives, and then took her to the home of one of their relatives in the mountains, where she was able to wait for the end of the war in the company of my Aunt Amélie Milhaud and her daughter Marcelle Carmona, who played a very active part in the Resistance.

Throughout my illness, which lasted several months, I continued teaching, my pupils coming to me in my bedroom. I was suffering from such a great deficiency of calcium that the doctors thought I should never be able to walk again. When I finally managed to crawl out of bed, there followed a prolonged period of re-education in the use of my limbs, during which I used crutches and a wheelchair. A friend of mine, the famous surgeon Dr. Eloesser, who is a great music-lover and proves it by tending musicians with disinterested care, prescribed penicillin, which was a new remedy still reserved for the armed forces. Gradually my pains left me and I was once again able to lead a normal life, though my health remained very precarious and I was unable to dispense with a car. That was what delayed my return to France for so long. I did not undertake any more journeys alone, except to Laramie, Wyoming. Allan Wilman, who teaches music in the University of Wyoming, had organized a series of annual concerts of contemporary music, the first of which he had reserved for me. I was to conduct my Cello Concerto, played by Wetzel, a Belgian soloist. As there were not enough students to form an orchestra, many of them having been called up, Allan Wilman recruited his players from schools sometimes very remote from Laramie, had them over for several week-ends of rehearsals, and lodged them in the university for the week before the concert. Thus my orchestra consisted wholly of young people filled with an abundance of goodwill and enthusiasm. How it warmed one's heart to see them!

On my way back to California by train I heard the news of Germany's capitulation. Already, ever since the liberation, I had been losing the feeling of exile. Contact with France had been re-established and we knew we should be able to go home again. What had largely contributed throughout the occupation to our sense of loneliness in California had been that, in spite of the affection of our American friends, news from Europe and the clandestine visits by members of the Resistance went no farther than New York or Washington. Unfortunately, the first letters to reach us from Europe brought news of bereavement: the death of my young nephew Jean Milhaud and more than twenty near or distant cousins in the German extermination camps. Then we received news of friends who had miraculously survived, letters still warm with affection and fidelity. Rosenthal conducted the first performance of *La Sagesse* in Paris, and almost at the same time Collaer conducted it in Brussels. A long succession of writers engaged on missions to the United States came to us in California and gave us details of the occupation and of the Resistance movement. Sartre visited war plants with a group of journalists and stopped for a few hours in San Francisco. What a joy it was to hear by word of mouth news of all our friends! Louise Weiss spent a few days with us; Duhamel, Thimerais, and Vercors gave lectures, Vercors creating a great impression by his humane and lofty ideas, though *Le Silence de la mer*, the first literary manifestation of the Resistance, had distinctly puzzled American opinion. Charles Trenet, a very vivacious singer and poet, brought us the rather crazy songs that everybody in Paris was humming.

Thanks to the tenacity, organizing genius, and unwearying devotion of Anne Logan Upton, head of the American Relief for France, the Théâtre de la Mode came to San Francisco and had a real success. When Yves Baudrier came, it was as if the whole family of musicians had been reunited. How glad we were to see him, though only for such a fleeting visit. He played us his own records made by his comrades. Already, a few weeks earlier, Jacques Scheffer had played us Poulenc's songs sung by Bernac, a record of Eluard reciting one of his poems, a heart-rending commentary on the liberation of Paris and the bells of Notre-Dame—all of which gradually helped us to feel back home in France.

The San Francisco Conference renewed our contacts with many friends and acquaintances, whom we greeted with a stream of questions after having been so long cut off from our compatriots. Violaine Hoppenot, whom we had last seen the day we left Lisbon, had now become a thin, emaciated girl with an expression in her eyes which was both piercing and remote, reminding one of the glorious years she had spent in the Resistance movement. With her came a throng of young diplomats and journalists, from the silent Beuve-Méry to the young hopefuls of the Quai d'Orsay and the press. They fell into the pleasing habit of calling regularly on us. These young people were joined by Professor Étienne Gilson, who was perhaps the youngest of them through his mental alertness, high spirits, and enthusiasm. Young authors were engaged to come to the Maison Française at Mills, and Georges Magnane was the first to tell us about the poets of the Resistance and about existentialism. Then came Claude Roy, whose youthful genius and ardor brought us a bright ray of French sunlight. Others who had played an active part in the Resistance also helped us to understand the spirit of the new France; we were particularly friendly with Rosine Bernheim, a young heroine from Vercors, who had been deported to Ravensbruck. As I wrote this, we were expecting to see Henri Troyat, whose novels and biographies have been published in English and have aroused very keen interest.

Daniel made some good friends in California, but it is especially in New York that he found friends and teachers to help him in his work. The first exhibition held by Corrado Cagli after his return from Europe, where he took part in the Normandy landings, the liberation of Paris, the Battle of Bastogne, and the invasion of Germany right up to the junction with the Red Army near Leipzig, consisted of a series of impressive drawings, done on the spot, of the freeing of Buchenwald, the wreckage of the Rhine bridges, and the shooting of spies. These scenes from the great tragedy were depicted with that sure technique which links Cagli's art directly to the masters of the Italian Renaissance. Corrado has a studio near Fabio's, and supervises his young friends' development with affectionate care.

The last two years before our return to France we left Daniel alone in New York for part of the winter. I conducted a few concerts there during the Christmas holidays. In 1946, it was the New York Philharmonic-Symphony Orchestra in *La Suite française* and *Le Bal martiniquais*. Since my illness I conduct sitting down, which does not inconvenience the players, but detracts from the enjoyment of the public. I gave a performance of my *Two Marches: Introduction* and *Marche funèbre*, on the Columbia Broadcasting network, and *Les Saudades* with the flexible and vivacious C.B.S. Orchestra. In 1947 with the same orchestra I made a recording of my First Symphony. A few days later Madeleine took part in *Perséphone*, conducted by Stravinsky. In spite of material difficulties, Claire Reis, supported in her efforts by various American composers, went on giving concerts of contemporary music. The League of Composers devoted two concerts to my work: one in 1941, when I played *La Cantate de l'Enfant et de la Mère*, and the other in 1947, when I selected a program of cantatas: *Les Amours de Ronsard*, *Les Adages*, *Pan et Syrinx*, and the *Cantate pour l'inauguration du Musée de l'Homme*, because music of this kind is rarely heard in the United States. Apart from the soprano, the tenor, and Madeleine, the players and singers were all pupils of the Juilliard School, where the concert was repeated. It was at this point that the tragic accident occurred to Francis Salabert, who was flying to attend one of my concerts. He had just taken over the business of poor dear Deiss. Peacetime tragedies were following hard on the griefs of the war. On the other hand, a fortunate chance threw us into contact with Philippe Heugel, who, with his brother François, is going to play an active part in his father's publishing firm. He had come to the United States to learn at first hand the problems with which publishing has to contend in this country.

I was already well acquainted with the music of Aaron Copland, Roger Sessions, and Walter Piston, but I am glad to be able to say that my stay in the United States enabled me to get to know their work even better. What strikes one immediately in Copland's work is the feeling for the soil of his own country: the wide plains with their soft colorings, where the cowboy sings his nostalgic songs in which, even when the violin throbs and leaps to keep up with the pounding dance rhythms, there is always a tremendous sadness, an underlying distress, which nevertheless does not prevent them from conveying the sense of sturdy strength and sun-drenched movement. His ballet *Rodeo* gives perfect expression to this truly national art. His recent symphony, written for the Koussevitzky Foundation, has more grandeur and a deeper lyricism, but the melancholy simplicity of its themes is a direct expression of his own delicate sadness and sensitive heart.

Roger Sessions's music is less direct and more complex, thoroughly thought out. Recently he carried out in the University of California at Berkeley, where he is a teacher, an experiment that seems to justify my impression. He composed an opera called *The Trial of Lucullus*, on a libretto by Brecht. The work contains pages of great beauty, but it is extremely difficult both to grasp and to perform. It was written, orchestrated, rehearsed, and performed in less than five months! The singers and the players were all students. On the same program Charles Cushing conducted an excellent performance of *L'Histoire du soldat*. He is a young composer who studied in Paris with Nadia Boulanger and has a profound knowledge of contemporary music. I have often had occasion to consult his library, and we always get a hearty welcome at his house. On the other side of the continent Walter Piston trains young men at Harvard. Like Roger Sessions he is reserved in character and immensely cultured. Of his recent works, I greatly admired his Third Symphony and his Sonata for harpsichord and piano, in which there are great qualities of zest and movement, dignity and economy in the handling of the dramatic element, and an excellent sense of proportion. Finally Virgil Thomson, who collaborated with Gertrude Stein, is the real American disciple of Erik Satie, and divides his time between New York and Paris, to the great benefit of cultural relations between the two countries.

I should also like to mention the sturdy, harsh music of Carlos Chávez, who often comes from his native Mexico to conduct in the United States. It is thanks to him that I went to Mexico to give a concert. He had trained a flexible yet disciplined orchestra there which was astonishingly skillful in playing contemporary music. What other musical ensemble could give within a single period of six weeks festivals of Stravinsky, Hindemith, and Milhaud conducted by the composers themselves? We were all three delighted by our trip to Mexico. Hardly had we crossed the frontier when we were overwhelmed by the truly Latin atmosphere in which we found ourselves. Deep down inside ourselves we discovered a past to which the revelation of the great monuments of pre-Columbian art, the churches and convents where baroque art has run riot, the tumult of the big Indian markets, the appearance of the villages, and especially the gentle charm of the landscape were all closely linked. Carlos Prieto made it easy for us to see all these marvels; he is an industrialist, and placed a car at our disposal. He loves music, as does all his family; his sister is a composer. In response to his request to write a piece dedicated to him, I wrote a Trio for strings.

I should not like to end this chapter without enumerating all the "Notes with Music" composed by me during my long stay in America: three ballets: *Moses* (*Opus Americanum No. 2*); *Jeux de printemps* for the eightieth birthday of Mrs. Coolidge, played in the Library of Congress, with choreography by Martha Graham; and *The Bells*, based on the poem by Edgar Allan Poe, produced in Chicago by Ruth Page and revived by the Ballets Russes de Monte Carlo. One opera, *Bolivar*, on the libretto after Supervielle—the subject of Bolívar suited me admirably because I wanted a libretto full of action, with a masculine hero. Moreover, the central idea of the play was that of liberation and freedom, which in 1943 occupied my every thought. I had already written some incidental music for this play when it was performed at the Comédie-Française, but I did not use any of this old material now. The text also had to be slightly altered to make it a suitable libretto for an opera. Supervielle, who was in Montevideo, sent me some "airs" with which the action might be interspersed, and Madeleine prepared a libretto, keeping as close as possible to the poet's beautiful words. The only alteration she made was in the ending when the dying Bolívar sees in a vision his young wife dead. Before this scene she inserted an aria for Bolívar writing his will in exile, and for this she used the actual words of his will.

I composed four string quartets: the Tenth ("Birthday Quartet") dedicated to Mrs. Coolidge; the Eleventh, for the twenty-fifth anniversary of the League of Composers; the Twelfth, dedicated to the memory of Fauré, for the centenary of his birth; the Thirteenth, dedicated to Madeleine, because thirteen has always been our lucky number. (I composed this in my hotel bedroom in Mexico.) In addition, I produced a few short chamber works: a Sonatina for two violins, composed for my pupils in a Pullman at the same time as a Trio Sonata offered to my wife and my son in memory of a trip to the East. For Germain Prévost, I composed two Sonatas for viola and piano and, because he loves friends, youthful faces, and music, *Quatre Visages* for viola and piano ("*La Californienne,*" "*La Wisconsinienne,*" "*La Bruxelloise,*" "*La Parisienne*"). For Alexander Schneider and Ralph Kirkpatrick, I wrote a Sonata for violin and harpsichord. Some virtuosos wish to make sure of being allowed to give the first performance of a new concerto, and for this reason I have usually had a fair number of orders, in executing which I have granted the soloist exclusive rights in each particular work for a period of twelve months. I composed a Concerto for two pianos for Vronsky and Babin, who gave the work its first performance in Pittsburgh with Fritz Reiner; a Clarinet Concerto for Benny Goodman, which he never played, though he performed the transcription of *Scaramouche* that I had made for him in 1941 from the saxophone version; Cello Concerto No. 2 for Edmond Kurtz, which was given its first performance by the New York Philharmonic under Rodzinsky; Violin Concerto No. 2 for Arthur Le Blanc, a Canadian violinist; and Piano Concerto No. 3 for Emile Baume. I also received some orders of a rather special kind: the prodigious musician Larry Adler, who is capable of playing the harmonica with one hand and accompanying himself on the piano with the other, asked me to compose for him a Suite for harmonica and orchestra, which he played for the first time in Paris. Fearing, however, that the suite might never be played again, once the soloist's exclusive rights had lapsed, I wrote another version for violin and orchestra, which was often played by Francescatti. Naturally the two versions are completely different, in view of the nature of the instruments for which each is written. I also wrote a Concerto for marimba, in which I used the vibraphone as well. Mr. Jack Connor, who planned to play it at St. Louis under the direction of Golschmann, is capable of playing the two instruments alternately or simultaneously.

When a publisher asked me for an easy piece suitable for a school band, I composed my *Suite française*, utilizing folk tunes from Normandy, Brittany, the Ile-de-France, Alsace-Lorraine, and Provence in order to familiarize students with the songs of the regions where the Allied armies were fighting for the liberation of my country. I made a symphonic version of the *Suite française* of which I have often given concert performances. After the first performance of this suite by the famous Goldman Band, Schirmer commissioned me to write a piece for the same type of orchestra. I wrote *Two Marches: In Memoriam* (in memory of Pearl Harbor) and *Gloria Victoribus*. I composed *Le Bal martiniquais* for two pianos (there is also an orchestral version of this work), and Gaby and Robert Casadesus made a recording of it. For the two pianists Gold and Fizdale I composed *Carnaval à la Nouvelle-Orléans*, using French tunes from Louisiana. I also composed a few songs: *Rêves*, *Cinq Prières*, *Poèmes de Supervielle*, *Les Chants de Misère*, by Camille Paliard, and *Six Sonnets écrits au secret* by Cassou, for *a cappella* choir. Of all the poems written about the Resistance, these sonnets are the ones I find most moving, for though born of circumstance, they have the same quality of permanence as the most beautiful examples of classical poetry.

Although my first two symphonies were composed for American musical societies (Chicago Symphony Orchestra and the Koussevitzky Foundation), my third and fourth were commissioned in France. Henry Barraud, director of Radiodiffusion Française, asked me to write a *Te Deum*, which I composed in the form of a choral symphony. It consists of four movements, one of which is for choruses singing without words, and a finale based on the words of the *Te Deum*. I received a letter from the French Minister of Education asking me for a piece of music to celebrate the centenary of the Revolution in 1848. I thought of writing my Fourth Symphony on the boat perhaps; for the time for my journey was coming near and we had already reserved our passage on a Norwegian cargo steamer sailing via the Panama Canal.

I was going to see my friends again. Some of them had done their best to preserve all the mementos of my past: Roger Désormière had rescued my piano and pictures, and, an even greater service, had paid the rent for my apartment all through the occupation; Honegger and Sauguet had stored all my papers and music; Poulenc kept all my works published by Deiss as soon as he heard the news of our poor publisher's arrest; Paul Bertrand succeeded, not without difficulty, in recovering the trunkful of manuscripts which I had sent to my brother-in-law in Domfront, representing the labor of thirty years. And in Aix, too, devoted friends looked after all my mother's silver and jewelry. The Germans looted both our houses: Le Bras d'Or was successively occupied by the Italians, the Germans, the F.F.I., the Americans, and the band of the French Air Force; L'Enclos was turned into a hospital and according to all accounts was in a pitiful state; but the walls were still standing, and that was better than nothing at all.

We planned to sail when summer school ended on August 13, 1947. I would be leaving behind me seven long years of life in the United States, for which I shall always be grateful to that great country. I should return to it again, in order not to abandon the work I had started there, but already in imagination I could feel the emotion that would well up in my heart as I saw the shores of my long-lost homeland looming above the horizon.

35

FRANCE AND THE UNITED STATES,

1947—52

THE TRIP by freighter was very pleasant. We boarded our ship at Alameda, on San Francisco Bay, very near Mills College. Crossing the bay in the waning twilight, passing under the huge bridges sparkling with lights, was an experience of unexpected splendor. Our first stop, at Los Angeles, allowed us two days with friends, and we had a brief visit with Stravinsky, who played for us on the piano the first act of *The Rake's Progress*.

Then we set out on our adventure, sailing south, keeping close to the shore. Our ship, though small, was comfortable. There were only twelve passengers aboard, all elderly and well-mannered. The serious illness of a stewardess caused us to put in at a port in Guatemala (shipping companies do not have to carry a ship's doctor when there are fewer than thirteen passengers). While they were carrying the unlucky girl ashore, we looked at the superb forests and yearned to enter the jungle. The ship got under way again, but engine trouble forced us to stop over in Panama for three days. What a delight to find ourselves again in a tropical city! The French Minister and his wife were kind enough to take us driving. One drives very fast on the Panamanian roads. We drove from one ocean to the other in a few hours, but as the road goes through deep forest and over mountains, we did not see the Canal. On our way back to the City of Panama we got out of the car to admire a fine view at the edge of the forest. All at once I heard the extraordinary night-sounds that had so impressed me in the Brazilian jungles thirty years earlier.

At last we resumed our journey. The passage through the Canal was extremely interesting. The ship moved very slowly and was detained at numerous locks—and then, crossing a large lake, it reached the sea. No incident thereafter; magnificent weather. We put our enforced leisure to work. Daniel wrote an essay on philosophy and Chinese poetry, and I composed the symphony that the French government had commissioned for the anniversary of the Revolution of 1848.

One night our radio picked up broadcasts from the big European stations. Next day we could see the English and French coasts. It seemed odd not to be going straight to France, but to be sailing on to Holland. Sight of the cliffs at Pas-de-Calais only increased our impatience.

At Rotterdam our friends Paul Collaer and Franz André, *chef d'orchestre* for the Belgian radio, were awaiting us. It was our first sight—and a very moving one—of friends from whom we had been separated for a very long time. It was, too, our first sight of the ruins of the war: the center of Rotterdam was only a vast empty plain.

Our ship had to wait several days at Rotterdam and Antwerp. We stayed with the Collaers until time to go back on board. We were much tempted to go on to Paris by train so as to get there sooner, but we had so many packages of food and so much furniture aboard that we could not let them go through the customs unaccompanied.

The Belgian radio took advantage of my brief stay in Brussels to have me conduct. They had the orchestral parts for *Protée*, and this renewal of contact with a European orchestra delighted me. When the piece had been played, Madeleine heard two ladies call out: "Not bad!" Times had changed: twenty-five years earlier this same work had provoked a notorious scandal. We boarded the ship again at Antwerp. Before getting outside the port, it had to sail down innumerable small canals; with land on both sides, one saw all around ships that seemed to be lying in the meadows. At long last we reached the Channel.

At Le Havre four figures were waving as we entered the port: our very faithful friends Annie Dalsace, Jane Bathori, and Andrée Tainsy—and, along with them, Madeleine's young pupil Jacques Denoel, the actor. Visitors were not permitted aboard ship, so we held long conversations by shouting down from the deck. The captain understood our impatience and was kind enough to let our friends spend the evening with us. Next morning, before disembarking, we saw my brother-in-law Étienne, his wife, and his son arrive. They had come all the way from Angers to welcome us. It was very affecting to see them again. Annie Dalsace drove us back to Paris in her car. Everywhere we found the tracks of war: Le Havre destroyed, whole sections of Rouen demolished—and France surviving, dearer to us than ever.

Our feeling of familiarity came back very quickly. It seemed impossible that we had been away so long. The moment Daniel got back, he climbed on his bicycle and went off. After the few days necessary for getting settled in our apartment, we went to Aix-en-Provence. Madeleine's mother was waiting for us with understandable impatience, as was our Aunt Amélie Milhaud. But my joy at seeing them was darkened by the pain of returning to Aix, where my parents had died during the occupation without my being present to look after and comfort them. They left a great void behind them. All at once my health declined, and I became very ill at the home of my aunt. This illness—one of the most severe of my life—obliged Madeleine to resume the duties of a night nurse. Nothing helped me, and I was in terrible pain. At this time I was notified that I had been appointed to a professorship at the Conservatoire Nationale de Musique in Paris. How could I return to the capital? It was impossible. My predecessor in the post, Henri Busser, considerately consented to continue his classes until I should be able to take over.

Radiodiffusion Française, which organizes the larger part of the musical and cultural life of Paris, had arranged a festival of my works to constitute my "homecoming concert." But the date of this performance coincided with my attack of illness, and my friend Roger Désormière conducted in my place. Once again I was able to marvel at the ability of this incomparable conductor. From my sickbed I heard the first European performance of my Second Symphony and the *première* of the Third (*Te Deum*), with chorus, which latter the radio had commissioned from me to commemorate victory.

In January 1948, by train and ambulance, I re-entered Paris. I was unable to walk, but at least I could resume relations with my devoted young French students. I had also founded in Paris an extension course for Mills College (which I teach whenever I return to France); by this means American students are able to work under me while earning credits in their American colleges. During my entire stay I was unable to walk. Our apartment was never empty; it was

The Six and Jean Cocteau, Paris, 1952
(STANDING: *Poulenc, Tailleferre, Auric, Durey;*
SEATED: *Honegger, Cocteau, Milhaud*)

*Virgil Thomson, Milhaud, Charles Jones, and Curtis W. Cate,
Santa Barbara, 1949*

*Armand Lunel, Milhaud, and Madeleine Milhaud
arriving at the Lydda Airport, Israel, 1952*

marvelous to see again our most faithful friends. Madeleine was very busy. Lise Caldaguès, who was in charge of recorded music on the radio, had given her an interesting job: a series of broadcasts on the relationships between poets and musicians. As Marinette and Rodolphe Fabbri, Daniel's old nurse and her husband, had come back to work for us, Madeleine was relieved of household duties and could spend more time on her professional work. She resumed as well her instruction in dramatic art at the Schola Cantorum.

During this period I wrote a new ballet, *'adame Miroir*, to a scenario by Jean Genet, for the Ballets de Paris of Roland Petit. The rather dramatic theme involved a labyrinth of mirrors, in the midst of which a doomed sailor finds himself face to face with Death. During the entire ballet his reflection, his double, attends him. I had myself carried to the theater and attended the final rehearsals of this ballet, mounted with great loftiness and emotion in the beautiful setting of Georges Delvaux, and the choreography by Jeanine Charrat.

In June the government arranged an official concert at the Théâtre des Champs-Élysées to celebrate the centenary of the Revolution of 1848. During it the first performance of my Fourth Symphony was to occur. Désormière was to conduct on the same program the admirable *Symphonie funèbre et triomphale* of Berlioz, as well as Beethoven's curious Fantasy for piano, chorus, and orchestra. I had missed my homecoming concert in November 1947; I resolved to risk the strain of conducting my Fourth Symphony. The joy of conducting its *première* personally more than repaid me for the difficulties and suffering it cost me.

Our 1948 departure for the United States took place in the midst of feverish activity. The night before we left, Daniel left for Italy to study painting—and the Opéra-Comique was giving the *première* of my ballet *Jeux de printemps*, with décor by Coutaud.

I was to teach a class in composition at Tanglewood, the home of the Berkshire Festival. My colleague was Aaron Copland, who is on the permanent staff, as well as being a director of the institution. Honegger had taught there the year before, and during his stay had become so ill that his life was in danger for several days. We were to occupy the room he had used, and I think that our charming landladies, the Misses Downes, must have formed a sorry picture of the health of Parisian composers when they saw me arrive, the year after Honegger, in a wheelchair that I was wholly unable to leave.

Under the encouragement of Serge Koussevitzky, the musical activity at Tanglewood was prodigious. In addition to the Berkshire Festival, during which the Boston Symphony played, there was an extremely good music school and a series of concerts and lectures. Every night we could go to a concert or an opera. Once more we met our old friend Mrs. Elizabeth Sprague Coolidge, who was presenting concerts of chamber music near by. She took us to a dance festival at Jacob's Pillow. In the country, in a huge barn that had been converted into a theater, Japanese and Negro dancers shared the program with performances of classic ballet. A few weeks later Mrs. Coolidge asked me to compose for this organization a work that could be both danced and performed as chamber music. I responded by composing the *Dreams of Jacob* for five instruments.

Later we left for California. We had been engaged to teach at the Music Academy of the West. This school is high up on a hill a short distance from Santa Barbara. Our terrace overlooked groves of lemon trees which spread out of sight down to the Pacific. This summer school was smaller than that at Tanglewood, but no less interesting, and we returned to it several summers in succession. The music director, Dr. Richard Lert, whom I had known at the Berlin Opera, had managed to develop a full orchestra from among the students at the school. It was fascinating to observe the progress of these young performers from one summer to the next. Santa Barbara was justly proud of its orchestra. Among the faculty members we found many old friends: Soulima Stravinsky, Charles Jones, Roman Totenberg, Martial Singher, and the violist Jascha Veissi. Madeleine gave a speech class in French and one in opera-production.

In September we returned to our house at Mills College. Teaching and work began. I wrote *Kentuckiana* for the Louisville Orchestra—an overture in the French style on twenty Kentucky airs. I prepared for the Juilliard School in New York a score for the *Jeu de Robin et de Marion*, after the music of Adam de la Halle (twelfth century). When I had completed these commissions, I turned to a rather special project. At the *première* of my Fourth Symphony in Paris, one of my friends had given me a small music notebook exquisitely bound in green leather and dating from about 1848. Nothing had been written in it. Each page contained eight staffs. I conceived the idea of using it to write two quartets that could be played separately, but which, when played concurrently, would form a third work, an octet different from the two component quartets. The first performance was given during the summer semester at Mills College by the Budapest Quartet and the Paganini Quartet. Hearing for the first time my two quartets played simultaneously was a very moving experience for me. I was fortunate indeed in having the services of two of the best American quartets. Several weeks later this "triple" work was performed by the students of the

Music Academy of the West. I was reassured that my score was not impossibly difficult, for the young students were able to give it a faultless reading.

Since then the Budapest Quartet has made a Columbia recording of this octet without calling upon the services of another ensemble. This was not easy. After having made separate recordings of the Fourteenth and Fifteenth quartets, they made a fresh recording of the Fifteenth while wearing earphones that conveyed the Fourteenth to them. They were thus able to obtain perfect synchronization.

I composed my Second Piano Sonata and dedicated it to Monique Haas, whom I greatly admire; and my Fourth Concerto for piano and orchestra for Zadel Skolovsky. When that astonishing virtuoso came to me from Mme Pierre Monteux to commission the latter work, he told me privately that he played octaves very well; I did not scruple to give him plenty of them all through that arduous composition. He played its *première* at Boston under Charles Munch, and then performed it in Paris under Désormière and in Brussels under Franz André. In 1949 he recorded it for Columbia in Paris under my direction.

My health during our 1949 stay in Paris was indifferent, but not so bad as it had been two years earlier. Radiodiffusion Française had commissioned from me a score for Blaise Cendrars's *Fin du monde*, which Madeleine had been assigned to broadcast. She included this work in an "Homage to Cendrars" program consisting of *La Création du monde*, Honegger's *Les Pâques à New York*, and readings of some of Cendrars's poems. Also for radio I worked on a project that I found most amusing: *Barba Garibo*. Armand Lunel wrote the text, a radiophonic dialogue interspersed with choruses and folk dances from Menton. *Barba Garibo* was presented during the Festival of Lemons, which the city of Menton observes each year. I was in such bad health that I could not think of conducting, and Eugène Bigot took my place. I decided, however, to make the trip with the help of hospital attendants, who took me from the train to my hotel and thence to the theater. The painter André Marchand had designed the sets and costumes, and the choruses were sung by the Capeline Mentonnaise and the Chanson de Montreux, the latter a Rhône-Swiss group. Our bedroom was filled with sunlight; the stay was pleasant in spite of everything. I found it delightful to chat with Armand Lunel among the ancient streets of Menton.

Some friends drove us to Aix. We stopped at Vallauris to see Picasso, who showed us a series of his astonishing ceramics. All along the road we ran across carnivals. Nice was bustling with preparations for its "Corso"; the mimosa festival was in progress at Saint-Raphaël; and Aix, when we got there, was crowded with people celebrating Mardi Gras. Not since my boyhood had I seen that hilarious crowd, all in masks, thronging the Cours Mirabeau. All that healthy happiness, the time-honored fireworks, the lovely Aix countryside, brought back to me my pleasant stay there so long before.

During the following winter I had one of the happiest experiences of my career. Paul Collaer arranged a broadcast, over the Brussels Flemish radio, of my *Euménides*. Even when I had been composing it, he had thought: "I shall have to produce this work one day." This opera, to the third part of Æschylus' *Oresteia*, was written between 1917 and 1923; it is so difficult that I never expected to hear it performed during my lifetime. The production was extremely scrupulous. The enormous chorus combined groups from the Flemish and French radio stations, as well as a Flemish village chorus. Franz André conducted orchestra, chorus, and soloists with

massive authority. I shall never be able to express my gratitude to the Belgian radio or to Collaer and André for this
undertaking.

When the Antwerp Orchestra and the Chorale Cæcilia
had presented the finale of my *Euménides* in 1928, notwith-
standing the excellence of their performance, the composition
had presented technical complications quite difficult to master.
Here, too, time had done its work: the performance, though
still demanding great subtlety, no longer presented any serious problem.

I was especially spoiled during that season, for in May
1950 the Paris Opéra put on my *Bolivar*. The performance
was remarkably skillful, thanks to André Cluytens, who
conducted the orchestra. The Opéra's best singers took part:
Jeannine Micheau, Hélène Bouvier, Roger Bourdin, and Gi-
raudeau. The production by Max de Rieux was superb, and
Fernand Léger's ten sets again attested to his great theatrical
artistry. We got a divided press. Certain reviewers outdid
themselves in hostility, going well past the boundaries of
criticism. They hoped to have the opera withdrawn, but the
public sided with me. *Bolivar* was played for two seasons,
and I had the pleasure of seeing it advertised when I arrived
back in Paris for the 1951–2 season.

I resumed my work with the cinema by writing music for a
documentary film on Gauguin by Alain Resnays and the
score for a long film by Nicole Vedres, who had been responsible for *Paris 1900* and *Life Begins Tomorrow*. This was designed to bring to the screen Jean-Paul Sartre and André
Gide, Le Corbusier, Picasso, Jean Rostand, and others. I did
not have time to orchestrate this score, so I entrusted the
work to Manuel Rosenthal before leaving for the United
States. For some years Madeleine had been director of the
Maison Française at Mills College. She had engaged for the

summer of 1951 René Lenormand and his wife, the actress Marie Kalff. We all sailed together. I think that this trip to America was one of the last pleasures of Lenormand, who died shortly after returning to France. Madeleine presented some scenes from his plays with her students at Mills. He was full of praise, but she was a little timid, as she had never before presented her students to an audience including the author. After the summer session at Mills, we went on to the Music Academy of the West for the first performance of my Sixteenth Quartet, a work that I had composed quietly, without Madeleine's knowing of it, and which was dedicated to her on the occasion of our twenty-fifth wedding anniversary.

I composed a rather important score for Shakespeare's *A Winter's Tale*, which Claude-André Puget had adapted for the Comédie-Française. This play had an unforeseen success: it was running again when I returned to Paris.

During the Christmas holidays, after spending a few days with our friend Florence Heifetz, we went on into the southern California desert, to Twenty-nine Palms. We had heard of this place because "General Lavine" had lived there. This old American acrobatic dancer had delighted Paris in 1910; it was he whom Debussy celebrated in the prelude *Général Lavine, Eccentric*. Had Debussy written this piece for Lavine? Nobody knows. The only certain fact is that the prelude was composed well after Lavine's departure, following his resounding success in Paris. I do not know what happened to him later. The San Francisco music critic Alfred Frankenstein discovered him at Twenty-nine Palms during the last war; he was running a small shop for manufacturing pins he had invented for attaching ribbons to army uniforms. His model had been adopted by the United States Army.

I took advantage of the desert solitude to compose my Seventeenth Quartet and to get to work on the Eighteenth, the last in the series. In 1920 I had, in fact, stated in an issue of *Le Coq*, a journal published by Cocteau: "I wish to write eighteen quartets." This paper often had a slightly pugnacious tone, at times an impertinent one. If my declaration appeared to mean "one quartet more than Beethoven," it was nevertheless not a young man's flippancy. I desired, in view of the æsthetic leanings of Cocteau—who was then busy glorifying "music with a punch," that of the circus and the music hall—to take up the defense (without seeming to do so) of chamber music, serious music, the music to which I have been faithful during my entire professional life. But the phrase haunted me: I often asked myself if I should ever complete my project. My Seventeenth Quartet, finished during Christmas week, is dedicated to my son for his twenty-first birthday.

I started work on my Eighteenth Quartet with a sense of solemnity and melancholy, for it would complete a cycle on which I had labored since 1912. I introduced in the final measures of this composition a theme that appears near the end of my First Quartet. But I did not spend my whole vacation working: we did a lot of driving about. As Twenty-nine Palms is near the Joshua Tree National Monument, we made numerous forays into that immense reservation, so oddly overgrown with joshua trees, half trees and half great plants, which assume fantastic shapes. The country had a strange, mad look. Before returning to Mills, we also traveled down to the region below Palm Springs, where date palms are cultivated. There the landscape altered completely: all nature was tamed and under control.

We went to New York for the Philharmonic concert at which Dimitri Mitropoulos conducted *Les Choéphores* with all his usual ardor and enthusiasm. Madeleine had the role of the *récitante*.

Once the school year ends, the weeks appear to slip by with incredible speed. One has to foresee departure and arrange for it while still at work. In June we went to Toronto for a few days. One of my students, Murray Adaskin, had got us an engagement with the Canadian Broadcasting Corporation for an orchestral concert and a chamber-music concert. In the latter Madeleine performed the *Cantate de l'Enfant et de la Mère*, and Frances James, Adaskin's wife, who is an excellent singer, sang some of my songs. We went with her and Murray to the Toronto Museum, which has one of the largest collections of Chinese antiques in America, an amazing wealth of bronzes, porcelains, terracottas—all burial objects recovered from the ground. It is a magnificent museum, but a museum of death. The Adaskins also drove us to Niagara Falls. Once more I realized that world-famous natural phenomena, like great monuments, deserve their celebrity. How could one fail to think so when confronted by those massive cascades crowned with clouds of mist?

During the summer term at Mills, we learned with sorrow that Arnold Schönberg had died on July 13, 1951, after a long cardiac illness. For this composer I had great respect and deep affection. I am happy that in his advanced years he was able to establish the tremendous influence of his twelve-tone theory throughout the world. He also had an incalculable moral authority, never consenting to compromise, and keeping his ideals unremittingly high. We had already been grieved by another death, that of Serge Koussevitzky. Earlier, during the winter, watching him conduct the Israel Orchestra with so much devotion on his return to the United States, we had been shocked by his face, his excessive fatigue. The morning after that concert he had taken to his bed. He had sent for me to tell me that he was arranging a great festival in Israel to commemorate the three-thousandth anniversary of

King David. He had asked me to write a large work for that occasion. He told me that I could choose my own collaborator. I thought immediately of Armand Lunel, for I find it very pleasant to work with him, as we can calmly discuss all problems without alienating him or risking the conflicts that spring from absurd touchiness. Koussevitzky's death grieved us deeply; all musicians will realize the extent of the services he rendered to music for so many years. He had already made the future of the Koussevitzky Foundation secure by placing it in the hands of the Library of Congress. Mme Koussevitzky will continue to administer this organization, which has commissioned so many works from composers all over the world.

During all periods musicians have been urged to compose for commission. Only the most perfected technique can undergo this discipline without constraint or loss of freedom. In such cases one is nearly always concerned with musical forms that one enjoys developing; and one is free to develop them while carrying out the requests of the commissioner. In the summer of 1951 I was asked to compose several works commemorating anniversaries: a *Concertino d'Été* for viola and nine instruments, which Robert Courte performed for the tenth anniversary of the Charleston, West Virginia, Chamber Music Society; a religious work for the United Temple Chorus, ordered by the Ernest Bloch Award Commission, for which I selected three fragments from the book of Proverbs: "*L'Ivrognerie et ses suites,*" "*Le Banquet de la folie,*" and "*La Femme forte.*" Coe College, in Cedar Rapids, Iowa, celebrates its centenary in May 1952; for this occasion I have written a religious cantata on passages from the Book of Daniel. During a four-week stay at Aspen, Colorado, Madeleine finished arranging the Biblical text for this cantata, which bears the title *Miracles of Faith*.

The Aspen Festival, to which is now attached a summer music school where we both teach, made quite a long stop for us. We settled down in this tiny town, which had enjoyed the highest prosperity in 1890, where Duse and Patti had won applause in the quaint little theater, and which now, thanks to the magic wand of Walter Paepcke, who has restored its position as a cultural center, was crowded with students, instrumentalists, singers, and composers. Some of them had already worked with us. The night of our arrival they serenaded us outside our apartment. The month of August, which we spent there, was marvelously exhilarating. Trips to the mountains alternated with concerts. We were surrounded with friends, including Claire Reis, Florence Heifetz, and her children. Jo Heifetz had studied composition with me in Paris; she had spent the winter there, and had become a member of our small Paris circle.

While in New York en route to France, we made a trip to West Point. I had been asked to compose a work for the one-hundred-and-fiftieth anniversary of the Military Academy. Captain Resta, the distinguished band-leader, wanted me to hear the ensemble for which I was to write the proposed piece. What was my surprise, on entering the rehearsal room of this famous band, to be welcomed with "Happy birthday to you!" It was actually September 4.

We had already agreed to stop off at Palisades on the way back from West Point. There our friends Arthur Gold and Robert Fizdale were living. These young pianists, who merit their international reputation, had twice requested me to write works for them: *Carnival in New Orleans* and the Suite, opus 300, with orchestra. They played the Suite in 1950 at the Venice Biennial with Herman Scherchen conducting. They again applied to me for a piece, and I composed for them the *Concertino d'Automne* for two pianos and eight in-

319

struments; of this they gave the first performance in New York in December 1951.

At Le Havre we had the happiness of joining our son, Daniel, who was there waiting for us. He had worked hard during his year away from us and had made great progress in his art. Thanks, I believe, to the high altitude of Aspen, my health had much improved, and I was able, for the first time in many years, to go to the theater and to travel for pleasure. I seized the occasion to make a motor trip to the Midi along the "Scholars' Road" and back, going through Burgundy, Provence, and Touraine. So many beloved sites and memories! There was another old project that I carried out: I visited my friends the Hoppenots at the Embassy in Bern during a concert tour of Switzerland. They had succeeded in transforming the official building of the French Embassy into a museum. In the midst of their remarkable collections, archæological remains and modern pictures, our old friends welcomed us.

The Centre de Documentation International de Musique put on in Paris an exhibition devoted to Les Six, which gave us a chance to see Jean Cocteau again. Manuscripts, photographs, letters, and models of sets and costumes composed an extremely striking exhibit and constituted, for the present generation, the mirror of an age already past. How gratifying it was for us all to meet again, the "six" once more together in untroubled friendship, as when we first began.

In 1952 Honegger and I shall both reach our sixtieth birthday. Claude Delvincourt, director of the Conservatoire, had the gracious idea of commemorating this by arranging a concert of our works. I was happy to conduct the Orchestra of the Conservatoire Students, a young, hard-working group, and to be connected again with Arthur; it seemed a symbol of our indissoluble friendship. Now we are getting ready for an

320

Easter trip to Jerusalem with Armand Lunel. We must, for the sake of the big work we are writing together, steep ourselves in the atmosphere of that remarkable land.

Now that my series of eighteen quartets is complete, I want to devote my next chamber-music works to the quite different problems posed by the quintet. My first, a Piano Quintet, was written to be performed for the Mills College centenary in May 1952 by the Hungarian Quartet and Egon Petri. The second, scored for quartet and contrabass, was commissioned by the University of Michigan for the Stanley Quartet. I have just completed an extended theatrical score for ten instruments. Jean-Louis Barrault wants to give Claudel's *Christophe Colomb* a stage presentation. This has created intricate and serious problems for me. When one has put the best one has into a composition, it is very difficult to adapt it to the instructions of a theatrical director, cutting down the effects, reducing the music to a sort of picturesqueness, to background music with only an occasional lyric passage.

As for my present work, I am engaged on a long ballet based on a scenario by Philippe de Rothschild. This will be produced next season at the Paris Opéra with costumes and sets by Dali, along with a performance of my opera *Medée*. Radio Italy has also commissioned me to compose a Fifth Symphony.

We return soon to the United States, as my teaching career involves a methodical alternation, in which one year in the United States regularly follows one year in France.

Paris, March 1952

LIST OF COMPOSITIONS

and

INDEX

Darius Milhaud

A LIST PREPARED BY ELENA FELS NOTH

DATE	OPUS	TITLE	DESCRIPTION	FIRST PERFORMANCE	PUBLISHER
1910–12	1	Poèmes de Francis Jammes	I: 9 songs; II: 7 songs		
1910–16	2	Trois Poèmes de Léo Latil	3 songs		
1911	3	First Violin Sonata	Violin, piano	S.M.I., Paris, 1913	Durand
1910–15	4	La Brebis Egarée (Jammes)	Opera, 3 acts	Opéra-Comique, Paris, 1923	Eschig
1912	5	First String Quartet	String quartet	S.M.I., Paris, 1913	Durand
—	6	Poèmes de Francis Jammes	4 songs; voice, piano		
1912–13	7	Sept Poèmes de la Connaissance de l'Est (Claudel)	7 songs; voice, piano; (No. 7 orchestrated)	Salon Automne, Paris, 1913	Mathot-Salabert
1913	8	Suite	5 numbers; piano	Brussels, 1914	Durand
—	9	Alissa (Gide)	8 numbers; soprano, piano	Paris, 1920	Heugel
—	10	Trois Poèmes de Lucile de Chateaubriand	3 songs; voice, piano	Paris, 1916	Mathot-Salabert
1913–14	11	Trois Poèmes Romantiques: I	3 songs; voice, piano	Aix-en-Provence, 1913	
—	12	First Symphonic Suite	Orchestra (also piano, 4 hands)	1914, Paris; Schmitz	Eschig

DATE	OPUS	TITLE	DESCRIPTION	FIRST PERFORMANCE	PUBLISHER
1913–14	13	Poème sur un Cantique de Camargue	Orchestra, piano	1915, Paris; Colonne-Lamoureux	Heugel
—	14	Agamemnon (Claudel)	Orchestra, soprano, chorus	1927, Paris; Straram	Durand
1914	15	Sonata for Piano and Two Violins	Piano, two violins	1915, Paris	Durand
1914–15	16	Second String Quartet	String quartet	1915, Paris	Durand
1913–19	17	Protée (Claudel)	Orchestra, chorus	1929, Groningen	Durand
1914	18	Le Printemps	Piano, violin	Vieux-Colombier, Paris, 1919	Durand
—	19	Trois Poèmes Romantiques: II	3 songs; voice, piano		
—	20	Quatre Poèmes de Léo Latil	4 songs; voice, piano	1915, Paris	Durand
—	21	Le Château (Lunel)	8 songs; voice, piano		
—	22	Poème du Gitanjali (Tagore-Gide)	Voice, piano	1915, Marseille	Revue Française de Musique (Edition de luxe.)
1915	23	Variations sur un Thème de Cliquet	Piano		
—	24	Les Choéphores (Claudel)	Soprano, baritone, orchestra, soloists, narrator, chorus	1919, Paris, Del-grange; on stage, Monnaie, Brussels, 1935	Heugel
1915–19	25	Printemps	3 numbers; piano		La Sirène-Eschig

DATE	OPUS	TITLE	DESCRIPTION	FIRST PERFORMANCE	PUBLISHER
1915–17	26	Quatre Poèmes pour Baryton (Claudel)	4 songs; baritone, piano	1922, Paris	Durand
1915	27	D'Un Cahier Inédit du Journal d'Eugénie de Guérin	3 songs; voice, piano	1921, Paris	Roudanez-Philippo
—	28	L'Arbre Exotique (Chevalier Gosse): Romance	Voice, piano		
—	29	Notre-Dame de Sarrance (Jammes): Cantique	Voice, piano	Festival Sarrance	
—	30	Deux Poèmes d'Amour (Tagore)	Voice, piano	1915, Rio de Janeiro	G. Schirmer
—	31	Deux Poèmes de Coventry Patmore	2 songs; voice, piano	1924	Heugel; Stols (Maestricht) (Edition de luxe.)
1916	32	Third String Quartet (in memory of Léo Latil)			To be issued posthumously by Durand
—	33	Sonata for Piano	Piano	1920, Paris	Mathot-Salabert
—	34	Poèmes Juifs	8 songs; voice, piano	1920, Paris	Eschig
1916–17	35	Deux Poèmes du Gardener (Tagore)	2 songs; 2 voices, piano		

327   *The Compositions of* DARIUS MILHAUD

DATE	OPUS	TITLE	DESCRIPTION	FIRST PERFORMANCE	PUBLISHER
1916	36	Child Poems (Tagore)	5 songs; voice, piano	S. M. I, Paris, 1919	Music Composer Corp.—Fischer
—	37	Trois Poèmes (Christina Rossetti, Alice Meynell)	3 songs; voice, piano (or small orchestra)	1916, Paris	
—	38	No. 34 de l'Eglise Habillée de Feuilles (Jammes)	Vocal quartet; piano, 6 hands		
1916–19	39	Deux Poèmes (Saint-Léger Léger, René Chalupt)	2 songs; vocal quartet	1921, Paris	Durand
1917	40	Second Violin Sonata	Violin, piano	1916, Rio de Janeiro	Durand
1917–22	41	Les Euménides (Claudel)	Opera, 3 acts	The finale: 1928, Antwerp; entire: I. N. R., 1949, Brussels	Heugel
1917	42	Le Retour de l'Enfant-Prodigue (Gide)	Cantata: 5 voices, 21 instruments	Concerts Wiener, Paris, 1922	Universal (Vienna)
—	43	First Symphony (Le Printemps)	Small orchestra	1918, Rio de Janeiro	Universal (Vienna)
—	44	Chanson Bas (Mallarmé)	8 songs; voice, piano	Vieux-Colombier, Paris, 1919	La Sirène-Eschig
		Suivies d'un verso Carioca (Claudel)	Voice, piano		
—	45	Deux Poèmes de Rimbaud	2 songs; voice, piano		

DATE	OPUS	TITLE	DESCRIPTION	FIRST PERFORMANCE	PUBLISHER
1918	46	Fourth String Quartet	String quartet	Delgrange, Paris, 1919	Senart-Salabert
1918	47	Sonata for Piano, Flute, Clarinet, Oboe	Piano, flute, clarinet, oboe	1921, Wiesbaden	Durand
—	48	L'Homme et son Désir (Claudel)	Vocal quartet, 12 solo instruments, 15 percussion	Swedish Ballets, Paris, 1921	Universal (Vienna)
—	49	Second Symphony (Pastorale)	Small orchestra	Delgrange, Paris, 1919	Universal (Vienna)
—	50	Poèmes de Francis Jammes: IV	4 songs; voice, piano	Vieux-Colombier, Paris, 1919	
—	51	Deux Petits Airs (Mallarmé)	2 songs; voice, piano	1921, Paris	Eschig
—	52	Deux Poèmes Tupis	2 songs; 4 women's voices, handclapping	Vieux-Colombier, Paris, 1919	
—	53	Psaume 136 (Claudel)	Baritone, chorus, orchestra	1928, Berlin	Universal (Vienna)
1919	54	Psaume 129	Baritone, orchestra	Concerts Hubbard	Universal (Vienna)
—		Poème de Francis Thompson	Voice, piano		
—	55	Les Soirées de Pétrograd (René Chalupt)	12 songs; voice, piano	Galerie Barbazange, Paris, 1919	Durand
—	56	Machines Agricoles	Voice, 7 instruments	1920, Paris	Universal (Vienna)
—	57	Second Symphonic Suite ("d'après 'Protée'")	5 numbers; orchestra	Colonne, Paris, 1920	Durand

The Compositions of DARIUS MILHAUD

DATE	OPUS	TITLE	DESCRIPTION	FIRST PERFORMANCE	PUBLISHER
1919	58	Le Boeuf sur le Toit (Cocteau): Ballet	Orchestra	Champs-Elysées, Paris, 1920	La Sirène-Eschig
		b. Cinéma-Fantaisie	Violin, orchestra	Benedetti, 1921	La Sirène-Eschig
		c. Tango des Fratellini	Piano or orchestra		La Sirène
1920	59	Trois Poèmes de Jean Cocteau	3 songs; voice, piano	Galerie Montaigne, Paris, 1920	La Sirène-Eschig
—	60	Catalogue de Fleurs (Lucien Daudet)	7 songs; voice with piano or 7 instruments	Conservatoire, Paris, 1922	Durand
—	61	Ballade	Piano, orchestra	New York City Symphony, 1923	Universal
1920-21	62	Sérénade en 3 parties	Orchestra	1921, Winterthur	Universal
1920	63	Cinq Etudes	Piano, orchestra	Golschmann, Paris, 1921	Universal
—	64	Fifth String Quartet	String quartet	S. M. I, Paris, 1922	Senart-Salabert
—	65	Feuilles de Température (Morand)	3 songs; voice, piano	1923, Paris	
—	66	Le Printemps: II	3 pieces; piano	Concert des Six, Paris, 1920	La Sirène-Eschig
1920-21	67	Saudades do Brasil: Dance Suite	Piano or orchestra; also piano, violin; piano, cello	Concert des Six, Paris, 1920; with orchestra, Champs-Elysées, Paris, 1921	Desmets-Eschig

The Compositions of DARIUS MILHAUD

DATE	OPUS	TITLE	DESCRIPTION	FIRST PERFORMANCE	PUBLISHER
1920	68	Caramel Mou (Shimmy) (Cocteau)	Piano or small jazz band, voice	Th. Michel, Paris, 1921	Eschig
1921	69	Cocktail (Larsen)	Voice, 3 clarinets	Galerie Barbazange, Paris	Almanach de Cocagne
—	70	Les Mariés de la Tour Eiffel: show by Cocteau with music by the Six: I Marche Nuptiale; II Fugue du Massacre		Champs-Elysées, Paris, 1921	
—	71	Third Symphony (Sérénade)	Small orchestra	Société de Musique de Chambre, Paris, 1921	Universal
1921	72	Psaume 126 (Claudel)	Male chorus	Harvard Glee Club, New York, 1922	Universal
—	73	Poème du Journal Intime de Léo Latil	Piano, voice	Concert Olénine d'Alheim	Eschig
—	74	Fourth Symphony (Overture, Choral, Etude)	Ten string instruments	1921, Paris	Universal
1922	75	Fifth Symphony	Ten wind instruments	Champs-Elysées, Paris, 1923	Universal
—	76	Sonatina for flute and piano	Flute, piano	Concert Wiener, Paris, 1923	Durand
—	77	Sixth String Quartet	String quartet	Pro Arte, Brussels, 1923	Universal

DATE	OPUS	TITLE	DESCRIPTION	FIRST PERFORMANCE	PUBLISHER
1922	78	*Trois Rag Caprices*	Piano or small orchestra	Concert Wiener, Paris, 1923	Universal
1923	79	Sixth Symphony	Vocal quartet, oboe, cello	Concert Wiener, Paris, 1924	Universal
—	80	*Quatre Poèmes de Catulle*	Voice, violin	1923, Paris	Heugel
—	81a	*La Création du Monde* (Cendrars): Ballet	Orchestra	Champs-Elysées, Paris, 1923	Eschig
—	82	*Récitatifs pour "Une Education Manquée" de Chabrier*		Ballets Russes Diaghilew, Monte Carlo, 1924	Enoch
1924	83a	*Salade* (Flament): Ballet	Orchestra	Théâtre Cigale, Paris, 1924	Heugel
—	84	*Le Train Bleu* (Cocteau): Ballet	Orchestra	Ballets Russes Diaghilew, Paris, 1924	Heugel
—	85	*Les Malheurs d'Orphée* (Lunel)	Opera	Monnaie, Brussels, 1926	Heugel
1925	86	*Six Chants Populaires Hebraïques*	Voice, piano or orchestra	Madeleine Grey, Paris, 1925	Heugel
1925	87	Seventh String Quartet	String quartet	Pro Arte, Brussels, 1925	Universal
—	88	a. *Hymne de Sion—Israël est Vivant*	Voice, soprano	Jane Bathori, Paris, 1926	Universal
		b. *Deux Hymnes*	Orchestra	Straram, Paris, 1927	Universal

DATE	OPUS	TITLE	DESCRIPTION	FIRST PERFORMANCE	PUBLISHER
1925	89	Esther de Carpentras (Lunel)	Opera, two acts	Radio Rennes, Paris, 1937; Opéra-Comique, Paris, 1938	Heugel
1926	81b	Suite de Concert de la Création du Monde	String quartet, piano	Baden-Baden, 1927	Eschig
—	83b	Le Carnaval d'Aix	Piano, orchestra	New York Philharmonic-Symphony, 1926	Heugel
—	90	Pièce de Circonstance (Cocteau)	Voice, piano	Jane Bathori, Paris, 1926	Ten copies not for sale
—	91	Impromptu	Violin, piano		Heugel
—	92	Le Pauvre Matelot (Cocteau)	Opera	Opéra-Comique, Paris, 1927	Heugel
1927	93	First Violin Concerto	Violin, orchestra	Poulet, Paris, 1928	Heugel
—	94	L'Enlèvement d'Europe (Hoppenot)	Minute opera	Baden-Baden, 1927	Universal
—	95	L'Eventail de Jeanne (Polka): Ballet	Ballet	Opéra, Paris, 1928	Heugel
—	96	Prières Journalières à l'Usage des Juifs du Comtat Venaissin	3 songs; voice, piano	Jane Bathori, Paris, 1928	Heugel
—	97	3 Caprices de Paganini	Piano, violin	Pro Arte, Brussels, 1928	Heugel
—	98	L'Abandon d'Ariane (Hoppenot)	Minute opera	Wiesbaden, 1928	Universal

The Compositions of DARIUS MILHAUD

DATE	OPUS	TITLE	DESCRIPTION	FIRST PERFORMANCE	PUBLISHER
1927	99	Le Délivrance de Thésée (Hoppenot)	Minute opera	Wiesbaden, 1928	Universal
—	100	Sonatina for clarinet and piano	Clarinet, piano	S. M. I, Paris, 1929	Durand
1928	101	La Bien-Aimée: Ballet	Orchestra	Opéra, Paris, 1928	Universal
—	102	Christophe Colomb (Claudel)	Opera	Opera, Berlin, 1930	Universal
—	103	Cantate pour Louer le Seigneur	Orchestra, soloists, chorus	Aix-en-Provence, 1928	Universal
—	104	Actualités: Film Music	6 numbers; small orchestra	Baden-Baden, 1928	Universal
—	105	Vocalise: Air	Voice, piano		Leduc
1929	106	Quatrain (Jammes)	Voice, piano	Festival Roussel	Revue Musicale
—	107	La P'tite Lilie: Film music		Baden-Baden, 1929	Universal; Tobis, Berlin
—	108	Concerto for Viola and Orchestra	Viola, orchestra	Concertgebouw, Amsterdam, 1929	Universal
1929–30	109	Concerto for percussion and small orchestra	Percussion, small orchestra	Pro Arte, Brussels, 1930	Universal
1930	110	Maximilien (Werfel-Hoffman-Lunel)	Opera	Opéra, Paris, 1932	Universal
—	111	Choral	Piano		
1931	112	Sonata for Organ	Organ	S. I. M. C., Berlin, 1932	Gray, New York

DATE	OPUS	TITLE	DESCRIPTION	FIRST PERFORMANCE	PUBLISHER
1931	9	Alissa (Gide): New Version	Voice, piano	Sorbonne, Paris, 1932	Heugel
1932	113	Deux Poèmes de Cendrars	2 songs; vocal quartet or chorus	League of Composers, New York, 1933	Deiss-Salabert
—	114	Deux Elégies Romaines (Goethe)	Female chorus or 4 solo voices	Sérénade, Paris, 1933	Deiss-Salabert
—	115	L'Automne	3 numbers, piano	Conservatoire, Paris, 1932	Deiss-Salabert
—	116	La Mort du Tyran (Lampridius-Diderot)	Chorus, percussion, piccolo, clarinet, tuba	Sérénade, Paris, 1933	Chant du Monde
—	117	L'Annonce Faite à Marie (Claudel): Play with incidental music		Salle Iéna, Paris, 1933	Deiss-Salabert
—	118	A Propos de Bottes (Chalupt): Play for children	11 numbers; voice, violins, cellos	Théâtre de Marionettes, Paris, 1933	Durand
—	119	Un Petit Peu de Musique (Lunel): Play for children	12 numbers; voice, violins, cellos	Triton, Paris, 1933	Durand
—	120	Le Château des Papes (Richaud): Play	Two pianos, trumpet, sound waves	1932, Paris, Atelier	
		b. Adages	Vocal quartet, piano or instruments	1934, Paris, Cité Universitaire	Deiss-Salabert
		c. Suite	Sound waves, piano	1933, Paris, Sérénade	
—	121	Eighth String Quartet	String quartet	Concert Coolidge, Asolo, Italy	Chant du Monde

The Compositions of DARIUS MILHAUD

DATE	OPUS	TITLE	DESCRIPTION	FIRST PERFORMANCE	PUBLISHER
1933	122	Devant sa Main Nue (Raval)	Female chorus or 4 solo voices	1933, Paris, Sérénade	Deiss-Salabert
—	123	Le Funeste Retour	Song	1933, Paris, Boeuf sur le Toît	Deiss-Salabert
—	124	Les Songes (Derain): Ballet	Orchestra	1933, Paris, Champs-Elysées	Deiss-Salabert
—	125	Liturgie Comtadine	5 songs, voice, piano, or small orchestra	1934, Paris, Ecole Normale	Heugel
—	126	Hallo Everybody: Film			Philipps
—	127	First Piano Concerto	Piano, orchestra	1934, Paris, Pasdeloup	Deiss-Salabert
—	128	Madame Bovary: Film	Orchestra	1934, Paris, Ciné-Opéra	Enoch
		b. L'Album de Madame Bovary	Piano	1934, Paris, Pupils of Mme Long	Enoch
		c. Trois Valses	Piano		Enoch
		d. Deux Chansons (Flaubert)	Voice, piano		Enoch
—	129	Quatre Romances sans Paroles	Piano	1935, Paris, Radio Luxembourg	Deiss-Salabert
1934	130	Pan et Syrinx (Piis-Claudel): Cantata	6 numbers; soprano, baritone, vocal quartet, five instruments	1934, Brussels, Pro Arte	Deiss-Salabert

DATE	OPUS	TITLE	DESCRIPTION	FIRST PERFORMANCE	PUBLISHER
1934	131	Ritournelle et Six Chansons (Moreno): Play, "Se plaire sur la Même Fleur"	Voice, piano		
—	132	Les Amours de Ronsard	Chorus or vocal quartet, small orchestra	1935, London, His Majesty's Theatre	Deiss-Salabert
—	133	Un Petit Peu d'Exercice (Lunel): Play for children	12 numbers, voice, violins, cellos	1937, Paris, Grand Palais	Durand
—	134	Exercice Musical	Pipe, piano	1948, New York, Juilliard School	L'Oiseau-Lyre
—	135	Concertino de Printemps	Violin, orchestra	1935, Paris, Concert Astruc	Deiss-Salabert
—	136	First Cello Concerto	Cello, orchestra	1935, Paris, Sérénade	Deiss-Salabert
—	137	L'Hippocampe: Film	Orchestra	Omnia-Ciné, 1935	Pathé Nathan
—	138	Tartarin de Tarascon: Film	Orchestra	1935, Paris, Ciné Marivaux	Pathé Nathan
—	139	Le Cycle de la Création (Sturzo): Play	Chorus, orchestra		
1935	140	Ninth String Quartet	String quartet	1935, Concert Coolidge	Chant du Monde
—	141	La Sagesse (Claudel): Theater	Orchestra	1945, Radio Paris; 1950, Rome, Opera	Heugel

The Compositions of DARIUS MILHAUD

DATE	OPUS	TITLE	DESCRIPTION	FIRST PERFORMANCE	PUBLISHER
1935	142	Le Cygne I and II (Claudel)	Voice, piano	1935, Petits Lits Blancs	
—	143	Quatrain (Flament)	Song		
—	144	Dixième Sonate de Baptiste Anet (1729); free transcription	Violin, piano	1935, La Chaux-de-Fonds	
—	145	Le Faiseur (Balzac): Play	Incidental music	1935, Paris, Atelier	
—	146	Voix d'Enfants: Film	Petits Chanteurs à la Croix de Bois	Paris, Ciné-Marignan	Echo
—	147	Pastorale	Oboe, clarinet, bassoon	Bourges	Chant du Monde
1935–6	148	Bolivar (Supervielle): Play	Incidental music	Paris, 1936, Comédie Française	
		b. Trois Chansons de Negresse	Voice, piano or orchestra	Paris, 1937, Concert Grey	Deiss-Salabert
1936	149	La Folle du Ciel (Lenormand): Play	Incidental music; sound waves, harp, voice	Paris, 1936, Mathurins	Heugel
—	150	The Beloved Vagabond: Film	Orchestra	Ciné-Marignan, 1936	Echo
—	151	Deux Chansons for Play: "Tu ne m'échapperas jamais"		Brussels, 1936, Théâtre des Galeries	Heugel
—	152	Bertrand de Born (Valmy-Baisse): Play	Incidental music	Orange, 1936	Deiss
		Moyen-Age Fleuri: Ballet	Orchestra, chorus, soloists		

DATE	OPUS	TITLE	DESCRIPTION	FIRST PERFORMANCE	PUBLISHER
1936	152	a. Suite Provençale	Orchestra	Venice, 1937; as ballet, Paris, Opéra-Comique, 1938	Salabert
		b. Trois Chansons de Troubadour	Voice, orchestra	Orange, 1936	Deiss-Salabert
—	153	Quatorze Juillet (Rolland): First-act finale of play	Incidental music	Paris, 1936	
		Introduction et Marche Funèbre	Orchestra	Paris, 1936, Philharmonique	Chant du Monde
—	154	Le Conquérant (Mistler): Play	Orchestra	Paris, 1936, Odéon	
		b. Fragments Dramatiques	Orchestra	Paris, 1936	Revue Musicale
—	155	Cantique du Rhône (Claudel)	Chorus a cappella, mixed	Paris, 1937, Sérénade	Elkan-Vogel
—	156	Arnal, ou la Lettre du Roi (Tagore-Gide): Play	Incidental music; piano, violin, clarinet	Paris, 1936, Mathurins	
—	157	Le Voyageur sans Bagages (Anouilh): Play	Incidental music	Paris, 1936, Mathurins	
		b. Suite	Piano, violin, clarinet	Paris, 1937, Sérénade	Deiss-Salabert
—	158	Jules César (Shakespeare): Play	Incidental music; instruments, percussion	Paris, 1937, Atelier	
1937	152c	Le Trompeur de Séville (Obey): Play	Recorded instrumental music	Paris, 1937, Porte Saint-Martin	

DATE	OPUS	TITLE	DESCRIPTION	FIRST PERFORMANCE	PUBLISHER
1937	159	Fête de la Musique (Claudel): Celestial Ballet	Orchestra, piano, vocal quartet, soprano solo	Recorded for World's Fair, Paris, 1937	
—	160	La Duchesse de Malfi (Webster): Play	Recorded incidental music	Marseille, 1937, Rideau Gris	
—	161	Roméo et Juliette (Shakespeare): Play	Recorded incidental music	Paris, 1937, Mathurins	
—		b. Suite d'après Corrette	Oboe, clarinet, bassoon	Paris, 1938, Sérénade	Oiseau-Lyre
—	162	Le Tour de l'Exposition	Piano	Paris, World's Fair, 1937	Deiss-Salabert
—	163	Liberté (Lenormand, Vildrac, etc.): Collective play	Overture and Interlude for orchestra	Paris, 1937, Champs-Elysées	
—	164	Cantate pour l'Inauguration du Musée de l'Homme (Desnos)	Vocal quartet, narrator, six instruments	Paris, 1937, Conservatoire	
—	165a	Le Médecin Volant (Moliere): Play	Incidental music; piano, clarinet or saxophone	Paris, 1937, Champs-Elysées	
—		b. Scaramouche	Two pianos or saxophone (or clarinet) and orchestra	Paris, World's Fair, 1937	Deiss-Salabert
—	166	Cantate de la Paix (Claudel)	Chorus, children's voices, male voices	Paris, 1937, Sorbonne	Schirmer
—	167	Cinq Chansons (Vildrac)	5 songs; voice, piano	Paris, 1937, Radio Française	Deiss-Salabert
—	168	Cantate Nuptiale	4 numbers; voice, orchestra	Marseille, 1937, Radio Marseille	Deiss-Salabert

The Compositions of DARIUS MILHAUD

DATE	OPUS	TITLE	DESCRIPTION	FIRST PERFORMANCE	PUBLISHER
1937	169	Main Tendue à Tous (Vildrac)	Chorus a cappella	Paris, 1937	Chant du Monde
—	170	Les Deux Cités (Claudel): Cantata	Chorus a cappella	Paris, 1937, Sérénade	Schirmer
—	171	Chansons de l'Opéra du Gueux (Gay): Play	Voice, orchestra	Radio Marseille, 1937	Salabert
—	172	Carnaval de Londres	Orchestra	Revue Musicale, Paris, 1939	Deiss-Salabert
—	173	Chanson du Capitaine (Bloch)	Voice, piano	Palais Sports, Paris, 1937	Deiss-Salabert
—		Java de la Femme	Voice, piano	Paris, 1937	Salabert
—	174	Mollenard: Film	Orchestra	Cinéma Normandie, Paris, 1938	Echo
—	175	Macbeth (Shakespeare): Play	Incidental music	Old Vic, London, 1937	
—	176	La Citadelle du Silence: Film, with Honegger	Orchestra	Ciné Olympia, Paris, 1937	Ariel
—	177	Hécube (Euripides-Richaud): Play	Orchestra	Champs-Elysées, Paris, 1937	
—	178	Poème de Corneille: Rondeau	Voice, piano		
—	179	Holem Tsaudi-Gan Hayom: Two Popular Palestine Songs	Voice, piano		Masada
—	180	Quatrain (Mallarmé)	Voice, piano		Nigun
—	181	L'Oiseau	Orchestra	O. S. P., Paris, 1938	

DATE	OPUS	TITLE	DESCRIPTION	FIRST PERFORMANCE	PUBLISHER
1937	182	Grands Feux: Cartoon film advertisement			Central Film, Zurich
	183	Prends cette Rose (Ronsard)	Soprano, tenor, orchestra	O. S. P., Paris, 1938	
	184	La Conquête du Ciel: Film	Orchestra	Cinéma Madeleine, Paris	
1938	185	Cantate de l'Enfant et de la Mère (Carême)	Narrator, string quartet, piano	Beaux-Arts, Brussels, 1938	Heugel
	186	Plutus (Aristophanes): Play	Incidental music	Atélier, Paris, 1938	
	187	Tragédie Impériale: Film	Orchestra	Cinéma Marignan, Paris, 1938	Choudens
	188	Fantaisie Pastorale	Piano, orchestra	O. S. P., Paris, 1939	Deiss-Salabert
	189	Les Quatre Eléments (Desnos): Cantata	Soprano, tenor, orchestra	O. S. P., Paris, 1939	Heugel
	190	Tricolore (Lestringuez): Play	Incidental music	Comédie Française, Paris, 1938	
	191	Médée (Madeleine Milhaud): Opera		Antwerp, 1939	Heugel
	192	Le Bal des Voleurs (Anouilh): Play	Incidental music: clarinet, saxophone	Théâtre des Arts, Paris, 1938	
	193	La Première Famille (Supervielle): Play	Piano, songs	Mathurins, Paris, 1938	Heugel

DATE	OPUS	TITLE	DESCRIPTION	FIRST PERFORMANCE	PUBLISHER
1938	194	Magali-Se Canto-L'Antoni-Le Mal d'Amour: Four Popular Songs of Provence	Voice, orchestra	Gaîté-Lyrique, Paris, 1938	Chant du Monde
—	195	Récréation (Krieger): Four Songs for Children			Silver Burdett
—	196	Les Otages: Film	Orchestra	Cinéma Marivaux, Paris, 1939	Choudens
1938-9	197	Concerto for Flute, Violin, and Orchestra	Flute, violin, orchestra	Radio Suisse-Romande, 1940	Deiss-Salabert
1939	198	Islands: Film	Orchestra	World's Fair, New York, 1939	G. P. O. Films, London
—	199	Trois Elégies (Jammes)	Soprano, tenor, strings		
—	200	Hamlet (Laforgue): Play	Incidental music	Atelier, Paris, 1939	
—	201	Incantations: Three Aztec songs	Chorus, male voices	Oakland, California, 1945	
—	202	Espoir (Malraux): Film	Orchestra	New York World's Fair, 1940	Echo
		Cortège Funèbre: Concert version	Orchestra	C. B. S., New York, 1940	
—	203	Voyage au Pays du Rêve: Radio play, musical adaptation		Paris, P. T. T., 1939	

DATE	OPUS	TITLE	DESCRIPTION	FIRST PERFORMANCE	PUBLISHER
1939	204	Cavalcade d'Amour: Film	Orchestra	Cinéma Marivaux and Colisé, Paris, 1940	Coda
—	205	La Cheminée du Roi René	Suite: 7 numbers for flute, oboe, clarinet, French horn, bassoon	Mills College, Oakland, California, 1941	Woodwind Music (Andraud), Cincinnati
—	206	Quatrains Valaisans (Rilke)	5 numbers; chorus a cappella	Paris, 1948	Heugel
—	165c	Scaramouche	Suite: 3 numbers for saxophone, orchestra	Radio-Paris, 1940	Deiss-Salabert
			Version for clarinet, orchestra	Rochester Symphony Orchestra	
—	207	La Reine de Saba: Palestine song	String quartet	Radio Jerusalem, 1939	
—	208	Gulf Stream: Film	Orchestra		
—	209	Fanfare	Orchestra	St. Louis Symphony Orchestra, 1940	
—	210	First Symphony	Orchestra	Chicago Symphony Orchestra, 1940	Heugel
1940	211	Couronne de Gloire (Gabirol-Lunel): Cantata	Voice, piano or string quartet, flute, trumpet		
—	212	Indicatif et Marche pour les Bons d'Armement: Record	Orchestra	Radio d'Etat, Paris, 1940	

DATE	OPUS	TITLE	DESCRIPTION	FIRST PERFORMANCE	PUBLISHER
1940	213	Cantate de la Guerre (Claudel)	4 pieces; chorus *a cappella*	University of Oregon, Eugene, 1947	Schirmer
	214	Sornettes (Mistral): Songs	Two children's voices		
	215	Un Petit Ange de Rien du Tout (Puget): Play	Incidental music	Théâtre Michel, Paris, 1940	
	216	Le Voyage d'Eté (Paliard)	Suite: 15 numbers; voice, piano	New York, League of Composers, 1940	Heugel
	217	Cours de Solfège—Papillon, Papillonette (Fluchère)	Songs: children's voices, piano		
	218	Tenth String Quartet (Birthday Quartet)	String quartet	Washington, D. C., Library of Congress, 1940	Salabert
	219	Opus Americanum No. 2 (Moses): Ballet Suite	Orchestra	San Francisco Symphony Orchestra, 1943	Elkan-Vogel
	220	Introduction et Allegro: Fragments of Couperin's La Sultane	Orchestra	St. Louis Symphony Orchestra, 1941	Elkan-Vogel
	221	Sonatine / b. Sonatine à Trois	Two violins / Violin, viola, cello	San Francisco, 1940	Mercury / Mercury
1941	222	Touches Noires (Black Keys); Touches Blanches (White Keys)	Piano, for children		Carl Fischer
	223	Quatre Chansons de Ronsard	Voice, orchestra	Waldorf-Astoria Hotel, New York, 1941	Boosey & Hawkes

DATE	OPUS	TITLE	DESCRIPTION	FIRST PERFORMANCE	PUBLISHER
1941	224	*Mills Fanfare*	String orchestra	Mills College, Oakland, 1941	
—	225	Second Piano Concerto	Piano, orchestra	Chicago, 1941	Heugel
—	226	Sonatine	Violin, viola		Mercury
—	227	Four Sketches: I *Eglogue*; II *Madrigal*; III *Sobre la Loma*; IV *Alameda*	Orchestra; or wind quintet; or piano, clarinet	C. B. S., New York, 1942; 1943	Mercury
—	228	Concerto for Two Pianos and Orchestra	Two pianos, orchestra	Pittsburgh Symphony Orchestra, 1942	Elkan-Vogel
—	101a	*La Bien-Aimée:* Ballet (new orchestration)	Orchestra	Ballet Theatre, Mexico City, 1941	Universal
—	229	*Pastorale*	Organ	National Cathedral, Washington, D. C., 1942	Gray & Co.
—	230	Concerto for Clarinet and Orchestra	Clarinet, orchestra	Marine Barracks, Washington, D. C., 1946	Elkan-Vogel
1942	231a	*L'Annonce Faite à Marie* (Claudel): New music for play	Orchestra	Mills College, Oakland, 1943 (Christmas)	
—	231b	*Neuf Préludes*	Organ	Paris, Salle Pleyel, 1948	Heugel

DATE	OPUS	TITLE	DESCRIPTION	FIRST PERFORMANCE	PUBLISHER
1942	231c	Cinq Prières	Voice, organ	Mills College Women's Choir, Oakland, 1943	Heugel
—	232	Eleventh String Quartet	String quartet	New York, League of Composers, 1942	Salabert
—	233	Rêves: Six songs	Voice, piano	Radio Brussels, 1945	Heugel
—	234	Suite	3 numbers; harmonica or violin, orchestra	Philadelphia Orchestra (violin), 1945; Salle Pleyel, Paris (harmonica), 1947	Boosey & Hawkes
—	235	Fanfare de la Liberté	Orchestra	Washington, D. C., 1943	
1943	236	Bolivar (Supervielle-Madeleine Milhaud)	Opera	Paris, Opéra, 1950	
—	236a	La Libertadora: Dance suite	Two pianos	Town Hall, New York, 1945	
—	236b	La Libertadora	Piano	University of Wyoming, Laramie, 1945	Deiss-Salabert
—	237	Songes: Suite	Two pianos	University of Wisconsin, Madison, 1944	Heugel
—	238	Quatre Visages	Viola, piano		

DATE	OPUS	TITLE	DESCRIPTION	FIRST PERFORMANCE	PUBLISHER
1944	239	Borechou-Shema	Voice, chorus, organ	Park Avenue Synagogue, New York, 1944	Schirmer
—	240	First Viola Sonata	Viola, piano	University of Wisconsin, 1944	Heugel
—	241	Cain et Abel	Narrator, orchestra	Hollywood, 1945	
—	242	Air de la Sonate	Viola, orchestra	University of Wisconsin, 1944	
—	243	Jeux de Printemps: Ballet	6 numbers; chamber orchestra Piano, 4 hands Large orchestra	Library of Congress, Washington, D. C., 1944 Radio Brussels, 1945; (as ballet), Paris, Opéra-Comique, 1948	Salabert
—	244	Second Viola Sonata	Viola, piano	Edgewood College, Madison, Wisconsin, 1944	Heugel
—	245	La Muse Ménagère: Suite	15 numbers; piano or orchestra	Radio Brussels, 1945	Elkan-Vogel
—	246	La Libération des Antilles: 2 creole songs	Voice, piano	Oakland, California, 1945	Leeds

DATE	OPUS	TITLE	DESCRIPTION	FIRST PERFORMANCE	PUBLISHER
1944	247	Second Symphony	Orchestra	Boston Symphony Orchestra, 1946	Heugel
—	248	Suite Française	5 numbers; symphonic band Piano, four hands Orchestra	New York, 1945	Leeds
—	249	Le Bal Martiniquais	2 numbers; 2 pianos Orchestra	New York, 1945 Radio Brussels, 1945 New York Philharmonic-Symphony Orchestra, 1945	Leeds
1945	250	Prière pour les Morts (Kaddisch)	Voice, chorus, organ ad libitum	Park Avenue Synagogue, New York, 1945	Schirmer
—	251	Elégie	Cello, piano	Town Hall, New York, 1945	Boosey & Hawkes
—	252	Twelfth String Quartet	String quartet	Washington, D. C., 1945	Salabert
—	253	Printemps Lointain (Jammes)	Voice, piano		
—	254	Introduction, Marche, Fête de la Victoire (to complete ballet version of Suite Française)	Orchestra		
—	255	Second Cello Concerto	Cello, orchestra	New York Philharmonic-Symphony Orchestra, 1945	Associated Music Publishers
—	256	Danses de Jacaremirim	3 numbers; violin, piano	Hollywood, 1948	Delkas-Leeds

The Compositions of DARIUS MILHAUD

DATE	OPUS	TITLE	DESCRIPTION	FIRST PERFORMANCE	PUBLISHER
1945	257	Sonata for Violin and Harpsichord	Violin, harpsichord	Town Hall, New York, 1945	Elkan-Vogel
—	258	Duo	2 numbers; 2 violins	Private audition, Alma, 1945	Mercury
—	259	The Bells (Poe): Ballet	5 numbers; orchestra	University of Chicago, 1946	
1945-6	260	Deux Marches	a. Orchestra	C. B. S., New York, 1945	Schirmer
			b. Symphonic band	Goldman Band, New York, 1948	
1946	261	Pledge to Mills (Hedley): Student song		Mills College, 1946	
—	262	Farandoleurs	Violin, piano	Conservatoire, Paris, 1946	Salabert
—	263	Second Violin Concerto	Violin, orchestra	Conservatoire, Paris, 1948	Associated Music Publishers
—	264	Prélude et Postlude pour "Lidoire" (Courteline): Play	Clarinet, bassoon, trumpet, accordion, harp, doublebass	Paris, 1946	
—	265	Chants de Misère (Paliard)	4 numbers; voice, piano	Radio Française, 1946	Heugel
—	266	Six Sonnets composés au secret (Cassou)	Vocal quartet or chorus	Basel, 1947	Heugel

DATE	OPUS	TITLE	DESCRIPTION	FIRST PERFORMANCE	PUBLISHER
1946–7	267	Sept Danses sur des Airs Palestiniens	Orchestra		Salabert
1946	268	Thirteenth String Quartet	String quartet	Washington, D. C., 1947	
—	269	Une Journée	5 numbers; piano	New York, 1946	Mercury
—	270	Third Piano Concerto	Piano, orchestra	Prague, 1946	Associated
—	271	Third Symphony	Orchestra, chorus	Radio Française, 1947	Heugel
—	272	The Private Affairs of Bel Ami: Film	Orchestra	Cleveland, 1947	United Artists
1947	273	Man Ray Sequence of "Dreams that Money Can Buy": Film	Orchestra	Brussels, 1947	
—	274	String Trio	Violin, viola, cello	Paris, 1947	Heugel
—	275	Carnaval à la Nouvelle-Orléans	4 numbers; two pianos	Michigan State College, Lansing, 1947	Leeds
—	276	Trois Poèmes (Supervielle)	Voice, piano	Conservatoire, Paris, 1947	Heugel
—	277	Méditation	Piano		
—	278	Concerto Marimba	Marimba, vibraphone, orchestra	St. Louis Symphony Orchestra, 1949	Enoch
—	279	Sabbath Morning Service	Baritone speaker, chorus, organ or orchestra	Temple Emmanuel, San Francisco, 1949	Salabert

DATE	OPUS	TITLE	DESCRIPTION	FIRST PERFORMANCE	PUBLISHER
1947	280	The House of Bernarda Alba (García Lorca): Play	Incidental music; flute, bassoon, oboe, percussion	Hollywood, 1947	
—	281	Fourth Symphony (1848)	Orchestra	Paris, 1948	Salabert
1948	282	Le Grand Testament: for radio	Orchestra	Paris, 1948	
—	283	'adame Miroir (Genet): Ballet	Orchestra	Paris, 1948	Heugel
—	284	Paris	6 numbers; 4 pianos		
—	285	Shéhérazade (Supervielle): Play	Incidental music	Avignon, 1948	
—	286	L'Apothéose de Molière: Suite	5 numbers; harpsichord, strings, flute, oboe, clarinet, bassoon	Capri Festival, 1948	Oiseau-Lyre
—	287	Kentuckiana	a. Two pianos b. Orchestra	Radio Française Louisville, 1949	Elkan-Vogel
—	288	Le Jeu de Robin et de Marion (Adam de la Halle): Play	Voice, flute, clarinet, saxophone, violin, cello	Wiesbaden, 1951	Marks
—	289	L'Enfant Aime ...	5 numbers; piano	University of Wyoming, Laramie, 1949	Leeds
—	290	L'Chob Dodi	Voice, chorus, organ	Temple Emmanuel, San Francisco, 1948	
1948-9	291	Fourteenth and Fifteenth String Quartets (can be played together as String Octet)	One or two string quartets	Mills College, 1949	Heugel

DATE	OPUS	TITLE	DESCRIPTION	FIRST PERFORMANCE	PUBLISHER
1949	292	*Naissance de Vénus* (Supervielle) Cantata	4 numbers; mixed chorus, *a cappella*	Radio Française, 1949	Heugel
—	293	Second Piano Sonata	Piano	B. B. C., 1950	Heugel
—	294	*Les Rêves de Jacob* (*Jacob's Dreams*): *Dance Suite*	Oboe, violin, viola, cello, doublebass	Jacob's Pillow Dance Festival, 1949	Heugel
—	295	Fourth Piano Concerto	Piano, orchestra	Boston Symphony Orchestra, 1950	Heugel
—	296	*Ballade-Nocturne* (Vilmorin)	Voice, piano	Town Hall, New York, 1949	Heugel
—	297	*La Fin du Monde* (Cendrars)	Orchestra	Radio Française, 1949	Heugel
1949–50	298	*Barba Garibo* (Lunel): *Suite des Chansons Mentonaises* b. *La Cueilette des Citrons*: Ballet	10 numbers; orchestra, chorus		Heugel
1950	299	*Gauguin*: Film	Orchestra	Menton, 1950	Royalty
—	300	*Suite Opus 300*	2 pianos, orchestra	Paris, 1950	Heugel
—	301	*Le Repos du Septième Jour* (Claudel)	Incidental music	Venice, 1950	
—	302	*Jeu*	Piano	Paris, 1950	Pierre Noel
—	303	Sixteenth String Quartet	String quartet	Santa Barbara, California, 1950	Heugel
—	304	*La Vie Commence Demain*: Film		Venice, 1950	Choudens
—	305	*Les Temps Faciles* (Marsan)	Voice, piano	Paris, 1950	

DATE	OPUS	TITLE	DESCRIPTION	FIRST PERFORMANCE	PUBLISHER
1950	306	Le Conte d'Hiver (Shakespeare): Play	Incidental music; preludes, dances, songs; orchestra	Comédie Française, Paris, 1950	
—	307	Seventeenth String Quartet	String quartet	Washington, D. C., 1951	Heugel
—	308	Eighteenth String Quartet	String quartet	Aspen, Colorado, 1951	Heugel
—	309	Concertino d'Automne	2 pianos, 8 instruments	Town Hall, New York, 1951	Heugel
—	310	Cantate des Proverbes	3 numbers; female chorus, instruments	New York, 1952	Mercury
—	311	Concertino d'Eté	Viola, chamber orchestra	Charleston, 1951	Heugel
—	312	First Piano Quintet	Piano, string quartet	Mills College, 1952	Heugel
1951	313	West Point Suite	3 numbers; band	New York, 1952	A. M. P.
—	314	Les Miracles de la Foi (Miracles of Faith)	Chorus, tenor, orchestra	Cedar Rapids, Iowa, 1952	Schirmer
—	315	Candelabre à Sept Branches	7 numbers; piano	Ein-Gev Festival, Israel, 1952	Israel Music
1952	316	Second Quintet	2 violins, viola, cello, double-bass	Ann Arbor, Michigan, 1952	Heugel
—	317	L'Anneau de Pourpre (Rothschild): Ballet	Orchestra		Eschig
—	278a	Suite Concertante	Piano, orchestra		Enoch

DATE	OPUS	TITLE	DESCRIPTION	FIRST PERFORMANCE	PUBLISHER
1952	318	*Christophe Colomb* (Claudel): new version for play	Incidental music		
—	319	*Petites Légendes* (Carême): 12 songs	Voice, piano	Aspen, Colorado, 1952	Heugel
—	320	*David* (Lunel): Opera			Israel Music

INDEX

OF PROPER NAMES

(separate index of Milhaud's compositions follows)

i

iv

xvii

INDEX OF MILHAUD'S COMPOSITIONS

REFERRED TO IN THE TEXT

*[Opus numbers given in brackets; further information
on each composition can be found after its opus number in the list of compositions beginning on page 325.]*

xix

A NOTE ON THE TYPE

IN WHICH THIS BOOK IS SET

This book was set on the Monotype in JANSON, a recutting made direct from the type cast from matrices made by Anton Janson some time between 1660 and 1687.

Of Janson's origin nothing is known. He may have been a relative of Justus Janson, a printer of Danish birth who practiced in Leipzig from 1614 to 1635. Some time between 1657 and 1668 Anton Janson, a punch-cutter and type-founder, bought from the Leipzig printer Johann Erich Hahn the type-foundry which had formerly been a part of the printing house of M. Friedrich Lankisch. Janson's types were first shown in a specimen sheet issued at Leipzig about 1675.